LEARNING CAPOEIRA

LEARNING CAPOEIRA

LESSONS IN CUNNING
FROM AN AFRO-BRAZILIAN ART

GREG DOWNEY
UNIVERSITY OF NOTRE DAME

Oxford   New York
OXFORD UNIVERSITY PRESS
2005

Oxford University Press

Oxford   New York
Auckland   Bangkok   Buenos Aires   Cape Town   Chennai
Dar es Salaam   Delhi   Hong Kong   Istanbul   Karachi   Kolkata
Kuala Lumpur   Madrid   Melbourne   Mexico City   Mumbai   Nairobi
São Paulo   Shanghai   Taipei   Tokyo   Toronto

Published by Oxford University Press, Inc.
198 Madison Avenue, New York, New York 10016
www.oup.com

Oxford is a registered trademark of Oxford University Press

Library of Congress Cataloging-in-Publication Data

Downey, Greg.
    Learning capoeira : lessons in cunning from an Afro-Brazilian art / Greg Downey.
        p. cm.
    Includes bibliographical references and index.
    ISBN-13: 978-0-19-517698-8 (alk. paper) — ISBN-13: 978-0-19-517697-1 (pbk. : alk.
        paper)
    1. Capoeira (Dance) I. Title.

GV1796.C145D69 2005
793.3'1981—dc22
                                                                2004054797

Printed in the United States of America
on acid-free paper

CONTENTS

PART 2: REMEMBERING

PART 3: PLAYING

PREFACE

Learning Capoeira: Lessons in Cunning from an Afro-Brazilian Art is an ethnographic study of *capoeira*, a genre that combines elements of martial art, dance, and musical performance. A descendant of slave arts, gangs' fighting techniques, and urban popular culture, capoeira is practiced today throughout Brazil and increasingly around the world. Ironically, many Brazilians now consider the art—once persecuted severely—a national treasure. Along with *samba* and international excellence in *futebol* (soccer), they see capoeira as evidence of a distinctive Brazilian dexterity and genius for movement, as well as a clear indication of African influences on their cultural patrimony.

Capoeira is typically played now as a game in which two contestants vie to control space, demonstrate superior mobility, and trip, kick, or head-butt each other to the ground at a moment of vulnerability. With players not allowed to use their hands to strike, to an uninitiated observer the game may resemble a combination of acrobatic dance, slow martial arts sparring, and musical performance. As they play, adepts harmonize their movements with an orchestra, while other practitioners comment upon the game through song. Learning capoeira requires a student to master all dimensions of the genre—acrobatic attacks, evasive defenses, musical instruments, traditional rituals, and improvised songs.

Contemporary teachers claim that training in capoeira transforms the novice. During apprenticeship, the discipline takes hold of devoted students, instilling in them what veterans call *malícia*, or "cunning," both within the circular *roda*, the "ring" where the game is played, as well as outside it. Veterans say that the art's distinctive swaying movement makes them more deceptive, that training heightens their awareness of potential danger, and that the defensive strategies they learn for the game transfer over to everyday life. For this reason, the book treats the art as a bodily discipline for transforming a person's perceptions, sense of self, and styles of interaction, rather than just an isolated performance. The book explores how physical training might affect experience and subjectivity, combining ideas from cultural anthropology, phenomenology, gender studies, psychology, and even neuroscience to make sense of what practitioners, called *capoeiristas*, report feeling.

Specifically, the book examines in detail how novices learn the art through imitation; how new skills, such as playing musical instruments, shape experience; the factors that affect the experiential texture of the game; and how practitioners describe different styles of moving. In Salvador, Brazil, where field research for this book was focused, many adepts were concerned about changes in capoeira practice. They argued about whether certain styles of moving were "whitened," losing touch with the art's African cultural roots, or if a revival of the traditional style had political significance. These debates, although they employed a language of ethnicity, class, politics, and history, revealed how capoeiristas felt when they tried to move in different ways, especially when they struggled to overcome their own physical inhibitions.

Learning Capoeira applies an innovative phenomenological approach to ethnography, providing a model for scholars and students alike, as well as an intimate portrait of an important artistic legacy of the African diaspora. Capoeira provokes us to consider more deeply how cultures might shape diverse forms of embodiment, and how bodily training conditions social interaction, the experiential quality of everyday life, and even physiological development. *Learning Capoeira* demonstrates how pervasive physical education is, extending beyond sports or games into the more mundane habits, sensitivities, and comportments that embed us in different worlds. This focused study of a living Afro-Brazilian tradition shows concretely how unspoken, non-symbolic dimensions of culture can shape people, discussing capoeira in light of findings about historical memory, music perception, environmental psychology, physiological change, and neurological plasticity. In an accessible and engaging style, *Learning Capoeira* demonstrates that ethnographic apprenticeship and experience-centered analysis can capture a distinctive cultural world—how it feels, what it looks like from within, and how its inhabitants learn to navigate it with cunning.

ACKNOWLEDGMENTS

This book was more than a decade in the making. In that time, I amassed more debts than possibly can be discharged in prefatory remarks, but some acknowledgments are in order. My graduate academic advisors—Jim Fernandez, Andrew Apter, and Phil Bohlman—provided inspiring role models and shepherded this project through its earliest, most fragile stages. In addition, while at the University of Chicago, I learned more than I can even recall at the feet of the resident "mestres," especially John and Jean Comaroff, Ray Fogelson, Bill Hanks, Bruce Lincoln, John MacAloon, and Nancy Munn. Preparing specifically to work and cope in Brazil, I was fortunate to receive critical assistance from Randy Matory, Tony Seeger, and Lowell Lewis. Since moving to the University of Notre Dame, I have benefited from the enthusiasm and support of all my colleagues, but a special note of thanks is owed to Roberto DaMatta for being such a strong mentor and for sharing his vast knowledge of Brazilian popular culture.

The book benefited from intellectual sparring with a number of colleagues along the way; I especially need to thank Karl Appuhn, Ira Bashkow, Maria Farland, Laurie Frederik, Shane Green, Jamie Jacobs, Carolyn Johnson, Anne Lorimer, Even Meceda, John Norvell, Christy Rudolph, Susan Seizer, and Hoon Song. From 2002 to 2003, when preparing the final draft, I was privileged to spend a year of sabbatical at the Pembroke Center for Teaching and Research on Women at Brown University. The year-long faculty seminar on "embodiment," guided by Anne Fausto-Sterling, was essential to this project; her influence will be felt on my work for years to come. Thanks also to Josh Kaplan, Rochelle Rosen, Gayle Salamon, Patricia Synnods, Debbie Weinstein, Elizabeth Weed, and all the seminar participants for their help and close readings of drafts of many chapters. When the manuscript was finally finished, Mark Harris (University of St. Andrews), Rob Lavenda (St. Cloud State University), and Kathryn Lynn Geurts (Hamline University), offered meticulous readings and many comments, both sympathetic and critical, that helped me to clearly define the book's goal and audience.

Field research in Salvador in 1992 and from 1993 to 1995 was undertaken with support from the Fulbright Foundation Institute for International Education and the Tinker Foundation. My apprenticeship in capoeira was again more intensive from 1998 to 2000, during tenure at the Society of Fellows in the Humanities of Columbia University; there I was able to enroll in the Academy of Capoeira Angola of Mestre João Grande. While in Salvador, the Centro de Estudos Afro-Orientais of the Univesidade Federal da Bahia sponsored the project—thanks to Jefferson Bacelar, Júlio Braga, and Afonso Florence—and the Instituto Mauá always opened its doors and its library to me. In New York and elsewhere, Bob Cooper has helped the project more than he will admit to with his generosity and enthusiasm for the work. The publication of the book was made possible in part by a grant from the Institute for Scholarship in the Liberal Arts, College of Arts and Letters, University of Notre Dame.

My gratitude is also owed to my editor at Oxford University Press, Jan Beatty, and her assistant, Talia Krohn; their support has been decisive and unswerving. Readers will join me in enthusiastically thanking Mestre Cobra Mansa for providing some of the beautiful pictures that add so much to this text, helping to explain movements that are difficult to convey in words. (For more information on Mestre Cobra's work and the International Capoeira Angola Foundation he founded, readers should go on-line to http://www.capoeira-angola.org/.) Thanks also go to Bessa Kautz for obtaining the cover photo. Kathy Cummins and Jake Weiler helped with editing and indexing.

In my field research and apprenticeship, I benefited from the extraordinary generosity and *malícia* of countless practitioners of capoeira. I cannot possibly name them all, but I would be remiss not to acknowledge the wisdom, patience, and good humor of Mestre Nenel, Mestre João Grande, Mestre João Pequeno, Jair Moura, Ângelo Decânio, Mestre Cobra Mansa, Bira Almeida (Mestre Acordeon), Mestre Jogo de Dentro, Mestre Dermeval, Mestre Nô, Mestre Camisa, Professor Ferreira, Mestranda Edna Lima, André Lacé, Carlos Senna, Mestre Lua, Mestre Canjaquinha, Mestre Bobó, and Mestre Curió (even though he threw me out of his academy). Although capoeiristas pride themselves in being suspicious and wary, the community was friendly, welcoming, and warm, almost to a fault (almost). Many more fellow players could be added to this list, but, at the very least, I have to thanks my instructors—contramestres Valmir, Boca do Rio, Paulinha, Poloca, and Pepeu—and fellow students like Rosângela, Cizinho, Marcio, Luís, Nise, and Marcos. They appear both by name and implicitly throughout this book. The members of the Grupo de Capoeira Angola Pelourinho, the Capoeira Angola Center of Mestre João Grande, the Fundação Internacional da Capoeira Angola, the Fundação Mestre Bimba, the Filhos de Bimba, Grupo Urucungo, Capoeira Angola Palmares, and the Grupo-ABADÁ in New York City provided hours of camaraderie as well as many hard lessons.

Of course, all errors are ultimately the responsibility of the author, even though the reader should be warned that capoeiristas are a wily bunch, not above yanking the chain of a foreign researcher for their own amusement. All translations from Portuguese are also the author's.

Finally, thanks to all those who have supported me morally on the long struggle to finish this work, to my colleagues at the University of Notre Dame, to my family—especially my parents Jeanne and Greg, and my brother Mike—and to Shari Nemeth, for her patience and gentleness during the writing process. Most of all, I owe an enormous debt of gratitude to Frederico de Abreu and my teacher, Mestre Moraes; if I have any insights to offer into the nature of capoeira, they were probably first spoken by one of the two.

Prelude: Playing Capoeira

The call to play the Afro-Brazilian game *capoeira* is the incomparable twang of a single-stringed musical bow, the *berimbau*.[1] Our *mestre*—our capoeira teacher—strikes the steel cord of the instrument twice, letting the bow reverberate and fade between each toll before settling into a steady rhythm. We students form the circular *roda*, or capoeira ring; our bodies fill the orchestra bench on either side of the mestre, and we follow the tempo he sets. The berimbau is first joined by additional berimbaus, tuned higher than the first, that interlock with its bass voice. Then the berimbaus are joined by two tambourine-like *pandeiros*, by a scraper, by an *agogô* (a double bell-gong), and by a tall drum known as an *atabaque*. The two *capoeiristas* (practitioners of the art) who will enter the roda first move in low and crouch down in front of the mestre, *ao pé do berimbau*, "at the foot of the berimbau." Their heads are lowered respectfully as they rest on their heels and watch each other warily out of the corners of their eyes.

To call our attention, the mestre shouts the first syllables of the opening solo *ladainha* or "litany": *Iê!* He sings a familiar verse about Salvador, the city in the state of Bahia, Brazil, considered to be the cradle of capoeira, listing landmarks: the names of famous churches and places where legendary rodas were once held during religious festivals. The song is thick with history. Each place named, every church and plaza, calls to mind stories told about capoeira practitioners in the early part of the twentieth century, before the art was safely ensconced as it is today in physical education departments and sports academies. The names recall a time when practitioners of capoeira were persecuted—a mounted police contingent once broke up rodas in Salvador—and the game was potentially dangerous—it's said that a fight might have been resolved with straight razors.

After the solo ladainha, our mestre leads the whole roda in call-and-response salutations. *Viva meu Deus!* he sings, and the group echoes back

1

the line. Some bow their heads or raise their hands to heaven. Our teacher sings thanks to his absent mestre for teaching him "the treachery of capoeira"; we, his students, likewise raise a hand to him in gratitude when we repeat the salute. Then he warns the players crouched before him: *Menin' é bom*, "The child's good," and *Sabe jogar*, "Knows how to play."

Galo cantou, "The cock crowed," he sings, *Co-co-ro-co. É hora, é hora*, "It's time, it's time." *Vamos embora*, "Let's go." *Pelo mundo afora*, "Out into the world. . . ." We echo back each phrase. The waiting pair gestures as if offering each other the floor, a picture of diplomacy and graciousness. They prepare themselves to play; they touch the ground, cross themselves, and whisper prayers. (One mestre told me that he always prayed, "Safety for us both; victory for me.") Players are reminded to be careful. Even if the game may resemble harmless play, it's said that capoeiristas have died in the roda as a result of betrayal, anger, or bad luck.

Following the salutations, the mestre sings the first lines of a familiar song: "Aye-aye-aye-aye, St. Benedict calls me!" All those assembled sing back in response: "Aye-aye-aye-aye." Guided by the rhythm and propelled by the singing, the two players slowly begin to test each other. Still crouching, they lean onto their arms and deliberately turn toward the center of the roda, holding their weight on their hands. One pivots around on his foot, his other leg trailing straight and outstretched in a slow *rabo d' arraia*, a kick called a "stingray's tail." His adversary rolls even closer to the ground, supporting himself on deeply bent arms. Accompanying the direction of the kick, his cheek grazes the floor. As the heel of his adversary's kicking leg passes close, he turns and rolls over to free his own leg for a deliberate counterattack.

The two capoeiristas weave around each other patiently on the floor, cartwheeling, crab-walking, spinning, and sliding close to the ground. The game resembles a slow motion, acrobatic pantomime of a fight. The attacks are more implied than actual. Most kicks pass close to the other player, forcing him to move and respond with a counterattack. The players jockey for superior position, demonstrating uncanny flexibility and balance rather than simply striking at each other. They attack the space around each other with their legs and head, using their arms merely to support their bodies. One gets the sense that each player is trying to herd the other one into an awkward position.

A kind of bodily conversation develops between the two, simultaneously cooperative and competitive, aesthetic and agonistic. Only hands, head, and feet touch the ground. The game looks choreographed, so smoothly do attack, counterattack, and counter-counterattack flow one into the next. The first passes of the game are deceptively slow, but they're a competition as certainly as the quicker and more overtly aggressive exchanges that follow. For now, the game develops low to the ground in a series of acrobatic evasions, sweeping kicks, bent handstands, spine-twisting back bridges, and cagy cartwheels.

When the rhythm quickens, the players open up their postures, and the game becomes more heated. Moving faster now, no longer staying so close to each other or the floor, they stumble and pirouette. Their legs suddenly reach out in kicks from unexpected angles. The capoeiristas look off-balance, smiling, their eyes wandering in a studied, deceptive disinterest that conceals complete concentration. They strive to trip each other or await the perfect moment of vulnerability for an artful counterattack.

Then one player unwisely cartwheels too casually over the other's *tesoura*, a leg "scissors" that slides along the floor at ankle height. When the reckless player reaches, extending to vault over the top of his adversary, he leaves his body exposed. The player doing the tesoura lunges into the upside-down victim's open belly with his forehead—a *cabeçada* or head butt. The target can't close his legs quickly enough to cover the "opening." The cabeçada sends the target tumbling, disjointed, to the ground. The cabeçada was perfectly timed and beautifully executed.

The mestre leans his berimbau into the roda to stop the game. The victim won't get a chance to retaliate, at least not during this game. He picks himself up off the ground as his partner exaggeratedly mimes helping to brush "dust" off his clothes. The "help" serves only to underscore who it was that fell to the floor (it may even be an approach for another takedown if the loser is insufficiently wary). Crowd and players alike chuckle and play with the interaction. As if to rub salt in a wounded ego, the mestre begins a new song: "My machete struck low," he sings. The chorus responds, "The banana tree fell down." His choice plays on the fact that a handstand—like the upside-down position in which the capoeirista was caught unawares—is called "banana tree," a *bananeira*.

The next pair is already moving to the foot of the berimbau to enter the roda. Games continue throughout the afternoon. Players usually are matched randomly; veterans play with beginners, men with women, adults with small children, although instructors avoid pairing really raw novices to prevent accidental collisions between nervous rookies. As a rule, however, a person arriving at the foot of the berimbau becomes the partner of whoever comes from the other side.

Finally, I'm next in line. The woman now playing the *berimbau gunga*, the deep-toned bow passed off to her earlier by the mestre, leans forward, and looks left and right along the bench of musicians. Her eyes summon me and another player who will be my partner to the foot of the berimbau. I walk to the shadow of the gunga crouched low to the ground, stretching my neck to relax myself for the impending game. Head lowered, I watch my adversary discretely out of the corner of my eye as he ties his long dreadlocks into a bundle to keep them from falling in front of his face. As I wait, I trace protective, "magical" patterns with my right hand on the floor at the foot of the orchestra. His slightly exaggerated patience and my apparent distraction are both head games, attempts to let the opponent stew and, at the same time, adjust our own dispositions so that our bodies will be as limber and responsive as possible. When he is ready, the gunga inclines between us and beats out a steady stream of open notes—"dun-dun-dun-dun-dun-dun. . . ." We both raise our hands up, saluting the berimbau and evoking protection from heaven. Then we reach out to shake hands. I'm a little surprised that he smiles as our glances graze each other. As she raises the berimbau, the leader of the orchestra sings out, *Olha lá, o moleque!* "Look there, the urchin!" The roda responds, *O molequ' é tu*, "You're the urchin!"

My partner and I gesture toward the middle of the roda, inviting each other to enter. I feel the opening space inside the roda roll out before us like sound expanding to fill the room. Crouched down, my body leans sideways. I watch the other capoeirista carefully but affect nonchalance as I lower the top of my head to the floor and cartwheel slowly into a tight, compact headstand. My adversary pushes himself with his arms, his feet sliding toward the center of the roda, so I rotate on my head deliberately, keeping my legs between my body and his as protection. His right leg languidly rises to kick, and he pivots toward me, against the direction of my cartwheel. His foot and calf slice into the space my body was descending into, forcing me to twist around and bring my hands to the other side of my head while my neck supports my weight. Even with my head on the ground, there's not enough space to finish the cartwheel under the kick. I lower myself down onto my elbow, catching it against my gut, shrinking before the oncoming attack into a position called a "fall on the kidneys," a *queda de rins*. I then lift myself off my elbow. My leg straightens, drawn into the exposed ribs on the back side of his kick. After his leg passes, mine swings inside and just behind his, prying open the space along his body, trying to open up his closed, protective posture.

As we circle and attack each other again and again, he's moving a little more quickly and aggressively than I expected. It's as if he's listening to the high-pitched, staccato *berimbau viola* instead of the measured bass voice of the deeper berimbau gunga. Or maybe he's just pressing me to see if I will get rattled, leaving my body tense and my movements jerky. I feel a smile on my face as I finish a cartwheel, leaning away from an

Mestre Cobra Mansa (foreground) and a student play at the celebration to open Cobra's academy in Washington, D.C. Cobra is doing a rabo de arraia *(stingray's tail kick) while his student rolls through a back "bridge," or* ponte. *(Photo by G. Downey)*

oncoming attack even before I see it. His head was clearly leading into another arching kick as he turned to avoid colliding with the soles of my shoes. I anticipate the kick and turn away from it instinctively, listening to the beat of the gunga, trying to let the deep reverberations guide and relax my body. I lean onto my arms in a low *negativa*, an evasive posture, ducking beneath the plane of the kick.

However, when his kicking leg rotates through to my waist, my opponent jumps slightly off his pivot foot, supporting his weight briefly on his arms, and switches the direction of the kick. As soon as the foot in front of me leaves the ground, the smooth circular flow of his momentum breaks. My head suddenly feels vulnerable when his feet leave the ground. My arm already protects my torso, but my head is turned to the side, exposed. When a "stingray's tail" kick swings around from the opposite direction, I need to escape again.

I move more quickly now, rolling away with the oncoming leg, switching to do a negativa to the other side. But this kick, too, is a feint. Again his weight lifts onto his hands, and the foot on which he was pivoting moves straight out toward my exposed hip. It is a backward-pushing attack, like a one-legged mule kick, called a *chapa d' costa*, and, if it catches my hip, could knock me over. It's not far to fall—I'm only inches from the ground—but everyone will see me land on my butt. My body folds and turns to roll away from him, splaying backward out of range and under his foot. My reactions grow more urgent and tense. I try to continue wheeling around so that I can reach my leg along the floor, beneath his extended chapa d' costa, to hook the foot that's left on the ground and wrench it from under him.

As I sweep my leg out, however, I sense no real opening or vulnerability. His weight isn't precariously balanced. His body isn't overextended. He's "closed." He gently pushes with one leg off the ground before my sweep and floats up into a handstand, leaving his leg extended to fend me off in case I follow up my clumsy attack. He makes me look bad. His head crooks slightly—almost ironically—between his arms as he looks at me upside-down. Having me on the run, leading me to move too quickly, is a tactical victory for him. In a sense, the tilted head provokes me, mocks me for getting flustered.

When he lowers himself out of the handstand, I begin to pace in a circle around the inside of the roda, discontinuing the exchange. The circling breaks the flow of our interaction, and he follows me. After a couple of trips around the circumference of the playing space, I turn to face him again. Pointing to the gunga, I take him back to the foot of the berimbau in front of the orchestra. The game restarts slowly, and I will try to take control of the pace. The game's just begun.

1   Inside and Outside the Roda

Capoeira (pronounced "ka-pooh-AIR-ah") is an Afro-Brazilian art that combines dance, sport, and martial art. When it is played as a game (rather than used for self-defense or performed in folklore shows), two players, called capoeiristas, enter a round playing area, the "roda" ("HOE-dah"), formed by the bodies of other players and musicians. There, they attempt to outmaneuver, trip, or strike each other while coordinating their movements to music that controls the tenor of the game. The legs and head are the principal weapons; the hands primarily distract opponents and support the body's weight. Players defend themselves by avoiding impact rather than by blocking strikes. In the tight confines of the roda, capoeiristas evade each other by using an extraordinary repertoire of dodges, cartwheels, and other acrobatic movements, some of them inverted, the body turned upside down on the arms or head. A player strives to control space, to evidence *malícia* or "cunning," to execute more difficult movements, to employ dramatic devices skillfully, and to show greater aesthetic sensitivity. At the same time, a player must avoid a sweep, trip, kick, or head butt that may knock him or her to the floor.

Capoeira training transforms practitioners' comportment in everyday life so that the cunning they learn in the game orients them outside it as well. Like many people who study martial arts or bodily disciplines such as tai chi or yoga, capoeiristas believe that changing the way students walk, breathe, stand, and carry their bodies affects their emotional lives, social interactions, and perceptions. This book is dedicated to understanding how that might happen in capoeira, and what anthropologists might learn from this sort of life-transforming physical education.

The following chapters explore how training affects devoted practitioners, but this introduction must serve another purpose: to help the reader understand what is at stake in the game, both for those who play it and for an anthropologist who studies it. The people I conducted research with are convinced that their art is valuable, to each practitioner individually and to Brazil as a whole. To play an African-derived art in a country with complex racial attitudes has political implications.

The longer I studied capoeira, the more I felt that to do justice to what players were telling me, I had to change the way I conducted research. Although the social issues discussed in this chapter, like race relations, class conflict, and Brazilian history, lurked nearby, I felt that my analysis had to stay close to the roda. Only by concentrating on the experience of learning could this book shed light on why players would devote so many hours, over so many years, and suffer so much to master this art. But before readers can explore the hard lessons that shape the capoeirista, they must be aware of how larger social issues in Brazil affect capoeira and its devotees outside the roda.

THE DEVELOPMENT OF CAPOEIRA

Observers often compare capoeira to a dance, a martial art, a sport, or a fight. It incorporates elements of each. Lowell Lewis (1992: 1) describes it as a "blurred genre," borrowing a phrase from Clifford Geertz (1983). The description captures well the art's indeterminacy, as well as players' continual renegotiating of their relation while they play. A good player is judged so according to multiple, sometimes contradictory, criteria. Dominance in the roda is as much psychological and artistic as it is a question of who winds up tumbling to the floor. For this reason, an inexperienced observer may find it difficult to judge who is "winning" a game, or even to understand what players are attempting to accomplish. With no codified system for determining a victor, games are typically inconclusive. The intensity, violence, playfulness, and attention paid to aesthetic considerations vary enormously from event to event, among players, even within the same game. The ambiguity is reflected linguistically; capoeiristas most often use the verb "to play" (jogar) and the noun "game" (jogo) to describe the activity, rather than more definite terms like "sport" or "fight" (cf. Lewis 1992: 1–9).

The origins of capoeira are much debated; capoeiristas commonly believe that it came from Africa or that slaves created the art in their struggle for liberty. Practitioners and scholars point to aesthetic dimensions of the art and song texts, as well as similar traditions throughout the African diaspora, as evidence of its African origins. Whether the practice should be considered "Brazilian," "African," or "Afro-Brazilian" is a point of contention for historians, anthropologists, activists, and practitioners alike.

In Rio de Janeiro during the nineteenth century, men of many ethnic backgrounds, called *capoeiras*, formed *maltas* or gangs.[1] These gangs controlled city neighborhoods, and politicians recruited them for intimidation at election time. After the fall of the monarchy in 1889, the new republican government persecuted the maltas so severely that they disappeared (many had fought on behalf of the crown). *Capoeiragem*—their acrobatic style of fighting, often employing razor blades, knives, or clubs—was virtually eradicated from Rio de Janeiro. The cities of Rio de Janeiro, Recife, and Salvador, and the area surrounding the Bay of All Saints in the state of Bahia all supported local traditions of capoeiragem.

In contrast to Rio de Janeiro, capoeira suffered less persecution in the state of Bahia, where rodas were held in public squares during saint's day festivals into the twentieth century. Unlike the battles of Rio's street gangs, these events resembled the contemporary game, with music, ritual, and (usually) restrained play. Beginning in the 1930s, a champion capoeirista in Salvador, Bahia, Mestre Bimba, or "Teacher" Bimba (Manoel dos Reis Machado), created an innovative "modernized" version of the art, *Capoeira Regional,* which featured a systematic pedagogy and an emphasis on self-defense.[2] His students spread the style as they moved out of Salvador. Capoeira Regional gradually replaced or incorporated regional variants of capoeiragem, especially after the 1960s.

The dissemination of Capoeira Regional reached groups in Brazil that previously had hated and feared the art, and even spread overseas. Although the advent of Capoeira Regional increased the art's status, some players argued that the innovations of Regional undermined the art's traditional aesthetics, mores, and wisdom, as well as the integrity of older styles, most noticeably the Bahian form that came to be known as *Capoeira Angola.* Other observers, especially those interested in seeing capoeira recognized as a sport by the state, claimed that Capoeira Regional made older styles obsolete. The innovative style allegedly was more effective, and traditional practice had lost its martial efficacy.

At the start of the 1980s, the status of Capoeira Angola increased during a broader efflorescence of Afro-Bahian popular culture. New students took up the traditionalist Angola style in unprecedented numbers, instructors came out of retirement, and the style gained renewed prestige. Mestre Pastinha (Vicente Ferreira Pastinha), a Bahian capoeirista who died in 1981, served as a point of reference for the traditionalists. Capoeira Angola practitioners held up his teachings as a paradigm of capoeira, unaffected by Mestre Bimba and other innovators. Some adepts, especially those linked to Afrocentric cultural groups, came to value qualities associated with the Angola style such as musicality, rather than speed and efficiency as self-defense. This interest in Capoeira Angola and Africanity sparked new arguments about racism and whose practice was authentic.

The *Grupo de Capoeira Angola Pelourinho* (or GCAP, pronounced "gee-CAP-y"), named for the historic Pelourinho district of Salvador, was central to the renaissance of Capoeira Angola. The group, with whom I worked most closely, drew attention to the political importance of bodily movement styles. Its members alleged that a concern with technical "efficiency" among practitioners of Capoeira Regional concealed a profound shift in the social significance of the practice. Like other critics, they characterized the emergence of Capoeira Regional as a "whitening" or "bourgeois-ization" that emptied the art of its essential racial, spiritual, and ideological implications. These controversial criticisms provoked capoeiristas to discuss the political significance of black culture, movement styles, and variations in bodily techniques.

BLACK CULTURE IN BRAZIL

Colonial Brazil, the final destination for many of the enslaved Africans brought to the New World, became, in 1888, the last American country to outlaw slavery. Although estimates vary, Brazil probably received almost as many slaves as all of Europe's West Indian colonies combined, perhaps two-fifths of the total number that crossed the Atlantic. Brutal living conditions and low fertility chronically checked the growth of Brazil's African community. Still, scholars point out that massive slave imports left Brazil with the second largest African-descended population in the world, smaller only than that of Nigeria. This population is spread unevenly across the country, concentrated in regions, like the northeastern state Bahia, that were once the site of plantations, mines, or other slave-based industries.

Salvador, in the state of Bahia, was the colonial capital of Brazil, and its port was a center of the country's once-mighty sugar-growing economy. The city fell into decline when sugar prices collapsed and the nation's political focus migrated south, especially when the Portuguese crown relocated to Rio de Janeiro to escape Napoleon's reach. The rise of coffee and manufacturing also shifted the country's economic center south. Salvador's fortunes rebounded in the latter half of the twentieth century following the discovery of petroleum and with recent growth in tourism, but the Brazilian northeast is still wracked by chronic poverty, droughts, and persistent social problems.

The state of Bahia, and Salvador in particular, has long been a stronghold of black culture in Brazil. As many as 80 percent of all Salvador's residents claim African ancestry, most describing themselves as racially mixed. Brazilians widely consider the city one of the most "African" in their country, however, not merely because of the ancestry of its population, but also because daily life there bears the mark of African influences, especially religion, music, cuisine, and popular culture. The high concentration of nonwhites in Bahia has long been a source of prejudice against its residents; as historian Kim Butler writes, "To a Brazilian elite that understood progress in European terms, Bahia was its antithesis" (1998a: 163).

Scholars following pioneers like Melville Herskovits, Arthur Ramos, Pierre Verger, and Roger Bastide in the study of the African diaspora place the state of Bahia alongside rural Haiti and maroon communities in Suriname and Jamaica as the sites where African cultural influences are most strongly felt in the Americas. Unlike these other places, Salvador is an urban area where African practices did not merely survive, but, in some cases, attracted large followings among the city's mixed-raced and European-descended inhabitants. For instance, the most prestigious houses of Candomblé, religious devotion to West African–derived spirits called orixás, often gained upper-class patrons, who financed elaborate possession rituals and shielded the houses from persecution. In some countries, African practices survived under slavery by hiding. In Salvador, Muniz Sodré (1983) suggests, African culture often openly "seduced" its oppressors (cf. Freyre 1986a).

Cultural mixing was facilitated, no doubt, by a large group of Bahians who considered themselves to be intermediate in color between black and white.[3] Scholars, activists, and politicians have long argued about the significance of Brazil's mixed population. Some activists see mixed-race Brazilians as a legacy of exploitation because Portuguese colonizers, who were disproportionately male, raped African women. Others treat the mulatto population as a sign of a Portuguese openness; whereas northern Europeans kept their distance from Africans and abhorred intermarriage, the Portuguese allegedly treated their slaves well, even married them, according to precedent established with "Moors" from North Africa. Some Brazilians proudly point to the complex color classifications they use as a sign of their tolerance, the outward manifestation of Brazil's lack of clear color lines. More radical analysts see the proliferation of terms other than preto ("black") for dark-colored people as the effect of racial prejudice so pervasive that African-descended individuals try to claim every degree of "lightness" they can. Others suggest that the large portion of Brazil's population that claims to be intermediate between "black" and "white" is the result of modern Brazilian cultural categories that, without regard for ancestry, classify people on the basis of their appearance.[4]

Regardless of whether Brazilian slavery was more severe or humane, and whether racial relations in Brazil are better than those elsewhere, outsiders have long interpreted the absence of legalized discrimination or obvious segregation as a sign of racial harmony. Over time, many Brazilians, including some Afro-Brazilians, came to take pride in the idea that they were exceptional, avoiding racism when so many countries were beset by ethnic division, resentment, and violence. The perception was so widespread that, following World War II, UNESCO sent a team of researchers to Brazil to explore how the country had overcome racism, hoping to identify a model for the rest of the world.

The team found, however, that the situation was not quite as portrayed by glowing accounts of Brazil's "racial democracy." In nearly every important realm of everyday life—from occupational and educational achievement to marital patterns, health indices, and media stereotypes—researchers amassed evidence of inequality.[5] Although intermarriage took place, working-class neighborhoods were multiracial, and all Brazilians might lay claim to being a little African during carnival,[6] dark-skinned Brazilians clearly faced injustice and exclusion of all sorts. Brazilians, however, had what Florestan Fernandes (1969) called the "prejudice of having no prejudice"; thus they were unable to see social conditions clearly and unwilling to admit inequality. Some researchers accepted an older argument that inequality was a hangover of slavery, a question of social class rather than race. Carefully crafted studies over the following decades showed that this was not so.[7] As researchers piled up overwhelming statistical evidence from cultural studies of persistent inequality, it became increasingly difficult to defend the position that Brazil was a truly egalitarian racial paradise, or would soon become one.

MOBILIZING THE BLACK COMMUNITY

Before abolition Afro-Brazilians repeatedly organized to fight for better treatment: there were slave rebellions, *quilombos* or escaped slave communities, and even black Catholic brotherhoods that cooperated to purchase the freedom of slaves. Following abolition, black Brazilians founded newspapers and organizations, leading to the establishment of the *Frente Negra Brasileira* (Brazilian Black Front) in 1931. When Brazil's *Estado Novo* (New State) outlawed political parties in 1937, the Frente Negra disbanded.[8] With officials vehemently denying that racism existed, anyone who discussed inequality between blacks and whites was likely to be branded a racist.

Direct repression, however, was not the only impediment to large-scale mobilization. Afro-Brazilian activists often claim that the official embrace of the country's African heritage, ironically, has long been a serious obstacle. Many middle-class, white Brazilians claim that the entire country is partially African, or has "one foot in the kitchen," as a former president joked (although the same people may assert that they *personally* have only European ancestors). The most obvious manifestations of African culture in Brazil, such as cuisine, samba, and carnival, have been adopted as symbols of the Brazilian nation, making it difficult to rally around them to fight against racism (Fry 1982: 47–53). Anthropologist Roberto DaMatta (1995: 273) points out that Brazilians say that they are all black or Indian at times because the logic of Brazilian nationalism suggests that the "three races" that make up Brazil exist as complementary but inclusive. Because all Brazilians are supposedly part African, by definition, they cannot be racist.

Such "logical" arguments aside, most now acknowledge that prejudice exists; they just cannot identify it in themselves or others when they see it. A national survey, for example, revealed that 89 percent of Brazilians agreed with the statement that whites are biased against blacks, but only 10 percent admitted that they were prejudiced (Rodrigues 1995: 11). The same research revealed that fully 87 percent, including many Afro-Brazilians, held negative stereotypes or agreed with statements subtly expressing prejudice against darker Brazilians.

Another obstacle to mobilizing is the complex system of color classification that Brazilians employ, with many terms for intermediate appearances between black and white. Marvin Harris (1952), one of the anthropologists who participated in the UNESCO study, found over forty different color terms in use in one rural community. Scholars suggest that Brazilians shift how they classify a person depending on appearance, on the relation to the speaker, and on the social context (cf. Harris 1964, 1970; Sanjek 1971). Anthropologist Livio Sansone (1992), for instance, found that, during the course of a single interview, a Bahian might use several different terms to describe his or her own color in response to different questions.[9]

Uniting all those of African descent—many of whom do not classify themselves as black—has proven difficult for antiracist groups (Hanchard 1994; Burdick 1998: 5; cf. Barcelos 1999; Marx 1998; Winant 1994). As Michael Hanchard (1999: 7) put it, "how does one spawn a movement based not only on a recognition of racial inequality, but also on a common racial identity in a society where there is presumably no such thing?" In contrast to the United States, where a "one-drop rule" classifies anyone with a single African ancestor as black and banishes all ambiguity, and legal segregation presented clear injustice against which to mobilize, the Brazilian system produced fluidity and ambivalence. With no clear-cut legal prejudice, no apartheid, no Jim Crow laws, and at least superficial celebration of African cultural contributions, one of the greatest challenges facing activists in Brazil has simply been the construction of a meaningful black identity. Getting traction in what Rebecca Reichmann (1999: 5) has referred to as the "shifting sands" of Brazilian racial identity continues to be a daunting challenge for activists (cf. Telles 1999).[10]

Michael Hanchard (1993, 1994: 99–141) warns of the dangers of "culturalism" when Afro-Brazilian organizations become so focused on celebrating African identity, music, and fashion that they lose sight of overarching political goals. Afro-Brazilian groups that are primarily political or activist, however, tend to remain small (cf. Crook and Johnson 1999). Cultural practices, like funk dances and Afrocentric carnival groups, seem to be the most effective way to rally large numbers of supporters. Popular culture movements have accumulated immense followings around symbols of black identity, both homegrown and imported, such as North American soul music, hair styles, new names for children, black pride rhetoric, reggae music, and Rastafarian fashion.[11] Political groups such as the MNU, or *Movimento Negro Unificado* (Unified Black Movement), appeal primarily to intellectuals and well-off members of Brazil's black community. Afrocentric carnival groups and explicitly black aesthetic movements, such as Black Soul in Rio, have more widespread appeal and, perhaps, greater influence over the long term.[12]

The revival of interest in Capoeira Angola in the 1980s, for example, can be understood only in relation to Salvador's carnival groups. With the country still under a military regime, *Ilê-Aiyê* was formed in 1974, the first *bloco Afro*, or "Afro" carnival group, in the historically black neighborhood of Liberdade. The controversial carnival organization took explicitly African themes for its musical compositions, paraded in African-inspired costumes, and advocated racial pride. Initially, the group provoked accusations of racism for excluding light-skinned participants and promoting Afrocentric themes. Over time, however, Ilê-Aiyê, as well as other blocos Afro such as the world-renowned *Grupo Cultural Olodum*, have become cultural fixtures in Salvador's carnival. They now feature prominently in Salvador's global promotion as a tourist destination, in spite of the Afrocentric groups' critical postures on a range of social issues (see Dunn 1992; Perrone 1992; Crook 1993; Vianna 1999: 100–106). The success of the carnival groups, and their grassroots outreach programs such as schools and neighborhood organization, encouraged a broader re-Africanization in Bahian music, fashion, arts, and popular culture, including capoeira (Risério 1981: 13; cf. 1999).[13] Although critics are quick to point out that the celebration of Africanity has not translated into increased political representation or marked economic gain for Afro-Brazilians, the change is impossible to ignore. If the dominant classes were once embarrassed by Salvador's African traditions, they now celebrate them with costly statues, in glossy brochures, and in their own political campaigns. For many Afro-Brazilians in Bahia, black culture has become both a full-time occupation and a medicine they hope will remedy the country's persistent racism.

However, even some members of Bahia's black culture movement seem vaguely uneasy with capoeira. Clearly, capoeira rodas are what Livio Sansone (1992: 162–163; cf. 1997) calls a "black space," a sphere where dark skin *may* grant a special legitimacy (cf. Rolnik 1989; Fry 1995). But capoeira now serves as a national symbol, part of the denial that racism exists; middle-class groups suggest that their acceptance of the art demonstrates that they are open and unprejudiced (see Yúdice 1994). In criticizing the symbols used to hide racism, many activists also reject cultural forms like samba and capoeira. These activists—ironically, much like condescending members of Brazil's dominant groups—consider capoeira to be merely *folclore*, a remnant of an idealized past used in the service of nationalism. Unlike the songs of carnival groups like Ilê-Aiyê or Olodum, for example, traditional capoeira songs do not seem to carry overt messages of racial pride or unity. Quite the contrary, some celebrate internecine conflict within the black community. The art is universally recognized as African derived, but it is also associated with street crime and violence. Although a GCAP poster claimed capoeira as Brazil's "first black movement," playing off the name of the Unified Black Movement, many activists worry that the art feeds into long-held stereotypes of Afro-Brazilians.

GCAP vigorously argued that capoeira was, in fact, an important part of the political movement against racism. The group advocated capoeira as a way to unify the Afro-Brazilian community, to teach discipline to its young people, and to pave the way for a more just social order. Yet this antiracist political agenda, however crucial to GCAP members and to Brazil's future, seemed to leave out important elements of the art I was learning. The large-scale social impact of capoeira practice might be to diminish prejudice, but the everyday influence of the art on practitioners was much more subtle, complex, and multifaceted.

RESISTING SOCIOLOGY, STRUCTURES, AND SYMBOLS

Tacit norms in the capoeira roda prohibit players from using some of the most common tactics in martial arts, or responding in ways that appear obvious in fighting or sport. These restrictions encourage participants to do the unexpected and to develop abilities that would otherwise be unnecessary. For example, confronted with a virtual ban on striking with the hands, capoeiristas create a universe of kicks and head butts. Barred from grabbing an adversary, leaving a confined playing area, or blocking an attack, adepts learn extraordinary evasive maneuvers, executing them acrobatically even in close quarters. Forgoing the obvious and creating artificial obstacles forces a capoeirista to develop cunning, creativity, and flexibility.

In some sense, this book is a result of a similar, confining set of self-imposed challenges: to discuss the experience of learning capoeira at a personal, experiential level. For this reason, readers familiar with anthropology will find many of the following terms, which orient our discipline today, largely missing after this chapter: *identity, symbol, representation, structure, discourse, imaginary, cultural logic, context, economy, politics, resistance,* and even *culture,* whenever possible. These concepts are clearly useful if one wishes to understand social phenomena of all sorts, including capoeira; the best accounts of the art in English, such as those by Barbara Browning (1995) and Lowell Lewis (1992, 1995), use them.

Many of these concepts, however, can lead ethnographers far away from everyday life and their own perceptions. The terms have a momentum of their own, and they are liable to lead a reader away from the roda, halting the analysis of capoeira practice and its effects at the individual level. These terms try to explain what is immediate by referring to social, political, historical, or symbolic realms that are far more difficult, if not impossible, to observe directly. The story about African influences and race relations in Brazil, for example, although it may be intellectually compelling, remains largely invisible in everyday life. Writing this discussion required layers of academic texts. One need not know this history, however, to feel palpably the weight of race and the traces of African influences in Salvador. Although the history helps us to understand the source of traditions, it may not illuminate very well how they are lived. Although we may learn that racism originated in slavery, for example, we do not know better how racism feels, how people get classified, or how people are affected by encounters with prejudice.

When I first traveled to Brazil, I hoped to show how debates about capoeira styles were related to larger social conflicts there. But day-to-day life in capoeira academies was devoted to the practice itself.

Students struggled to develop proficiency; players tried to figure out how to do movements they liked; and teachers worried about how they might better help their students to learn the art, or grew disappointed when their efforts went awry. When I proposed to study capoeira more than a decade ago, I treated it as a performance to analyze, as if the game were a symbolic text or a manifestation of larger social forces. The closer I came to the art, the less comfortable I felt ignoring what was most important to practitioners: learning it, teaching it, and developing their abilities. Players and teachers treated capoeira like an open-ended project, one that required them to retool continuously the way that they carried themselves. I had imagined capoeira would be about self-definition in relation to society or declaring allegiance to a group; instead, it is about perception, interaction, and skill, what players want to do, the habits they hope to break, and how training might affect each individual. The challenge of becoming a capoeirista, as well as my colleagues' enthusiasm, quickly drew me in as I struggled alongside them to learn.

Debates about the social meaning of style or whether a practice was truly traditional—ideal material for social analysis—paralleled an even more heated discussion: how did diverse training techniques affect the game and a player's everyday behavior? Practitioners were concerned with the proper form of training not merely because they sought to preserve a "right" form of the art. They believed deeply that the discipline's effects on the devotee varied depending on how the art was performed, including details that might seem inconsequential to an outsider. When they sang about capoeira's history, complained about how other groups did the art, or discussed what a ritual signified, they tried to affect play, or were indicating sensual qualities of the game, a player's style, or how a gesture was performed. For example, when they talked about how a certain style was "modern" or "whitened," they were using terms that referred to palpable qualities in the movements and music. The techniques might, in fact, be quite old or performed by dark-skinned Brazilians. Instructors' pedagogical reflections and debates about style, together with observations and my own apprenticeship, provided avenues to develop a phenomenology of the bodily transformations brought about by capoeira.

A PHENOMENOLOGICAL TURN IN ETHNOGRAPHY

Phenomenology is the study of experience, of how things appear in consciousness, and what contributes to making them appear the way that they do. This varied school of thought emerged in European philosophy during the twentieth century, exemplified in such diverse writers as Edmund Husserl, Martin Heidegger, Jean-Paul Sartre, Simone de Beauvoir, and Maurice Merleau-Ponty. Although these thinkers disagreed on a host of issues, all wrote that to understand how objects in our consciousness come to appear as they do, it was necessary to step away from familiar, abstract modes of thought. Temporarily "bracketing" or suspending our everyday assumptions about the nature of reality might allow us to more acutely notice how things appeared. In the process, we could better understand how we come to know anything, or to *be* in the distinct way that we exist.

Capoeiristas claimed that how one experiences things like social interaction and life in the streets could be affected by skills and styles of acting. They implied that perception could be trained and that people's experiences of the world might differ widely. Wizened instructors insisted that they saw differently because of their training, knew how to hear things others did not, and inhabited their bodies in distinctive ways. Trying to understand how experience itself might vary—before it was labeled or interpreted or talked about—I found that other anthropologists facing similar challenges had brought phenomenological philosophy to bear on ethnographic research. Anthropologists such as Thomas Csordas, Robert Desjarlais, Michael Jackson, William Hanks, Tim Ingold, and James Weiner had explored experience in various settings, speculating about how a specific set of cultural practices might affect fundamental dimensions of the way we perceive everyday life.[14] This book follows in their footsteps, providing what I hope will be an accessible, compelling, intentionally one-sided ethnography—that single side being a phenomenological one—that will inspire students, anthropologists, and capoeira practitioners alike to think more deeply about how experience might be shaped by physical training.

Any work that attempts to bridge a gap between intellectual disciplines (and the chasm between contemporary ethnography and phenomenology is not small) must strive hard to be accessible. Some technical specificity will be sacrificed in the effort. Just as anthropologists may find our contemporary lexicon used sparingly in this book, a reader conversant in phenomenology will also find that the text rarely uses its specialized, technically sophisticated language. Phenomenological terminology can sometimes appear mystical to the uninitiated reader. Phenomenological thinkers have a long tradition of standing common words on their heads in the effort to return "to the things themselves," as Edmund Husserl famously advocated. If a reader becomes interested in phenomenology, the endnotes provide sites to explore the philosophers who inspired this analysis. This book intends to show a distinctive contribution that a phenomenological approach might make to anthropology without exhaustively explaining it.

In moving toward "the things themselves"—in this case, cartwheels, kicks, rhythms, songs, exercises, and rituals—and focusing on how they affect the practitioner, this ethnography swims across strong currents in contemporary cultural anthropology. For many anthropologists, ethnographic analysis must *not* simply be content with the appearance of "things themselves"; this is merely superficial description, not analysis. Rather they explore the "meaning" or social importance of any cultural practice. Typically, this significance is not immediately present in appearances. Instead, what anthropologists find before themselves is seen as a reference to deeper ideas, a cultural product of an underlying structure, a projection of economic arrangements, or the local signs of a larger political struggle. For some forms of cultural analysis, the crowning achievement of study is not to capture the "things themselves" in their peculiar immediacy. The palpable surface of everyday life is treated like a thin skin spread over deeper phenomena. These anthropologists diligently work to uncover hidden structures, or to follow threads of meaning that link what is before them to more distant ideas in webs of references.[15]

I was once convinced that cultural anthropology was the study of meaning-making; it was how I explained my discipline to nonanthropologists. Capoeira convinced me that to understand human differences, especially varieties of experience, I had to be ready to let go of the assumption that experiential reality was made *entirely* of "meaning." Clearly, we encounter symbols in everyday life, and some events and modes of perceiving can lead us to refer to things that are not present. But not *all* experience is made of reference, symbol, or discourse, nor do we require meaning to experience all things that we do. The classic example of this in philosophy is pain: it might be made meaningful, but one will certainly not remain numb to it simply because it is meaningless. Stretching the word "meaning" to say that immediate experience has something like "embodied meaning" needlessly distorts the object of study, assuming that it is like a symbol when it might not be. To treat all of culture under the banner of "meaning," as if daily life became perceivable only because we constantly looked up definitions or recalled other experiences, flattens the lived world as though a film of representation lay between us and everything perceptible.

This book, then, is emphatically *not about meaning*, if meaning is understood to be references, symbolic significance, or discursive sense. Rather, it is about training, perceptions, appearances, behavior, and their effects—sometimes phenomenological, physiological, or even neurological. Meaning comes into play, and symbols certainly influence experience, such as the way that singing affects how the game of capoeira feels. But if some forms of anthropological analysis look from the *outside in* at a practice like capoeira, seeing it as reflecting a broader context, this book looks from the *inside out*, asking how the world looks after one has spent enough time in the roda.

When capoeiristas talked about history, race, class, or tradition, capoeira had shaped their understandings, what they disclosed to me about their everyday experience, or how they sought to influence my perceptions. Instead of the world being made of language, for example, my fellow capoeiristas used words, including what resembled social analysis, to share what they perceived. Some sought to help me to see the world as they did, and coached me to walk, look, and hold myself like a capoeirista. They trained my body, let me join in their games, and struggled to share their feelings and skills. They were so eloquent at times that their words were poetry that called me to live alongside them and play in the roda.

PLAN OF THE BOOK

The first part of the book, "Learning," examines the apprenticeship process through which capoeiristas develop the skills that they bring to the roda. Chapter Two continues the discussion of phenomenology that started in this chapter, specifically considering the importance of bodily training in shaping our perceptions and comportment. Chapter Three examines capoeira education, exercises, and teaching arrangements, and discusses the group with which I trained. In addition, since apprenticeship served as my primary research method, this chapter asks how ethnographic research might be adapted to environments like a capoeira academy, where the researcher is not the only person trying to learn new skills.

The second section, "Remembering," describes how practitioners evoke the origin and development of capoeira. Chapter Four presents two framings of the art's history: the first as an epic of lawlessness and fighting prowess, and the second as a long saga of resistance to slavery, oppression, and racial prejudice. The chapter reflects upon how shared historical "memories" affect the experience of playing and simultaneously express dimensions of contemporary experience. Chapter Five examines how the violent past is invoked in song at the same time that singing moderates the game—calming the overexcited, goading the lackadaisical, and playing humorously with the participants.

The third part of the book, "Playing," analyzes the most important forum for demonstrating capoeira prowess: the roda. Chapter Six describes instrumental music. Capoeira training includes an apprenticeship in listening that inflects how adepts hear the berimbau, the art's most distinctive instrument. Chapter Seven considers how ritual sequences and gestures in the roda create tension by implying that the techniques of capoeiristas hold the potential for sinister violence. This section argues that phenomenological analysis may allow us to better understand the compelling ambivalence of capoeira "play."

How capoeira training might affect a devoted student's everyday comportment and perceptions is the subject of the fourth part, "Habits." Chapter Eight discusses malícia, or cunning, and how capoeiristas understand its relationship to the art's swaying movement style. How a growing awareness of vulnerability is instilled in students is discussed in Chapter Nine, as well as players' attempts to "close" their bodies against attack. Players allegedly take the comportment and composure they develop in the roda out into their daily lives. Chapter Ten specifically considers how this might occur, using as examples secrecy, wariness, and techniques for seeing.

The fifth part, "Changes," looks at the ways in which capoeira styles have developed in the recent past, specifically at accusations that some styles have become "whitened" (embranquecido) and assertions that doing traditional Capoeira Angola might raise political consciousness. Both the final chapters discuss how sociological changes in style, allegedly brought about by shifts in the community playing, reveal how players experience the game. A conflict arises when students attempt to move in ways that violate the learned inhibitions they have developed over their lives.

Training a person to play capoeira, ideally, transforms the student's visceral sense of self and the way he or she sees the world. Capoeira is not unique in this regard. On the contrary, different bodily training regimens, in a range of places, shape how people move, perceive, and carry themselves. Physical education for perception is a crucial foundation for every way of living in the world. This book seeks to show that culture does not stop at the skin, nor does it reside solely in the mind. Taking seriously how different ways of standing, moving, and acting animate us, inform our perceptions, and enliven our sense of ourselves requires an emphatically embodied form of anthropology.

2 THE SIGNIFICANCE OF SKILLS

To play capoeira, novices must master many techniques: acrobatic kicks, deceptive feints, powerful head butts, dynamic handstands, spectacular cartwheels, and slippery evasive maneuvers. Adepts learn the choral responses to traditional songs and become proficient with several musical instruments; in the process, they incorporate the art's rhythms so deeply that they dance beautifully when they play, however heated competition becomes. Ideally, players develop an aesthetic sensibility as well so that, when they lead the music and singing, they choose songs that enrich the game. In learning to anticipate another player's attacks, novices become acutely sensitive to an adversary's movements and aware of their own bodies' vulnerabilities. Adepts also acquire a theatrical sense, learning to judge how their interactions appear to an audience. They use dramatic gestures, ritual sequences, and physical humor to make performances entertaining. Although outside observers understandably are fascinated by the uncanny abilities of veteran players, studying capoeira from the perspective of practitioners means recognizing the awkwardness and challenges that they have overcome on the way to developing skills.

Apprenticeship can be a lengthy process. Many masters of capoeira claim that one never stops refining one's abilities.

The game demands many talents, but adepts often assert that a student does not simply learn an isolated body of skills. New bodily techniques must be coupled to the perceptual abilities that tell a player when and how to use them. Although novices may practice actions in isolation, players are quick to point out that a technique is not really mastered if a person cannot draw on it while playing. In a sense, movement must change from being the goal of devoted training into the means through which a capoeirista can interact, as practice makes proficiency.

The art transforms students. The skills they learn ostensibly affect how they conduct themselves and perceive the world outside the roda's confines. Players become new sorts of social, experiential, and physical actors: capoeiristas. The art is a way of life for the truly devoted. Author and practitioner Cesar Barbieri (1993), for example, titled his book about capoeira *A Brazilian Way of Learning to Be*. Ubirajara Almeida (Mestre Acordeon) likewise writes: "Capoeira is not an outfit that we wear in certain moments or for special occasions. Capoeira is our own skin. It is with us at every moment" (1999: 93). Adepts who wear capoeira as their skin and embody the art fully have a characteristic appearance and what Brazilians refer to as a *jeito*, a "way"—a distinguishing savvy and flair evident even in the way they walk. This chapter examines how capoeira affects a student by reflecting on the relation between students' bodies, training, and how adepts experience the world.

A CAPOEIRA CLASS

Training sessions with the Grupo de Capoeira Angola Pelourinho usually lasted an hour and a half. They were led by one of the group's *contramestres* ("foremen," or assistant teachers)—Valmir, Boca do Rio, Poloca, Pepeu, or Paulinha, the only woman contramestre—or by our mestre, Pedro Moraes Trindade, whom we called Mestre Moraes. Three or four days each week, the group came together in an upstairs room of the slowly decaying Forte de Santo Antonio Além do Carmo in Salvador's historic district to learn and play Capoeira Angola. The small fort had once defended the city from the Dutch, later serving as a prison before being converted into a center for popular culture. A couple of dozen adult students assembled after work (children trained during the day), changing into tennis shoes, black pants, and yellow T-shirts silk-screened with the group's logo.[1]

The classes always began the same way; the instructor shouted, *Gingando!* We all started to *ginga*, from the verb *gingar*, meaning "to sway" or "to rock" like a wave, the basis of the game's movement. Although the ginga is initially learned as a simple four-count box step, we were encouraged to vary it until little remained of the original pattern except its sinewy texture. As the students grew warm and loose, variations in the ginga became more elaborate. Unlike some academies I visited, in GCAP we did not do the basic step in unison; only if a technique like a cartwheel could lead us to collide did we do it together. Instead, students varied their rhythms at will, and the class became a seething laboratory for movement. Each student had to remain constantly aware of the surrounding space to prevent collisions and to thwart surprise attacks. A student might stray close to a neighbor just to

Pairs of students train together at the Grupo de Capoeira Angola Pelourinho—a laboratory for learning movement. (Photo by C. Peçanha)

test the colleague's level of wariness. Even while practicing, we had to remain on guard.

The instructor then called out to change the basic exercise, making the swarm of movement a little less chaotic, as students all tried similar techniques at their own pace. Our instructor might shout, *Embaixo!* (Below!), sending us into very low gingas, knees deeply bent and bodies stooped to beneath waist level. Or the drill leader might tell us to *Quebra!* (Break!) our gingas to encourage us to interrupt the regular rhythm of stepping with sudden pauses or syncopated steps. The exercises changed without stopping—anyone that paused was chastised: *Embora!* (Move it!).

With the simple directions *Isso... isso... isso...* (This... this... this...), an instructor might demonstrate a sequence of moves; we were to imitate the combination, making our own variations in timing and technique. Or our teacher might shout the name of a movement. An instructor might hold us in a negativa, like a push-up turned sideways and frozen at its lowest point, to strengthen our arms, or might simply do a kick, the whole class moving to "escape" it. Once we got started, our instructors checked students individually. They moved through the practice area, offered criticism ("Keep your head down," "You're wide open!"), and sometimes tested a technique by performing a possible counterpart—swinging a kick low over a *rolê*, or sideways roll, or providing their own bodies as a target for a student practicing a backward *chapa* kick.

Our teachers typically encouraged us to move deliberately, perfecting our balance and technique. A novice quickly discovered that slowly executing movements improved one's form. The unhurried pace exacerbated any flaw; only obvious strain could compensate for an imbalance in a leisurely cartwheel or in an excruciatingly slow "stingray's tail" kick. Our instructors intentionally tortured players who were visibly using force instead of proper form, repeating a drill until muscles grew too tired to cover for their errors. Only by learning how to sense when our bodies were in the right positions could we do these movements fluidly and effortlessly. In response to this training, our bodies adapted. My muscles strengthened and stretched, I lost weight, and distinctive calluses formed on my palms, just below my middle finger. Using my hands like feet on the hard concrete floor of the training area gradually left its mark.

Later in the class, the students might pair off to play variants of the game. Sometimes we executed elaborately choreographed exchanges of *golpes* (strikes) and *saidas* ("escapes" or evasive maneuvers). A sequence might include the players trading *tesouras*, for instance, a leg "scissors" in

Mestre Bobó (standing) defending himself after doing a tesoura, *or "scissors." His adversary slid between his legs and counterattacked with a heel kick. Seated in the first row on the far right is Mestre Curió.   (Photo by C. Peçanha)*

which an attacker slid along the floor to trap an adversary between scissoring legs. The target could escape by cartwheeling over the outstretched legs or by sliding even lower under them. Or we might be forced to play a variant of the *jogo de dentro*, the "inside game," in which we had to keep one hand on the ground at all times. The arbitrary limit kept us closer to the ground, making interaction even more grueling. After most classes, I pulled off my sweat-soaked uniform, satisfied simply to have endured another training session without keeling over from fatigue.

All this training prepared us for rodas held every Saturday night and every other Sunday afternoon. These were our chances to play using all the techniques we learned. A roda typically lasted two hours, and although our teachers might play several times, a student could expect to play only one or two games. Even if the hours had been divided evenly, with two dozen players present—and there were sometimes more—a student could expect to play only ten minutes for every two hours spent in the roda. The rest of the time one sang or played an instrument. Unless students ignored teachers' disapproval and played elsewhere (as I did), they might spend less than twenty minutes in the roda all week. Although other groups played more often, holding brief rodas at the end of every session, all schools spent far more time training than playing. Understanding capoeira as practitioners experience it requires paying at least as much attention to training as to the moments when that training is put to the test.

SKILL AND SENSITIVITY

As students become more proficient, capoeira affects how their bodies function: muscles grow stronger and more limber, tendons lengthen, breathing becomes easier, endurance increases, and techniques can be executed with greater and greater speed. But more importantly, students develop movement skills as they play in the roda. They repeat the techniques of the game over and over again to become fluent. Movements that once demanded their complete concentration become a repertoire of reactions summoned instinctually, almost unconsciously, in response to an adversary's actions (cf. Wacquant 2004). Examining this change—how an awkward task becomes, over time, a basis for acting—helps us to grasp the peculiar dexterity that capoeiristas develop.

Typically, to learn a new technique, a player first watches it and then tries to imitate it. For some of the simpler movements, especially those resembling everyday actions, the initial attempt may closely resemble its model. But for many techniques, especially those that demand completely alien motions, odd postures, or new uses for limbs, novices often

badly flub their first tentative attempts. Instructors may break a movement into steps, dividing a fluid whole into a series of stages or target
postures. New students follow haltingly, seemingly at odds with their
own bodies, sometimes unaware when they are in the wrong position.
They struggle to control their myriad body parts all at once. Or they
focus on one piece at a time, trying to pick out crucial elements at critical
moments: "keep your head down, look between your legs, hands flat on
the floor, rotate on your foot, kick with your heel ... no, *no*, the *other* foot!"

In his phenomenological study of embodiment, Drew Leder (1990:
30–32) describes how learning any skill often means treating one's own
body as if it were an object to be manipulated. For instance, the leg that
a moment ago carried a person effortlessly around the room suddenly
must be positioned consciously: where the foot is placed, how deeply
the knee is bent, whether the hip is twisting, all demand attention.
Learning the skill means that this explicit awareness is gradually ef-
faced, and the practitioner becomes *less* focused on the body. The better
we know how to perform a skill, the more unaware of it we become: "A
skill is finally and fully learned when something that was extrinsic,
grasped only through explicit rules or examples, now comes to pervade
my own corporeality" (ibid. 31).[2]

Even though skills are usually learned through repetition, neurosci-
entist Nicholai Bernstein warns that "it is wrong to consider a motor
skill as an imprint or a trace somewhere in the brain" as if it were a
"motor formula or a motor cliché" (1996: 180–181). Bernstein argues that
repetitive exercises do not lead to the acquisition of skill because they
produce constant, repetitive actions. Instead,

> *Repetitions* of a movement or action are necessary in order to *solve a
> motor problem* many times (better and better) and *to find the best ways* of
> solving it. Repetitive solutions of a problem are also necessary be-
> cause, in natural conditions, external conditions never repeat them-
> selves and the course of the movement is never ideally reproduced.
> Consequently, it is necessary *to gain experience relevant to all various
> modifications* of a task, primarily, to all the impressions that underlie
> the sensory corrections of a movement. (ibid.: 176, emphasis in the
> original)

Because conditions change, accomplishing what appears to be a similar
movement requires constant self-monitoring and ongoing readjustment
rather than flawless repetition.[3] For example, to do the "same" *aú*, or
cartwheel, players may have to adjust for numerous reasons: fatigue,
moving more or less quickly at the start, a change in hand placement

that shifts the balancing point, an incline in the floor, or a slight difference in the initial jump. Skillful action depends upon astute perception of relevant information about the body's position and an ability to compensate that can only be learned by varying the action in training, not by perfect repetition. My instructors in GCAP seemed to recognize this and encouraged students to avoid "robot capoeira," that is, repeating any movements too uniformly. Far from being regarded as skillful, too-faithful repetition was considered dreadfully boring, counterproductive for learning, and anathema to a cunning game.

Learning the aú, then, actually requires being able to produce an infinite variety of variations, appropriate in different situations. When we did a cartwheel in the roda, for example, our instructors warned us that we had to be ready to stop or change direction, instantly, at any point. If we were attacked, we might have to sink into a headstand or fall backward into a "bridge" to roll away. We might have to abruptly truncate the cartwheel's trajectory if near the edge of the roda, turn to keep sight of a fast-moving opponent, leap far to avoid a "scissors," or even launch toward an adversary if we spotted an opportune moment to attack. Dexterity, in Bernstein's (ibid.: 21) words, was the ability to rapidly find a motor solution to "unexpected, unique complications in the external situation." This dexterity made the aú more than just a single move; it became a realm of movement possibilities that could be mobilized to suit situations that arose in the roda. A player cannot perceive whether an action is right, or how to adjust to any of the myriad things that might require accommodation, before he or she gets the "feel" of the accompanying movement. Learning a physical skill requires that one develop both the necessary body techniques, robust and modifiable, and the sensory skills that they depend upon.

In addition, a player has to develop perceptual abilities to know *when* to execute the technique. For example, tripping an adversary requires the skill to do a *rasteira*, a leg sweep, as well as the acuity to read quickly an adversary's positioning and anticipate a kick that will leave the supporting leg vulnerable to being swept. Tim Ingold (2000: 353) points out that a skill resides in the relation a person comes to perceive with the environment, recognizing the opportunities this relation presents, and possessing the active response patterns to make use of them (cf. Ostrow 1990: 11). Without perceptual skill, an untrained person cannot exploit the vulnerability in a posture. As Ingold puts it, "progress from clumsiness to dexterity . . . is brought about not by way of an internalisation of rules and representations, but through the gradual attunement of movement and perception" (2000: 357).

In the Grupo de Capoeira Angola Pelourinho, Mestre João Pequeno catches another capoeirista with a well-timed rasteira, or leg sweep. But the victim, on the left, is already counterattacking by stamping toward the attacker's leg. (Photo by C. Peçanha)

For this reason, many capoeira exercises seem to train perceptual skills and bodily reflexes as much as they develop movement techniques. A head butt or *cabeçada*, for example, is a simple movement. Perceiving a vulnerability sufficiently in advance that a player can exploit it, and launching the head butt before an adversary can counter it, however, demands the acuity of a virtuoso. Players practice choreographed sequences of attacks, escapes, and counterattacks in pairs, but not so that they will automatically perform these sequences during the game; if they do mindlessly repeat them, an instructor is liable to deride them for unimaginative, mechanical play. Rather, capoeiristas train their dispositions so that they will perceive an adversary's vulnerabilities in motion, respond swiftly, avoid attacks, adjust their positions, and counterattack—all in virtually the same movements. According to Mestre Itapoan (R. Almeida 1994b: 83), the objective of training sequences in Mestre Bimba's academy, for example, was to create a "consciousness in the student" of the necessity to respond to any attack by first avoiding it and then initiating a counterattack. An adversary's precarious balance when kicking too high, ribs left open when vacillating in the midst of a kick, an unguarded belly when moving too quickly to a cartwheel—all are sensed acutely by a veteran as opportunities, and the perception invites a trained response.

LEARNING TO WALK

Capoeiristas are convinced that when they learn how to perceive another player's vulnerabilities, dodge under a benção or "blessing" kick, or counterattack into an oncoming "hammer" kick with a perfectly timed head butt, they are acquiring skills that bleed over into everyday life. They are reshaping their comportment until capoeira becomes their skin, as Mestre Acordeon put it. To make sense of these claims, it's important to consider the role of a person's body in shaping his or her sense of everyday life.

Western thought is often said to be marked by a strong "mind–body dualism," that is, a propensity to see the body and mind as separate, even antagonistic forces, which makes the relation of our own bodies to our thoughts difficult to grasp. In recent decades, scholars in disciplines ranging from anthropology, philosophy, and the arts to medicine, neuroscience, and psychology have increasingly argued that only by taking embodiment into account can we understand how people think, perceive, and behave.[4] Our bodies are the foundation of our thoughts, providing the physical site for thinking as well as experience that shapes our understanding. Many scholars have not been sensitive, however, to the fact that varied training regimens can shape radically different styles of embodiment. Physical education, broadly understood, may take hold of people's bodies and transform how they are inhabited. Capoeiristas suggest that the art they practice does just that.

For example, in a newspaper column provoked by the christening of a school in honor of Mestre Pastinha, folklorist and anthropologist Ordep Serra (1988) reminisced about his first lesson as Pastinha's student. His column focused on how ambitious instruction can aspire to reshape a student's style of embodiment down to the simplest everyday movements. Serra writes:

> I still remember the first time that I went to the academy as a student. After I paid a little informal acceptance fee to matriculate, the mestre ordered me to "do one lap" around the studio. . . . As a mere spectator in that same place, I had already watched the exhibitions and exercises of the capoeiristas many times. I knew that there was a moment in the game in which the contenders jogged in a circle, as if in a little race where they pursued each other. The pace is quick, and it always ends with some type of strike, a surprise attack, a counterattack, or a small,

semi-ritualized trap. Instead, the mestre recommended to me that I walk normally, and he remained there observing, sitting on his bench with a subtle smile on his lips. I obeyed, a little tactlessly and unenthusiastically. At the end, he told me to stop and asked:
"How old are you, son?"
"Eighteen," I responded.
"That's good. It's about time for you to learn to walk!"
It was his first lesson, one that I did not understand soon, totally. . . . Only much later did I realize that one of the most refined secrets of capoeira is made concrete in the walk, a secret that a perfect naturalness and a certain nonchalance hides quite well. In truth, when one succeeds in building into routine movements the profound rhythm, the concealed electricity, a flexible readiness for the unexpected, the whole art ripened. . . .
From the manner in which Mestre Pastinha spoke, I had the half-magical impression that the exercises of apprenticeship were a species of invocation, a call. If I would exert myself, capoeira would reveal itself in the end, as though emerging, luminous, from the fibers of my body.

The secret of capoeira, Serra suggests, actually lies outside the bounds of the roda, as he puts it, "made concrete in the walk," when routine movements were suffused with the "profound rhythm" developed in training. Serra describes how the art's exercises provoked his body to change. Because perception is grounded in the body and its behavior, teaching a person how to walk anew—that is, retraining basic styles of moving and habits—might conceivably have the far-reaching effects on everyday life that adepts like Serra describe.

THE BODY'S ROLE IN EXPERIENCE

The world provides more sensations than we can possibly perceive, infinite perspectives from which we might approach it, and countless standards that we might use to take its measure. Our bodies structure what we perceive. We have two eyes on the same side of our head, so we see only what is in front of us. We can hear what is behind us, so anything that happens in this half of the world may exist as sound, but not in the realm of sight. When we are provoked by a loud noise to spin around, what was once the center of our visual world slips beyond its borders.

We hear vibrations in the air within a specific range of frequency and intensity, so a dog whistle or distant whisper is inaudible. We walk upright, pushing against gravity, so "down" and "up" have basic, existential significance for us. "Down" and "up" become important cognitive categories (see Johnson 1987), and we must also learn to take gravity and verticality into account if we are to accomplish even the simplest tasks (see Berthoz 2000). Our bodies provide the scale of our world; without technological enhancement, we can perceive things only in certain proportion to ourselves, nothing too enormous or too minuscule. The same stairway may be a point of access or an obstacle depending upon how our size, strength, and mobility take its measure.

But the lived world, that is, the world as we experience it, is not shaped merely by the gross limits on our anatomy (which may themselves be altered by training or technology[5]). Our sensual worlds are, more importantly, shaped and imbued with corporeal sense through our actions, habits, and potential interactions with what we perceive. Drew Leder offers examples of how our potential for action—what phenomenologists call *motility*—affects how things appear: "We see chairs that offer up the prospect of rest, food that may be eaten, a cold rain that bids us stay inside. The sensory world thus involves a constant reference to our possibilities of active response" (1990: 17–18).[6] A person's possibilities for action help generate the primary qualities of things in the sensed world. Leder thus describes the body as "first and foremost not a located thing, but a path of access, a being-in-the-world" (ibid.: 21). Along similar lines, Merleau-Ponty suggests that the ability and compulsion to engage actively in the world imparts significance that underlies, and even precedes, conscious thought: "Consciousness is in the first place not a matter of 'I think that' but of 'I can'" (1962: 137).[7]

The ways we can interact with the lived world color it even when we don't actually act. Tools offer possibilities to those who know how to use them, printed texts for those who can read them; even when we choose not to take advantage of those options, they define objects for us in an immediate sense. A chair remains, to experience, a potential place to sit even though the stack of books that accumulates on it over months may slowly erode my recognition that this option remains.[8] For this reason, our actual interactions with the sense world do not alone shape how we sense it; as Merleau-Ponty describes, "the normal person *reckons with* the possible" (1962: 109, emphasis in the original). The body's potential for engagement undergirds the experiential world, providing a constant reference for perception, a basis for patterns of interaction, and a crucial, albeit often unexamined, element in our sense of self and others (cf. Ostrow 1990; Young 1990; Behnke 1997b; Weiss 1999).[9]

If our perceptions are based upon our habits and skills, as this discussion suggests, most of us will recognize immediately that this corporeal point of reference can differ widely. Marcel Mauss (1973) long ago pointed out that the "techniques of the body" vary across cultures, even for such basic tasks as walking, spitting, eating, sleeping, swimming, climbing, or having sex. A mat that my body may read as "to-walk-across-and-wipe-my-feet" might read in someone else's perception as "place-to-put-shoes-after-taking-them-off" or even "place-to-sit-and-relax." A plumber's tools, a painter's brushes, or a trombonist's instrument may call out to their hands, but mine are deaf to their summons. For a skateboarder, a stairway railing or concrete bench might offer palpable opportunities for physical sensations that thrill them, even though a nonskateboarder is numb to their potential existence. Across cultures, the gaps may be even greater. Although perception is bodily based, it is clearly not biologically determined, genetically predestined, universally shared, or "natural."[10]

Even though anthropologists widely recognize that differences in techniques of the body exist, they do not tend to take account of them when they discuss sense experience. They seem to assume that the senses are untouched by differences in the body's uses. Only our "interpretations" of experiences or the "meaning" of a sense varies, these approaches suggest, not the way our organs take in information, or how behavior can shape what gets sensed.

In fact, our senses are molded by the input we subject them to in observable physiological ways. For example, infants gradually lose the ability to discern distinctions, even on a neurological level, between speech sounds that they do not hear in their native language. Misuse can damage ears and eyes, as the predominance of near-sightedness in certain professions and widespread hearing loss from loud music attest. Experiences affect how later experiences feel, even immediate sensations. Long-distance runners, military recruits, yoga practitioners, and students in medical school alike report that their experiences of pain, discomfort, and fatigue change through training.

Regardless of whether we realize it, we are all engaged in life-long projects of bodily self-cultivation—diet (of food and other stimuli), habits, persistent emotional states, common activities, postural patterns—that profoundly affect our physiology and perceptions. Dedicated training and repetitive behavior can gradually reshape a person's very neurological structure. Studies using brain imagery find that professional violinists, for example, have larger portions of the cerebral cortex devoted to the sensing and control of the fingers on the left hand, the ones used to finely manipulate the instrument's strings (Ratey 2001: 156).

Behavior can also shape our perceptions in the moment, even before repetition leaves traces on our physiology. Because our senses are part of active "perceptual systems," to use an expression from James Gibson (1966), sensing is not just passive reception, but an active seeking out of important stimuli. With only the central part of the retina, the eye's fovea, able to take in fine detail, for example, our scanning patterns affect what we see well. These patterns vary widely, among individuals or in a single individual depending on emotional state, fatigue, or even seemingly irrelevant factors, such as whether we think we are looking at the face of a person who is "rich, sad, or well-coifed," or has big ears (Berthoz 2000: 196). Social norms and expectations govern how one should and does look, and at what. Posture and personality can influence perception through the behavior that they induce. The downcast eyes of a humble comportment leave certain things routinely unseen; skittish, uneasy surveillance can increase the variety and volatility of stimulation that a person receives. Basic patterns of mutual gaze and shared attention in infants may even shape a child's development (see Sheets-Johnstone 2000).

As bird-watchers, ocean navigators, fossil hunters, pickpockets, farmers, and building inspectors are well aware, many skills require that a person learn how to look in order to perceive relevant information. Jugglers, for example, must learn to watch the highest point of the trajectories of thrown objects, and to catch them, it is necessary to develop the sensory–motor coordination to use that information to anticipate quickly where the objects will fall. If they try to follow each object with their eyes, they take in too much redundant information about a single one; an unschooled pattern of looking makes keeping multiple objects aloft impossible. Skills become part of what Iris Young (1990: 16) calls the "general structures of experience" that distinguish a person's way of being-in-the-world. These structures are often behavioral: the habitual ways that the individual interrogates the world, picks out relevant information, and measures what he or she experiences.

People wear their flesh in distinct habitual styles; they "in-habit" different skills that shape their perceptions. According to Tim Ingold (2000: 416; cf. 1991), anthropologists have not been sufficiently sensitive to this practical dimension of life in culture, what he calls "enskilment." Ingold suggests that these abilities critically underwrite important cultural differences (cf. Lave 1990: 323). Treating capoeira as a field for developing distinctive skills, and considering how those skills might shape experience, allows us to better understand what it might feel like to do capoeira. But adepts like Ordep Serra suggest that we must also look outside the game, turning from what members of GCAP called the "little roda" to the "greater roda"—everyday life—to notice all the ways learning how to walk like a capoeirista might shape perceptions.

LEARNING TO FALL

Although many of our basic movement techniques develop during youth, the learning of skills continues for most people throughout life. New professions and pastimes, evolving social roles, and even deteriorating abilities for which we must learn to compensate, all require new bodily skills. At the same time, as we develop our styles of moving, customary postures, and habitual activities, we may gradually forfeit the ability to move in unaccustomed ways. Our bodies become inflexible, and peculiar postures may feel uncomfortable, insecure, or even emotionally upsetting. Infants invariably have greater flexibility, for example, than all but the most well-trained adults, and youngsters usually seem less inhibited when attempting a novel activity. Gradually we abandon to disuse much of our potential for physical action. To recognize this process, one need only recall how one of the most important early movement patterns—crawling—becomes painful, embarrassing, or even physically impossible over time.

Capoeira instructors insist that the art they teach transforms devoted students, in part, because they must reclaim corporeal potential that they have abandoned. Mestre João Pequeno, for example, once pointed to a crawling child and said that capoeira had arisen from this simple movement; the little boy's mother had been his first mestre. In fact, students in the academy where I trained did have to learn how to crawl and move about dexterously on all fours (although our "rediscovered" skill was modified by a prohibition against putting knees on the ground). Part of the pain of learning arises from trying to reclaim neglected physical capacities. Adult students in GCAP frequently envied children who took up the art—they seemed to suffer less from inhibitions and held to bad habits less tenaciously.

More than just a limited repertoire of skills added to previous proficiencies, then, capoeira ostensibly reforms how novices occupy their own bodies at a basic level. Like other forms of physical discipline, capoeira training reforms a person's habits to change the way the student lives in the world.[11] Capoeira serves as a physical discipline for "making a body" (Behnke 1997b: 187) and throws into high relief how changes in everyday behavior might bring self-transformation. To borrow a phrase from Michel Foucault, capoeira is a "technology of the self" (see Martin, Gutman, and Hutton 1988; cf. Foucault 1988). The art consists of a cluster of exercises through which students, with the help of others, cultivate themselves. Whether or not they know where apprenticeship might lead, novices place themselves under an instructor's guidance, trusting that they will transform themselves through disciplined practice.

To say that the practices are clustered, however, does not mean that we can easily condense the effects of training into a single idea or structure. Each skill is important and takes ahold of the body in a particular way. The adept is remade slowly, one skill (or group of related skills) at a time, rather than all at once, as in a rite of passage. If we examine the learning process closely, we can see specifically how a capoeirista's training might affect life outside the roda, as abilities, perceptual skills, and incremental changes in embodiment provide an evolving foundation for experience.

The subtle, unexpected way in which training might affect a student was brought home for me one evening, when I had resumed training intensely in New York City, almost five years after leaving Bahia. Because I was teaching, I often went to Mestre João Grande's capoeira academy straight from my office. I usually carried two bags, one slung over each shoulder, so that I could quarantine my sweaty uniform from my lecture notes and research materials after class. On one cold evening, as I left a crowded subway train at the 14th Street station, my foot caught on an iron panel. A work crew had left a hole in the subway platform, covering it with a heavy metal plate that snagged the edge of my shoe. Hemmed in on all sides by hurried commuters, my arms bound by the two backpacks, I started to pitch forward.

Neurologists and psychologists who study motor ability note that the vestibular system, anchored in a twisting group of ear canals, helps humans to maintain a balanced and upright position. When we trip over a curb or slip on ice, fluid in those ear canals suddenly accelerates, and we sense that we are falling. The vestibulospinal reflex, the reactions our body makes to keep us from falling, is considered one of the most basic reflexes: we jerk our heads upright, throw out our arms, and change posture to fight against falling or, if unsuccessful, prepare to crash. Some neurologists argue that this reflex is especially quick because it makes use of stereotypical movements, learned early and initiated by the vestibular system itself, without conscious decision making (see Berthoz 2000: 43–44).

That night on the subway platform, I did not seem to have a vestibulospinal reflex. Instead, I remember distinctly sensing that my foot was caught and that I was falling, but, for some reason, tipping past vertical seemed no cause for alarm. Maybe because I had done innumerable cartwheels and negativas and my body knew how to catch myself right before landing, I didn't throw out my arms. It seemed obvious on a visceral level that my foot had to go back the way it came to free my shoe; the feeling was as immediate as when one reaches out to catch a tipping glass or moves a paddle to return a serve in Ping-Pong. I remember falling slowly, probably a couple of feet while I pushed my foot the opposite way, loosening the rubber sole from the grip of the metal plate. I ended up walking out of the potential mishap, taking a giant step to balance myself. If I had tensed up, jerked my arms, yanked at my shoe, or grabbed a bystander to catch myself, without doubt, I would have crashed to the ground. But I had neither the physical reflex that would seem to be normal nor the emotional start that often comes from tripping.

I'm not sure what happened that evening, but I am convinced that hours spent falling over in capoeira moves delayed my vestibulospinal reflex momentarily, allowing me time to free my foot. Alain Berthoz (2000: 193) suggests that mechanisms inhibiting motor actions—like the one that seemed to delay my reflex—may be one of the primary conditioning devices that affect a person's neurological development. He offers a case in which a flautist, conditioned to play her instrument behind a row of string musicians, was unaffected by distracting movement in her visual field in his laboratory (ibid.: 220–221). Berthoz hypothesized that the musician had learned to suppress a very basic reflex as part of adapting to the orchestra seating, and that this skill modified her perceptions in his tests.

In the same way, I suspect capoeira training affected me when I tripped, creating a space for action where I might not previously have felt one. Years of physical training could affect even the most basic, almost instantaneous reactions. "A capoeirista doesn't fall," practitioners often say, "but if he does, he falls well." After years of training, I too fell well. Although this change appears humble, even inconsequential, I suspect that it, together with myriad other seemingly minor changes brought about by capoeira training, can have far-reaching effects on students' perceptions. To trace out this transformation, and to understand the significance of skills, we must follow students as they learn capoeira, taking small steps into their worlds of cunning.

3 Following in a Mestre's Footsteps

One of the most far-reaching changes in contemporary capoeira was the spread of formal classes in schools, gyms, and community centers. Instead of clandestine instruction (see Dias 2001: 103–106), when Mestre Bimba registered his sports center with the Bahian state government in 1937, he opened a new era of specialized, public classes. Prior to this, one could learn capoeira only by frequenting the open rodas where "toughs" played, imitating the action and gleaning a bit of advice from time to time. With the advent of the academy, capoeira became legal: what had been a crime was transformed into physical education. Mestre Bimba's classes attracted many middle- and upper-class Bahians, some of them university students. They brought with them organizational skills and expected a systematic pedagogy. From Bimba's collaboration with his students, the academy's curriculum and training methods developed (see Barbieri 1993: 81–82). This model of instruction grew increasingly influential, even among capoeiristas who explicitly criticized Mestre Bimba and his students on other grounds.[1]

The shift in the educational environment changed the methods students used to learn the art: before the academy, students watched, imitated, and learned by doing. Learning was unsystematic, and the curriculum flexible, determined by what a student wanted to learn as well as by a veteran player's guidance. Instruction was tailored to the student's individual situation. In modern academies, students employ a range of preexisting exercises, standardized methods, and choreographed training sequences set in a systematic progression. Whereas students once observed and copied at their own pace, learning techniques in no particular order, novices in an academy now encounter an elaborate structure of apprenticeship. Multiple teaching methods exist alongside each other in modern academies. Students learn by imitating and through fixed training exercises. Mestres lead group exercises, but they also take the time to diagnose individual students' problems. Some instructors are very eloquent coaches; others are more taciturn, teaching almost entirely by example. The various teaching methods shape players' experience of the game and influence what a teacher actually passes on to a student during apprenticeship.

The variability inherent in capoeira training guarantees that the art itself is no single thing. Rather, students reinvent capoeira in their own idiosyncratic fashions, even under the watchful eye and steady hand of a mestre. This creative tendency intrinsic to skill development puts intriguing questions before an anthropologist interested in the art, especially one using his own apprenticeship as a research method. Each capoeirista develops an idiosyncratic version of the art, making it all the more essential that a researcher study from within to observe the forces that shape the proficiencies that emerge in each adept.

THE ADVENT OF THE ACADEMY

Every veteran practitioner I talked to believed the move from informal learning to academies brought a fundamental change to capoeira. On the one hand, all practitioners are pleased that *capoeiragem*, once punished as vagrancy, became accepted as a form of physical education, sport, and "culture." This change has, in the words of one mestre, "raised capoeira from the mud," ending decades of persecution. Schools made the art more widespread than ever, attracting tens of thousands of students throughout Brazil and around the world.

On the other hand, the change also leaves some practitioners ambivalent. Critics of the academy system argue that market competition increased infighting among instructors, prompted unfit practitioners to set themselves up as teachers, and encouraged innovations motivated by profit. Some conservative mestres, for example, charge that colored cords, modeled on the belt systems to show advancement in Asian martial arts, have been introduced because tests for promotion allow instructors to charge special fees and motivate students to pay their dues. (Promoters of belt systems argue that they rationalize the learning process and allow instructors to better tailor instruction to students' skill levels in large classes.)

On an immediate level, the advent of academies divided capoeira space. Ironically, even though capoeiristas are often proud of their art's roots in street gangs and urban violence, some now disparage *capoeira da rua* (street capoeira) for being rough, ugly, and unrefined (e.g., Felix 1965; Pastinha 1988: 23–24). Teachers in Salvador warn their students away from public rodas because they are "dangerous" and "street capoeiristas" are dodgy characters, likely (I was solemnly told) to be small-time drug dealers or pickpockets preying on tourists. The ambivalence was painfully obvious, when one instructor who proudly bragged that he had been tested in the street, in the very next class, threatened to expel a student for playing in an informal roda in Salvador's tourist district.

Redefining capoeira as education affected social relations in the roda and the way novices enter the community of practice. Whereas prominent players were once known as *bambas* (tough-guys) or *disordeiros* (troublemakers), they are now called *mestres* (teachers) or *professores*.[2] The geography and weekly calendar of capoeira had previously been oriented by landmark rodas, presided over by legendary bambas. Gradually replacing this, a new educational landscape emerged around academies, punctuated by extensive class schedules, periodic "graduation" ceremonies, and capoeira "baptisms," when the public was invited to see students receive colored cords marking their progress. Although players still identify the roda rhetorically as the defining moment of capoeira practice, the primary setting in which capoeiristas are formed shifted to the structured instructional session, the *aula* (class) or *treinamento* (training).

Some critics wonder whether capoeira can survive being transplanted from the street to the academy (e.g., E. Costa 1969: 27). Sociologist and practitioner Júlio Tavares (1984: 76), for example, asks how an art that lives in the claustrophobic confines of a fitness center can ever retain a link to traditional practice, sprung from a need for self-defense. Tavares also points out that the game was originally a playful "vagrancy" practiced in moments stolen away from work. In contrast, academy capoeira is regulated and rationalized like wage labor, with fixed class periods and money exchanged for time as the student pays for training.

In addition, capoeira academies altered the ratio of students to veterans. In Bimba's academy, he was the only mestre, and yet, according to his students, his teaching method "was very artisan-like; he liked to instruct student-by-student and teach certain movements" (R. Almeida 1994b: 80). As classes grew larger, teachers contrived methods to teach wholesale, rather than customizing instruction for each student. Mestre Itapoan (ibid.) writes about

... what we see now: classes with 100, even 200 students, where it is necessary to adopt a collective teaching method. Like classes of aerobics, the instructor remains in the front performing the movements, and the students, through imitation, try to perform them. This is an extremely impersonal environment and only those who are really adept "survive" in the art.

Faced with so many students, instructors relied increasingly on unified movements and simultaneous exercises. Although some observers claim that students no longer learn through imitating, my impression is that imitation dominates more than ever in mass classes; what has diminished is the amount of direct interaction between teacher and student. To understand what a student might learn in capoeira, then, one must look closely at imitation.

MOVING LIKE A MESTRE

Traditional capoeira songs are often said to contain the accumulated wisdom of generations of adepts. One of the more curious lines heard regularly in capoeira solos that suggests the dynamic of imitative training is the following: *Foi eu. Foi meu mestre. Foi meu mestre mais eu.* "It was me. It was my mestre. It was me in addition to my mestre." Sung just before the start of a game, this odd passage alludes to the complex relationship between disciple and teacher, and to the origins of a novice's proficiency. Practitioners widely believe that capoeira education depends upon imitation and that students are indelibly marked by their mestres' styles. But they also assume that educational mimesis, or copying, is never quite perfect. Although capoeira may appear uniform to a naïve observer, adepts see vivid diversity in the ways people play, shaped by the dynamics of instruction and each individual's abilities. An individual's style is thought to be an amalgamation of the teacher's with the student's idiosyncratic variations: "Me in addition to my mestre" (or multiple mestres, as the case might be).

The unintended role of imitation in creating stylistic diversity struck me when I moved to New York City and began to train at the academy of Mestre João Grande. João Grande, a former student of Mestre Pastinha, had taught my mestre, Moraes. Ironically, as I made my way to Manhattan, far from Salvador, I was climbing the genealogy of instruction from disciple to master. João Grande recognized the influence of his student on my body so quickly that, in jest, he called me "Moraes" or "GCAP."

Verbal instruction in João Grande's academy was limited. The mestre spoke little English, and his Brazilian students told me that his deeply accented rural Portuguese could be difficult even for them to understand. The academy had students from Brazil, the United States, Europe, South America, Africa, and the Caribbean. Even a shifting contingent of devoted Japanese students, some of whom spoke neither Portuguese *nor* English, came to learn from the renowned mestre.

In this environment, João Grande taught primarily through demonstration and imitation. He gestured to start exercises and sometimes pinched a sleeve or cuff gingerly and pulled to correct gently an individual's position. Students watched closely and did their best to copy his intricate combinations. If someone struggled, João Grande might do the movements in front of the student slowly so the novice could mirror the mestre. Even with his Brazilian students, he said little during class, preferring to show techniques or offer very brief comments. Veterans helped new students to learn their teacher's distinctive movement repertoire or whispered a few words of advice on the sidelines.

The students' ability to learn from João Grande through imitation impressed me deeply. One young American, John, had developed a subtle "old school" playing style in only a few years, something that practitioners may fail to acquire after a far longer period. John spent many hours with the mestre but spoke little Portuguese. In spite of the language gulf, the student had internalized a startling range of João Grande's distinctive movements: the mestre's odd head bobs, straight-legged steps, sudden jerky movements, characteristic shoulder wobbles, a hoarse, tight-throated singing style, even elements of the mestre's style of dress. Intentionally or not, John had internalized the odd kinesthetic quirks and signature gestures of his teacher, echoing the older man's distinctive corporeal character. Anyone who knew João Grande would recognize his influence as soon as John moved.

What made this particularly intriguing was that many of João Grande's kinesthetic traits were adaptations to old age, compensating especially for the effects of almost five decades of capoeira and manual labor on his knees. Indeed, John's style differed markedly from that of other disciples, including my Bahian teacher, who had learned from João Grande when the senior mestre was younger. John had incorporated a movement style, quirks and all, from an old man with whom he couldn't easily converse. And João Grande, in spite of his conscientious fidelity to tradition and reputation as a pillar of Capoeira Angola, was inspiring a range of playing styles as his own game slowly changed and developed. Some observers even told me that variety in students' styles was the very hallmark of a great mestre's inspiration.

IMITATIVE LEARNING

Although John was something of a mimetic prodigy, and Mestre João Grande's academy privileged imitation more than many, imitating seems to be the rule rather than the exception when one learns any physical skill.

Merlin Donald (1991) argues that imitation is the most basic form of human intelligence, echoing Aristotle's assertion in the *Poetics* that the ability is "natural to man from childhood."[3] Aristotle goes so far as to claim that "one of [a human's] advantages over the lower animals [is] . . . that he is the most imitative creature in the world, and learns at first by imitation" (1448b 5–9).

Learning through imitation is difficult to explain if one assumes that all behavior is guided by, or learned through, conscious thought. When sociologist Pierre Bourdieu (1990a: 166) outlines his agenda for the study of sport, he submits that:

> The problems raised by the teaching of a bodily practice seem to me to involve a set of theoretical questions of the greatest importance, in so far as the social sciences endeavour to theorize the behavior that occurs, in the greatest degree, outside the field of conscious awareness, that is learnt by a silent and practical communication, from body to body one might say.

One question raised by this "practical communication" is exactly what is being passed from the person teaching a skill to the person learning it. As Bourdieu describes, "There are heaps of things that we understand only with our bodies, outside conscious awareness, without being able to put our understanding into words. . . . Very often, all you can do is say: 'Look, do what I'm doing'" (ibid.).

Learning skills through practical communication requires that beginners, especially prodigies like John, have perceptual abilities to simulate in action what they see others doing. Theorists like Samuel IJsseling (1997: 31) seem to take for granted that imitation is a visual matching task. They assume that imitation involves imagining a picture of one's own body, as if seen from the outside, and comparing this mental self-image to the model, as if people imitated by comparing their own movement with an ideal in an imaginary mirror.

Phenomenological analysis of imitating suggests that the process does not require a visual image of the self. When students ask capoeira instructors about techniques, even the most accomplished teachers often have to repeat the movement in question, freezing part way through to observe what they themselves are doing. This inability to translate easily an action they know well into a visual image, without doing the action, implies that capoeiristas may not possess visual images of themselves when they master a skill. They know well how a movement feels and how to do it without knowing how it looks. In addition, although some well-equipped academies have mirrors, most instructors recommended strenuously that players not train by watching their own reflections too intently. Too much attention to one's reflection detracted from a student's ability to perceive an adversary and distorted a technique, making it "for show" (*para mostrar*) rather than integrated into interaction. To varying degrees, students emulate movements directly, without focusing too intently on their own bodies' position. I noticed this ability most in its absence, when I tried to instruct a young man in Chicago who seemed oddly incapable of mirroring my actions. After he did a technique incorrectly for months, no matter how often it was demonstrated to him, I finally corrected the error explicitly in a way that he understood. He grew incensed; why had I hidden "the trick" from him for so long? A handful of other students had easily picked up the critical detail, however, long before I figured out how to explain it. A failure in mimetic learning had forced me to study my own movements carefully to make the detail explicit. For all the students but this one, teaching had proceeded through imitation, without the instructor (me) knowing exactly what he was doing.

Veteran students even prey upon novices' inclination to imitate. Some veterans suggest that new students have an almost unthinking inclination to mirror an adversary's motion. For example, a wily veteran may do a repetitive ginga knowing that novices often follow an opponent's rhythm. As soon as the student successfully synchronizes the two players' steps, it becomes frightfully easy for the experienced person to anticipate the student's actions. Likewise, when learning to avoid the *meia-lua de frente* (front crescent moon kick), new students almost invariably do the negativa, the appropriate dodge, in the wrong direction, leaning their heads into the oncoming kick. Some of the quickest studies seem the most prone to make this error. The tendency to move in the wrong direction, so pervasive that it was a standing joke, might arise because the windup to the kick involves the attacker leaning slightly to one side. If the escaping student mirrors the attacker's preparatory lean, his or her face will be in the path of the kick. As they learn, students have to suppress an inclination to imitate their attacker's windup.

Some neurological studies suggest that mimetic abilities make use of how neural architecture tends to develop. Studies of infant imitation, for example, have found that newborns less than one hour old are sometimes capable of mimicking basic facial expressions, long before they could possibly possess any visual image of themselves.[4] Colwyn Trevarthen and his colleagues (1999: 130, 142) suggest that "naïve and immediate" imitating in infants is a result of "intermotive attraction." That is, infants seem inclined to copy gestures because different channels of sense experience are put together by their brains. Evidence from neuropathology supports this theory. In a pathological condition called "imitation behavior," individuals with lesions in specific areas of the brain's frontal lobes are compelled to imitate other people's actions, such as hand gestures, even when these injured persons are instructed not to do so.[5] The ability seems to run rampant when it is not actively suppressed.

Research on primate brain activity, like studies of pathology, indicates that neurological dimensions of perception might facilitate mimesis. Italian researcher Giacomo Rizzolatti and his collaborators discovered that some of the same neurons were active when a macaque both executed an action and observed similar movements performed by a researcher. These "mirror neurons" link an observed action with performance of that action by another; similar structures have been located in humans.[6] The goal here is not to explain away mimetic ability by reducing it to neurons. Instead, findings in neuroscience corroborate other sources, including ethnographic research and phenomenological analysis: tight links between perceptions of others' actions (alteroception) and our own bodily sense of self (proprioception) seem to facilitate learning by imitation. Far from being a complicated imaginary task executed through visual matching, various research findings suggest that mimetic learning is a potential inherent in the way that humans perceive and in neuroarchitecture.

Learning entirely new skills by imitating, however, may pose serious challenges. Although mimesis plays a role, in many cases it is insufficient alone, and a teacher's duties extend far beyond just advising, "Do what I'm doing." In these cases, instructors may coach students, trying to make explicit what they understand in nonconscious ways. Coaches often do not translate implicit knowledge directly into articulated form, however; they may not even know how. Rather, effective coaching often acts indirectly, creating experiences and shaping perceptions that guide a student's own discovery of a skill (cf. Wacquant 2004: 102). In this case, verbal coaching and gestures must help a player to discover what he or she cannot simply imitate.

COACHING THE BANANEIRA

A capoeirista often spends a great deal of time in the roda in handstands, which Brazilians call *bananeira* (banana tree). In contrast to the handstands performed in Olympic gymnastics, when a capoeirista is inverted, the body is not held straight up. The bananeira ideally should be "closed," I was taught, the knees clenched to the chest, or the body bent so that the legs dangle protectively in front of the torso. My teachers warned that an extended bananeira, like the one in gymnastics, left a player too vulnerable.

A player also needs to relax and breathe normally while in the bananeira so that the position is not rigid. The best capoeiristas could walk about on their hands and kick their legs down to ward off attacks. Unlike gymnastics, in which contestants are rewarded for holding still and symmetrical, the bananeira is a dynamic position that may appear wildly off-balance. Mestre Moraes said that a bananeira was an opportunity to get off one's feet and rest while playing, which seemed preposterous to me while I was struggling mightily—and still failing— to maintain my balance.

A bananeira also differs from a handstand in gymnastics in that a capoeirista must keep from turning his or her face toward the floor or craning the neck backward. Players do the bananeira with their bellies toward an adversary, looking right at their opponent. Done wrong, a player looks at the ground and is unable to see incoming attacks. The head position makes the bananeira especially difficult. Keeping chin to chest and watching an adversary during a handstand completely inverts the inner ear, a locus of the sense of balance. Instructors never tired of

Mestre Cobra Mansa does a bananeira *and brings down one leg to fend off an opponent, "closing" the bananeira against attack. (Photo from the collection of C. Peçanha)*

reminding students to maintain proper form, even though they might grow exasperated with their slow progress.

One day before class in GCAP, after a half-hour of failed attempts had left me increasingly frustrated, one of the group's assistant instructors approached me. He had studied my bananeira, how I launched from the ground, teetered, and fell as soon as the force from my kick off the ground dissipated. "You're doing it wrong," he told me. He pantomimed my motion: he held his arms up, bent over, and pitched himself onto his hands, body straight, out of control. His legs catapulted his body toward a handstand as if, with just the right amount of force, the kick would land him right at the equilibrium point.

He held up one finger signaling I should watch closely. Then he did another exaggerated pantomime, this time to focus my attention on crucial corrections. He bent over at the waist and planted his hands emphatically on the ground. He then looked between his legs and gently pushed off the ground so that his weight shifted slightly onto his hands. His legs unfurled deliberately toward the ceiling.

After he walked around on his hands for a few seconds, he told me offhandedly: "Just stand up!" The advice stuck with me. It seemed so simple, even though it made no sense to me in an immediate, experiential way. I could not find physically, with my own body and movements, what he was telling me to do, although I could understand what he said. He tried to use words to pull together things that I knew—such as how to "just stand up" on my feet—to help me create a new skill.

Finally, several months after returning from Brazil, I suddenly had the sensation of "standing up" on my hands while doing the exercise my instructor had shown me. The abrupt shift was not a result of improved physical ability; if anything, my strength and stamina were deteriorating as I wrote my dissertation. My bodily motion was virtually the same as innumerable failed attempts that preceded it. And yet my experience of the bananeira changed completely. As my teacher suggested, I felt myself "standing up" on my hands. When I "stood up," my center of gravity perceptibly moved over my hands and then rose, as if I had simply put my feet underneath my body before standing up from the ground. My instructor's words came together with my experience. During this bananeira, I was struck by the novel sensation of using my fingers as toes, rocking slightly from the heels of my palms to my fingertips. My hands adjusted like feet under a teetering body, splayed fingers and the balls of my hands compensating with increased pressure to weight shifts. As my mestre had told me, I remained relaxed and loose even though I was balanced upside down.

The story stuck with me because of the power of the simple words: "Just stand up!" When I finally succeeded, the words were waiting for me, capturing evocatively my new sensation. I had seen countless handstands before he corrected me, but, as Mestre João Pequeno warned, if just watching was enough to learn, every stray dog that hung around an academy would be a mestre. When my instructor studied me, he recognized that I could not succeed unless I changed my perception of the technique. His advice did not treat my body as an object. Instead, he tried to shift my corporeal understanding of my movements. He realized from watching me that I did not share his perceptions. His deceptively simple words were a kind of poetry disclosing how to take up the bananeira with my own body.

By describing coaching as a form of poetry, this analysis highlights the power of words to "disclose being," in the words of Martin Heidegger (1971a). Dimensions of lived reality to which we may be numb or deaf come vividly into attention through poetry. James Weiner writes: "Poetry coheres the evocative power of imagery, rather than the referential power of words; by holding fast to the object, it shatters the conventions that insulate us from experience. Metaphor is a play on words; poetic image is additionally a play on the world" (1991: 13). When coaching is poetry, a phrase upsets the usually lax linkage between experience and language, disrupting a student's complacency. A phrase strikes us as poetry in everyday use because it powerfully evokes an experience that we have had, or jolts us into perceiving things in a new light. Thus, good coaching is a form of applied poetic phenomenology: an analysis of how things are experienced that may facilitate a shift in an athlete's perceptions.

The instruction "Just stand up!" was certainly poetry to me. The words rang true; initially, however, they had been out of reach of my immediate understanding. If anything, over time, the words *came to be true to me* because my experience shifted to meet them. When I finally managed to perceive them as real, I had an exhilarating sense of revelation. I found the bananeira in myself. Through repeated attempts, I came to experience directly the "standing up-ness" of a well-executed bananeira and the "bananeira-ness" latent in my own body. My instructor had pointed the way by sharing, poetically, how he lived the movement.

COACHING AND DEVELOPING SKILLS

Everyone's experience of learning the bananeira is different. Skills cannot be passed to another person, but must be rediscovered anew by each novice. No matter how many times my instructor did the handstand, it would not rub off on me directly, nor could it be handed on like a relay baton. I had to find the bananeira myself by playing it around in my body until I could feel it.

Anthropologist Andrew Lock (1980: 1) has used the term "guided reinvention" to describe how children "come to invent and use language." With language, adults provide an environment rich in stimuli, including distorted, simplistic, and emphatic speech, that helps a child to "invent" language for him- or herself. Tim Ingold (2000: 353–354; cf. 1998) suggests that an important implication of Lock's observation is that

> [e]ach generation contributes to the next not by handing on a corpus of representations, or information in the strict sense, but rather by introducing novices into contexts which afford selected opportunities for perception and action, and by providing the scaffolding that enables them to make use of these affordances. This is what James Gibson called an "education of attention" [quote from J. Gibson 1979: 254].

Coaching ("Just stand up!") cannot contain an experience or skill. In fact, the final realization of what the words meant, in a direct experiential sense, had to wait for several months until my skill level caught up to them. But the words were part of my learning environment, structured by instructors and veteran students.[7]

Referring to the learning process as a discovery or reinvention (rather than, say, a transmission or enculturation) highlights that students do not learn exactly what a teacher knows. Capoeiristas widely recognize that the skill of the apprentice is not identical to the master's. Training offers opportunities to perceive things and develop skills; it does not inject an unvarying body of tacit knowledge in the student. A teacher, like João Grande with his slowly aging knees, does not pass an unchanging "thing" to his students. Even in the same classes, what each student discovers is different. Ejgil Jespersen (1997: 183) suggests that sports apprenticeship inevitably has "centrifugal" creative tendencies because athletes continually endeavor to improve their own performance and draw on multiple role models. Calling capoeira "culture," if this means an unchanging body of knowledge, conceals the constant innovation inherent even in the rediscovery of the "same" practice, as when each student invents anew how to do a bananeira.[8]

In addition, the use of nonimitative teaching techniques like training exercises or drills can lead to unintended innovation. Divorced from the game, extra training may not teach skills similar to those that a player would develop simply by playing or imitating. If exercises are ill conceived or badly designed, they can even develop habits detrimental to the game. Some players criticize teachers who enthusiastically adopt techniques from physical education, like calisthenics, weight training, or stretching, saying that these exercises don't develop the proclivities, instincts, or abilities that players need in the roda. Group calisthenics, for example, teach unified, repetitive movements that are anathema to the cunning unpredictability idealized in capoeira.

A breakdown in learning was vividly illustrated in a class I attended on the outskirts of Salvador. An instructor led his students to do an exercise that he called a "negativa." The negativa is usually one of the first defensive techniques students learn. In the version I was taught, a player first crouches down and then leans to the side, away from an incoming kick, coming to rest very low on the hands. Some players appear to be lying down when they perform the technique although they are actually balanced on their hands and feet.

This instructor, however, demanded that his students *fall* forward, sideways, and backward, without crouching to prepare. They simply tilted over like chopped trees and crashed to the ground, catching themselves on their hands just before impact. Controlling this fall or slowing

Mestre João Pequeno tries to coach a student in the fundamentals of doing a rabo de arraia. He directly manipulates the student's body into a better position. (Photo by C. Peçanha)

one's descent was impossible. The instructor called out the direction, and his young charges obediently toppled over, some wincing as they came down hard on their wrists. He repeatedly discouraged students from reaching out their arms to decrease their momentum, seemingly determined to maximize the force with which the novices struck the ground. The collisions, students against concrete floor, resounded through the training area. Other training techniques did not make sense, but this exercise was stupefying, almost perverse. It appeared dangerous, both during practice and in a game. This form of negativa violated one of the most basic tactical principles of capoeira: while falling, students could not stop, change direction, or shift techniques if an adversary's attack turned out to be a feint. The toppling students were committed to a single course of action.

Puzzlingly, the teacher himself did not do the negativa this way when he played. Yet when asked about it, he insisted that it was the proper way to perform the movement. I was baffled. Couldn't the instructor see the disparity between the training exercise and the technique that he used in the roda? What was the relationship between this movement, repeated innumerable times judging from how the students greeted it, and the way they actually did play? Did they overcome this training, or did they do the "innovative" movement in games? There seemed to be a fundamental breach in the transmission of the art.

Coaching and individual discovery can cause capoeira to develop in different directions, even into different styles. (In contrast, assembling at capoeira "baptisms," visiting other academies, and emulating the same role models are activities that pull adepts closer, requiring them to develop skills so that they can play together in the same rodas or win their elders' approval.) Although teachers argue about who truly practices an authentic form of capoeira, the centrifugal tendencies of apprenticeship assure that variation is inevitable. The more fully a student embraces the art and pours his or her own creativity into the game, the more likely capoeira is to take new forms, albeit unintentionally. As a mestre cautioned me, "There is no capoeira, only *capoeiras*." Capoeira is not a single "thing."

APPRENTICESHIP AS A RESEARCH METHOD

This book depends heavily on my firsthand experience learning capoeira at the Grupo de Capoeira Angola Pelourinho. When I first arrived in Salvador, I trained in multiple academies. Several mestres warned that this was unsustainable: conflicting instructions would lead me to develop an incoherent style. Their concerns quickly became moot, however, when I was thrown out of one school (because I took classes elsewhere) and found it too physically grueling to keep up with training schedules at multiple academies. Forced to choose, I opted to join GCAP because I liked how the group played and because membership offered certain opportunities. Mestre Moraes and his students stimulated intense debate about the political implications of capoeira styles. Understanding the group's perspective was essential because so many people were reacting against GCAP. When other practitioners heard that Moraes was my mestre, many emphatically shared their own views on his controversial ideas, such as his argument that Capoeira Regional was a "whitened" version of the art. Mention of the group's name often provoked heated discussions about race, movement style, and the political role of capoeira, a valuable research tool I happened upon inadvertently.

Although these discussions helped assure that no single group entirely shaped my understanding of capoeira, my intimate relationship with GCAP itself also led me to depart from their particular interpretation of the art. The longer I trained with the group, the more inconsistencies appeared between its political rhetoric and the art as members were teaching it.

Capoeira training, in my opinion, is much richer than even the most well-developed political ideology, and the one GCAP professed is among the most penetrating. Capoeira teaches contradictory principles and very specific bodily and perceptional skills that cannot be converted into explicit verbal forms. Verbal explanation often seemed to be another game with the same cunning playful tactics as capoeira, like an improvised song composed to suit the circumstances, rather than the eternal "truth" about the art.[9] When I had attended enough classes, and came to roll my eyes at familiar myths and well-worn diatribes like any other adept, players sometimes gave up telling me *about* capoeira. Instead, they gossiped with me, corrected my game, compared notes on playing, or asked me about classes in my academy.

At times, my roles as ethnographic observer and practicing participant conflicted. When they did, I usually set down my notebook, opting instead for a good game or to join the orchestra. I trusted that what I learned by participating actively was more important and elusive than anything that could be recorded passively. This tendency to privilege participation certainly reduced the volume of material I collected. Joining in deepened my relationships with other practitioners. We shared a passion: capoeira. As in boxing, described by Loïc Wacquant (2004: 16), capoeira play may be individual, but "apprenticeship is quintessentially collective." Because of my practical immersion in the art, other capoeiristas did not offer the kind of "experience-distant" comments or abstract explanations of the art's significance that they often gave to spectators.[10] Instead, they shared their experiences, sometimes to correct and coach me, and sometimes simply to appreciate our mutual obsession. In the ongoing project of apprenticeship, they were my teachers, critics, and confederates.

Ethnographers have long recognized that apprenticeship can be a useful field method. Esther Goody (1989: 254–255) and Michael Coy (1989: 2) both suggest that apprenticeship is not only an excellent way to learn a skill; it is also an ideal way to *learn about* it, and to *learn about how one learns*.[11] Field research always requires that the researcher learn how to function effectively in an unfamiliar setting. Where better to gain entry and to study what a milieu demands than at a site where others are doing the same thing?

As a member of GCAP from 1993 to 1995, I was required to attend, at least, mandatory two-hour training sessions on Tuesday and Thursday, and a weekly roda Saturday evening. Every other weekend, we had an additional roda on Sunday afternoon. When I told Mestre Moraes about my research, he cut me short: "To me, you're another student." He offered me no special privileges. Although Moraes discouraged his students from playing elsewhere, I invariably did, joining rodas (but not training) in a circuit of other academies that welcomed me, more when I traveled outside Salvador and ran less risk of being caught. For several months when I arrived, I trained at a competing academy on Monday, Wednesday, and Friday nights, but my overlapping loyalties were discovered, and the rival mestre noisily expelled me. Outside of classes and rodas at GCAP, I took instrument lessons, observed other classes, occasionally helped to teach in GCAP's many children's programs, and, rarely, managed a pickup game on the beach or in a street roda. In all, I probably trained, played, or participated in rodas from ten to twelve hours each week while in Salvador. When I returned to the United States in 1995, I played and taught capoeira intermittently in Chicago and, when I moved to New York City in 1998, I finally trained again in earnest under Mestre João Grande.

The corporeal sensibility developed in my apprenticeship was the basis from which to evaluate what I heard, read, and observed. Anthropologist Maurice Bloch (1998) suggests that most ethnographies are based on similar forms of nondiscursive knowledge. Bloch admits how central cultural apprenticeship was in his work:

> I am fairly sure that the way I proceed in giving an account of the Malagasy cultures I study is by looking for facts, and especially for

statements, that *confirm* what I already know to be right because I know how to live efficiently with these people. . . . Like other anthropologists, I then pretend that the linguistic confirmations of these understandings, which I subsequently obtain from what my informants say, are the *basis* of what I understand, but this is not really so. My knowledge was established prior to these linguistic confirmations. (ibid.: 17, emphasis in the original)

Ultimately, each person's discoveries in apprenticeship are unique. One young capoeirista told me, "Capoeira Angola is the sea, and each person dives in at a different place." He suggested not only that the art was vast and deep, but that every venture from the shore—although all left one equally wet—revealed a different part of the art's immensity to one's experience. Similarly, Mestre Pastinha famously said: *Ninguem joga do meu jeito. Cada qual é cada qual.* The phrase loses its alliterative elegance in translation, but it means roughly, "No one plays in the same way I do. Each person is unique."

Like any other player, I discovered my own capoeira, reinventing the techniques that I saw others doing with their guidance. Far from making discussion of capoeira impossible, this process of inventing is exactly what this book explores: what forces draw practitioners together, like shared rituals, collective song, and oft-told stories, and which others lead them far afield, until some can scarcely play together. Each person who discovers capoeira seeks to enter the roda to play with others. Like the moment of recognition that comes from making "Just stand up!" real to one's body, an effective phenomenology does not exhaust all the possibilities of experience. Instead, it ideally resonates with our own experience at the same time that it bathes it vividly in a new light.

4   HISTORY IN EPIC REGISTERS

Having a conversation about capoeira in Brazil without turning to its past was difficult. When players explained to me the rituals preceding play, the form of the roda, the significance of specialized terms, or the meanings of song lyrics, they often made reference to key moments in capoeira history—persecution, deception, danger, betrayal, and struggle. For example, the type of front kick called the *benção* was said to be a parody of the hypocritical "blessing" given to Africans by cruel priests who preached that slaves should accept a fate ordained for them by God. Players told me that they stood in a circle around the game because, in decades long past, this concealed the game from the prying eyes of authorities. During classes, a teacher was liable to stop an exercise to show his students how a technique could be transformed into a lethal variant. We were told that these hidden versions of techniques belonged to more violent moments of capoeira history. Whenever a question scratched the surface of the art, history was liable to spring up, as if every gesture had its own genealogy.

All aspects of capoeira practice are, of course, to varying degrees and depths, the products of history. However, some of the "historical" explanations offered by practitioners seem patently absurd—ingenious, but improbable at best. For example, players sometimes explained that the prohibition on hand strikes in capoeira arose when slaves' hands were bound. According to this explanation, slaves developed complex kicking and head butting techniques because they only had their feet and head free to fight (see Evleshin 1986: 7). While few veterans take this explanation literally, all are familiar with it, and many novice players hear it when they ask about the restriction. But why would a martial art adapt to the moments in which enslaved laborers had their hands shackled, rather than the long hours they presumably spent unshackled in order to work? And why wouldn't slaves forced to wear heavy metal cuffs not use them to bludgeon an adversary? Many capoeira techniques, such as handstands and cartwheels, demand just as much mobility of the arms as punching. And wouldn't slaveholders worried about Africans fleeing be more likely to shackle a slave's ankles than his or her hands?

Many adepts seem acutely aware that capoeira history may be a creative endeavor as well as an archival one. Some regard the skilled fabrication of "historical" explanations with no small amount of amusement, chuckling when I tried to cross-check a particularly good yarn some other mestre had spun ("He told you *that?!*"). Mestre Gato, a member of Bahia's "old guard," is reputed to have said, "A capoeirista is creative. If he doesn't know, he'll make it up on the spot." Author and practitioner Ângelo Decânio called historical explanations of capoeira "lies"—"lies" of poetic license, exaggeration, and epic, he explained, not lies told with an intention to deceive. Let the listener beware.

Players' "historical" explanations for their art borrow from academic discussions of capoeira, but the traffic is hardly one-way. Stories cross back and forth quickly between academic and popular realms, no doubt partly because most students of capoeira history are also disciples of the art. The voracious imaginations of capoeiristas follow close on the heels of historians, quickly incorporating their findings into poetic readings of the rhythms, textures, and gestures of the game. For this reason, this chapter does not draw a hard distinction between written history, oral histories, and song texts; all influence each other in practice.

Although some historical explanations appear dubious, the enthusiasm with which capoeiristas embrace history reveals that they experience the game as profoundly connected to the past. Capoeiristas feel the past vividly through rituals, songs, and gestures that seem to echo from days gone by. Shrouded in mystery, the art seems to be bursting with history. The histories they tell do not create the impression of historical depth; they justify it and give it shape (cf. Casey 1987: 221). Various stories lend detail and texture to a conviction that arises out of practice.

Paying attention to the phenomenology of memory in capoeira, to the way that an awareness of the past arises in the experience of playing, helps us reframe the fierce argument that surrounds its origin: whether the art should be considered "African," "Brazilian," or "Afro-Brazilian." Ultimately, which adjective one chooses has profound political implications because the debate is not merely about credit for the art's creation, but also about the treatment of black culture in Brazil. By instead paying attention to how players experience history, however, we can ask questions that do not resolve eventually into this political calculation. For example, we may better understand how practitioners can hear such different histories commemorated in the same game, and why history itself is so often the register they use to explain the art as it exists around them in the present.

Although they may disagree vehemently, players with a variety of understandings of the art still play together. By focusing closely on how history is evoked, on the style and tone in which the past is remembered, this chapter and the next show how very different histories contribute to a similar experience of the art. In the end, these histories share an essential quality: they create emotional gravity by linking the roda with a past of violent struggle. They suggest that under a veil of playfulness and music lies a brutal legacy of conflict. This chapter explores two versions of capoeira's history: a "notorious" epic of untamed violence, focusing on morally ambiguous gangs, thugs, and tough guys; and a "liberatory" saga of the art's use to combat oppression, racism, and injustice.

A NOTORIOUS HISTORY OF OUTLAWS

"Notorious" versions of capoeira history construe the modern art as the heir to an epic tale of untamable violence and heroic outlaws. The notorious imagination of capoeira history is rich in detail, although sometimes shallow, consisting of little more than a litany of famous names and fragmentary accounts of legendary feats. At times, capoeiristas are portrayed as directing violence against their oppressors, but this style of remembering embraces moral ambiguity. Modern practitioners celebrate even internecine conflict among *capoeiras* and acts that reveal their ancestors in unflattering tones. These histories present capoeira heroes not as agents of social change, but as individual fighters noteworthy for their extraordinary physical prowess. The past demonstrates the courage and resiliency of Brazilian outlaws, especially the mythological *malandro*— the legendary rogue or hustler who survived alone in Brazil's urban streets on his cunning.[1]

Narratives of epic capoeira violence paint these conflicts in individualist terms (in contrast to the collective campaigns recounted in liberatory histories, explored shortly). In discussions of capoeira under slavery, for example, notorious accounts focus on a paradigmatic struggle between a lone escaped slave and the *capitões do mato*, heavily armed bounty hunters sent on horseback to recapture fugitive Africans. The theme of the story is that an unarmed individual with capoeira techniques at his disposal prevailed against improbable odds. These stories sometimes take the putative origin of the word "capoeira," from the indigenous term for a type of scrub vegetation in which escaped slaves could have hidden, as an artifact of this historical moment (cf. Capoeira 1992: 16–18).[2] Some assert that the unusual, acrobatic kicks and evasive techniques of the art were developed to avoid the firearms of a bounty hunter, to attack decisively, and then to flee into the backlands to hide.

Notorious accounts of capoeira in the nineteenth century, however, tend to be dominated by a discussion of the *capoeiras* in Rio de Janeiro. The "maltas," gangs of urban *capoeiras*, were territorial and organized by neighborhoods. Modern capoeiristas celebrate the maltas in histories and song—groups are even named for the gangs, especially the two largest, the Nagoas and the Guaiamus, who split control of Rio de Janeiro's underworld (see Dias 2001; C. Soares 1994: 39–94).

The Brazilian Penal Code of 1890 made it explicitly illegal to perform "in streets or public plazas the exercises of agility and physical dexterity known by the name of *capoeiragem*" (Capoeira 1992: 43; cf. Bretas 1989: 57; Dias 2001: 80). The *capoeiras* had long been treated as a problem of urban disorder, like drunks or vagrants (cf. Hollaway 1989, 1993). The respectable public feared *capoeiras*, and the police actively persecuted them.

Throughout the nineteenth century, historian Carlos Soares (1994: 7) writes, the maltas were the "privileged target of the violence of the State," the "scourge" of the authorities responsible for maintaining order. Newspaper accounts from the end of the century refer to the gangs as "the terror, the panic, the impalpable specter of the people." One journalist insisted that the maltas had to be broken up if responsible citizens were to sleep peacefully "without seeing the flash of the terrible razor in their dreams" (the newspaper *Novidades*, cited in Bretas 1989: 57). Whereas duels fought with razors may once have scandalized Rio's residents, modern celebrations of this period see the weapon as a symbol of both the fearlessness and the formidability of the *capoeiras*.

The *capoeiras* also used their violent skills on behalf of the Brazilian state. Various songs refer to how *capoeiras* distinguished themselves in the war against Paraguay in the 1860s. At the end of the 1880s, when republicans fought the Brazilian monarchy, the *capoeiras* supported the crown. Because Princesa Isabel had liberated the last slaves, many Afro-Brazilian *capoeiras* joined the *Guarda Negra* (Black Guard) against republican forces (see Freyre 1986c: 10–12; C. Soares 1994: 225–238; Dias 2001).

After the republicans prevailed in 1889, new police chief Sampaio Ferraz made eradicating the maltas the centerpiece of his campaign to cleanse the capital of vice (J. Moura 1985). Disregarding the social connections of many prominent *capoeiras*, Ferraz aggressively attacked the maltas. His campaign against the maltas was so intense that it provoked a political crisis in the young republic. Ferraz arrested the famous *capoeira*

Juca Reis (José Elísio dos Reis), son of the Count of Matosinhos, a republican stalwart and owner of the newspaper *O País*. The minister of foreign relations, Quintino Bocaiúva, threatened to resign if the *capoeira* was not freed. Ferraz refused to relent, and Reis was deported (Bretas 1991: 252–253; C. Soares 1994: 300–301; Dias 2001: 130–132).[3]

Discussions of the *capoeiras* in Rio de Janeiro almost all point out that the gangs were not merely the targets of police persecution; in many cases, *capoeiras* allied with elite groups.[4] Throughout the nineteenth century, *capoeiras* maintained strong ties with the military and police; many free *capoeiras* entered the Brazilian National Guard, gaining a degree of police immunity for prior (and future) offenses (C. Soares 1994: 247–253). The head of the Royal Police Guard, Major Miguel Nunes Vidigal, persecuted the maltas, but he was also well versed in the use of the razor, and the kicks and head butts of capoeiragem (A. Santos 1993: 49). Even Sampaio Ferraz, the police chief who broke the maltas, was adept (although he was felled against a marble table by his friend, the poet Luís Murat, secretary general of the State of Rio de Janeiro, in an impromptu duel of capoeiragem at the Café Inglês [J. Moura 1985: 93]). Knowledge of capoeiragem was widespread among the men who most ruthlessly attacked the gangs. In addition, *capoeiras* often served as *capengas*, bodyguards and companions for young *bon vivants* of the imperial elite.

THE BAMBAS OF BAHIA

Although a few of Rio de Janeiro's *capoeiras* survive by name in popular histories, modern practitioners tend to recall them as anonymous gangs. Beginning in the twentieth century, the principal plot line in these histories shifts from Rio to Salvador, Bahia, and becomes peopled with distinct individuals. Modern capoeiristas commemorate these heroes in song, and their names are familiar, even though little more may be known about these figures than the verses of the songs that mention them.

Authorities persecuted capoeira in the state of Bahia, especially in the 1920s.[5] The art emerged from the period more robust than in Rio de Janeiro, however, perhaps because police attacked Rio's gangs more vigorously, or because a playful form of capoeiragem was woven into the texture of Bahian popular festivals. In Salvador, capoeira practitioners held rodas at regular locations over long periods of time, a tradition that some maintain, often with support from the city's tourist industry. According to contemporary understandings, these rodas were meeting places that attracted stable groups of *bambas*, tough guys who habitually came to *vadiar* (to "engage in vagrancy," "idle," or "hang out"), an older way to describe capoeira.

In popular narratives, the geography of capoeira shifts at the turn of the twentieth century. The roda as a ritual emerges and marks sites in Salvador, many of which are recalled in song: the port of Salvador, especially in front of the Church of Our Lady of the Immaculate Conception; the Mercado Modelo (the "Model Market," where rodas are still held for tourists); church plazas, such as the Terreiro de Jesus (also still a site for tourist capoeira); Salvador's old red-light district and the "lower city"; neighborhoods like Liberdade, where the black population was traditionally concentrated; on outlying hilltops, such as Engenho Velho de Brotas or the heights of Chame-Chame; and in the interior towns of Santo Amaro, Cachoeira, and Nazaré das Farinhas and the Ilha (Island) de Maré in the Bay of All Saints.

Perhaps the most famous heroic bamba associated with capoeira in Bahia is Besouro, hailing from the interior town of Santo Amaro da Purificação. Besouro (Manuel Henrique) was reputedly invincible in combat, his "closed" body magically immunized against metal blades. Legend holds that Besouro was so bold that he took firearms from police officers in pitched battles and later returned the weapons to the police station. Reportedly confronted by forty armed men, he escaped—because of magical invulnerability, according to some; others claim that he turned himself into a beetle and flew away. He borrowed his nickname, "Besouro Mangangá," from a beetle with a poisonous sting. Many attempts to kill him failed, but eventually, already famous at the age of 27, he was stabbed to death with a horn knife in the town of Maracangalha (see Pires 2002). Biographical details are sparse, but references to Besouro in song are frequent. Eight of the songs Waldeloir Rego (1968: 123–124) collected are about him, and I heard many, including some of the most popular verses.

Traditional songs make reference to a variety of capoeira heroes. Some songs include biographical information, but most are little more than invocations of a renowned name. Almost invariably, histories of capoeira—especially those written by practitioners—offer extensive lists of the names of famous capoeiristas, sometimes pages long, with minimal narration (e.g., Pastinha 1988: 23–26; J. Moura 1991: 36–37, 43, 61; Coutinho 1993: 65–66). For example, in Mestre Bola Sete's discussion of "the *capoeiras* of Bahia," he includes almost five hundred names of contemporaries and predecessors (J. Oliveira 1989: 23–38).

The rosters of heroes, some with evocative *appelidos* or nicknames— Samuel "Beloved of God," "Seven Deaths," Antonio "Pig-Mouth,"

Maria "Twelve Men," "Traitor," Antonio "Devil"—together with place names, do more than simply preserve skeletal histories of fallen heroes and landmarks of their struggles. These lists evoke an epic age, a violent past in which distinguishing good and evil is not a primary concern. The events blur; the names roll off the tongue or past the eyes. The tales blend together: a *capoeira* kills for the love of a woman, capoeiristas fight *Yanquis* sailors stationed in Salvador during the Second World War, thugs duel with razor blades, capoeiristas flee police cavalry. . . . History recalled as a list of names and fragmentary stories of prowess in battle allows the past to pile up without chronology into an intense but ahistorical sense that the roda has seen the passing of many powerful figures. The past gets murkier just as it becomes overstuffed with conflict. The stories turn to epic, the names legend, and the state of war eternal in a myth-saturated yesteryear.

THE CLOSING OF THE "HEROIC CYCLE"

Scholar Muniz Sodré considered his former capoeira teacher, Mestre Bimba, to be "one of the last great figures of what we might call the heroic cycle of Blacks in Bahia."[6] Born November 23, 1900, in Salvador, Bahia, Manoel dos Reis Machado transformed capoeira, both through his own accomplishments and by creating Capoeira Regional. He symbolically closed the age of epic violence; himself a veteran of the mean streets, he introduced capoeira into the closed halls of the athletic academy.

Mestre Bimba worked as a carpenter, dockworker, and day laborer. He is said to have learned capoeira from Bentinho, an African ship's captain with the Bahian Navigation Company, and the brutal techniques of *batuque* from his father, Luis Cândido Machado. His father was a champion of the Afro-Bahian challenge dance, batuque, in which one dancer tries to trip or knock down a stationary adversary (also sometimes called *pernada*).

As he grew, Mestre Bimba became frustrated that capoeira was not afforded equal status with jujitsu, boxing, and *luta livre* (free-style wrestling). He was disgusted by what he viewed as the impoverished capoeira seen at public festivals, in which participants competed to pick up with their mouths money thrown into the roda by spectators. As he began to teach capoeira in the 1920s, his admirers insist that Mestre Bimba developed the aggressive potential latent in capoeira, incorporated throws and trips from batuque, and, after observing other styles of fighting, created countermeasures derived from capoeira techniques. These modifications formed the core of Capoeira Regional (R. Almeida 1994b: 17).

Mestre Bimba vaulted into the public eye in a series of exhibitions beginning in 1934. Through Bahian newspapers, he offered an open challenge in 1936 to any who questioned the superiority of his fighting techniques, suggesting that skeptics bring their doubts to the ring. The matches were short and brutal, earning him the nearly forgotten nickname of "Three Blows" (*Três Pancadas*), because it was alleged that no adversary could withstand more (J. Moura 1991: 21; cf. Abreu 1999).

These fights attracted a growing number of young men to Mestre Bimba's classes, even youths from segments of Bahian society that had previously considered capoeira to be an urban blight or archaic folklore. Their parents may have looked down on the art; the young men wanted to learn how to fight from the city's champion. Students at the federal university in Salvador, especially those in the medical, legal, and engineering schools, flocked to his classes. In 1937 the secretary of education, health, and public assistance allowed Mestre Bimba to register his sporting academy, the Center of Regional Physical Culture (from which the name "Capoeira *Regional*" reputedly arose). The police still persecuted capoeira, but the "modern" period of the art had dawned. Students with high social standing entered the roda. Even the general public recognized Machado as *mestre* or "teacher." Ironically, the word "*capoeira*" still denoted a thug, thief, or political enforcer for many Brazilians. Following Mestre Bimba, capoeira became a symbol of Brazilian national identity. As Gladson de Oliveira Silva suggests (1993), capoeira passed from "the plantation to the university" almost entirely within the lifetime of one man.

The transformation of capoeira's social position was complete when, on July 23, 1953, the governor of Bahia invited Mestre Bimba to perform during an official reception for the Brazilian president, Getúlio Vargas, in the governor's palace. After the presentation, Vargas declared, "Capoeira is the only truly national sport," and allegedly invited the mestre to train his private guard (R. Almeida 1994b: 44).[7]

In 1972, frustrated that the state did not sufficiently reward his contributions to popular culture, Mestre Bimba left Bahia for Goiânia, the capital of the interior state of Goiás. There, the government and a former student promised the aging mestre a formal position in the public school system (R. Almeida 1994b: 57–58). The promised support never materialized, and, when he died on February 5, 1974, he was said to have been left hungry and betrayed. A group of Mestre Bimba's students erected a monument to their teacher and moved his remains to Bahia for reburial in 1978, even though, when alive, the mestre vowed angrily never to return to the state.

Mestre Bimba looms large in the living history of capoeira. His former disciples continue to recount episodes from the mestre's life and to transmit his lessons (e.g., U. Almeida 1986, 1999; R. Almeida 1994a; Decânio n.d.a.). His admirers commemorate him in innumerable songs, name schools for him, place his portrait on myriad posters and T-shirts, eulogize him in biographies, and consider him to be the most important authority in the capoeira community. Although his students frequently speak nostalgically, as if they shared the life of the *capoeiras* in their youth, they all assume that the violent age of the maltas is definitively passed (e.g., U. Almeida 1986: 111–123; cf. J. Moura 1991: 47–51; R. Almeida 1994b: 63–68). The notorious heroic cycle has ended. Mestre Bimba provides an incarnate link to this epic period, assuring contemporary practitioners through his own street fights and feats in the prizefighting ring that the capoeira they practice is grounded in the heroism of the original *capoeiras*. To have learned capoeira under Mestre Bimba is to have come into direct personal contact with the heroic cycle of capoeira history, to have brushed up against this violent age. Apprenticeship to the mestre serves as a badge of authenticity, so much so that some seem to exaggerate grotesquely their teacher's violence.

For his detractors, Mestre Bimba is either a tragic figure or a traitor. They describe him as charismatic, sometimes even conceding that he was a great practitioner of the traditional art; but above all his critics hold him responsible for corrupting the capoeira community. Either he or his students are blamed for betraying the struggle against oppression, the most important overarching theme in the liberatory mode of imagining capoeira history.

THE LONG STRUGGLE FOR LIBERATION

The members of the Grupo de Capoeira Angola Pelourinho recall the past as a saga of struggle against enslavement, cruelty, and exploitation, in which capoeira traditionally served as a weapon of the weak. Notorious accounts of capoeira history close the chapter on heroic violence; in the liberatory epic, however, members of GCAP imply that the long-fought war against racial oppression continues. Just as Brazilian society is said to inherit a recalcitrant racism, GCAP casts itself as an heir to a legacy of resistance. Whereas some adepts revel in the outlaw image of the *capoeiras*, members of GCAP claim that Afro-Brazilians were more often simply on the wrong side of unjust laws. The notorious version of capoeira history tends to be amoral, even cynical; history in a liberatory register reverberates with strong moral undertones. This moral reading of capoeira's role in Brazilian history buttresses the Grupo de Capoeira Angola Pelourinho's political and cultural authority. It provides a persuasive rationale for the group's many projects, such as teaching capoeira to street children and in impoverished neighborhoods, and it imbues with authority the group's distinctive way of practicing Capoeira Angola. Preserving an African art is cast as a way to resist aggressive collective amnesia about slavery and the racist erasure of Afro-Brazilian contributions to Brazil's culture.

The liberatory framing of capoeira history reaches deeper into the past than the notorious version—to colonial Brazil, and even to the African communities from which slaves were abducted. For those interested in the *capoeiras*, old police records and newspaper archives may corroborate references to maltas. In contrast, early episodes of capoeira's development on plantations and in communities of escaped Africans are virtually invisible in historical records. The members of GCAP argue that this invisibility is not an accident; selective social memory is a technique for racial oppression. They tell an apocryphal story about Finance Minister Rui Barbosa, the republican stalwart who burned the archives recording slave transactions in Rio de Janeiro in 1890 (cf. Butler 1998b: 7). Although patriotic histories allege that the official sought to erase the shameful stain of slavery, most historians also note that he protected Brazil's new republican government from indemnity claims by slaveholders who had lost their human "property" in 1888. Members of GCAP pointed out that the arson made uncovering the history of slave life, including the development of capoeira, even more difficult (see GCAP 1993: 7). This forces modern researchers to study painstakingly every fragmentary description of slave life in a traveler's account, every clue to slave culture in an old engraving, every reference by a folklorist to a potential ancestral art, and every mention of Africa in an old song.

The liberatory saga recounted by GCAP consists of four primary episodes: the art's African origin, the slaves' struggle against their masters, the government's persecution of urban *capoeiras*, and the survival of Capoeira Angola in spite of the creation of Capoeira Regional. One reason that GCAP has become so influential among capoeira practitioners is that this account has such compelling moral force. It is a saga of ongoing struggle against racial injustice, a Manichean confrontation between good and evil.

AFRICAN ORIGINS AND SLAVE RESISTANCE

Like many scholars of the African diaspora, capoeiristas often claim that the art is firmly rooted in African soil. For members of GCAP, capoeira arose from the African dance *n'golo*—also called the "Dance of the

Zebras." The n'golo dance accompanied female initiation among the "Bakóongos" in what is now Angola, according to GCAP histories (1989: 35; 1993: 6, 16). Young men allegedly performed the competitive dance, and the one judged champion could take a bride without paying bride wealth.[8] As evidence of the connection to Africa, members of GCAP point to the frequent mention of "Luanda," the capital of Angola, in capoeira songs. They recall that the traditional form of the art was once known as *Capoeira* de *Angola*—capoeira "of" or "from" Angola. Instead of an etymology of the term "capoeira" from indigenous languages,

A student decorates berimbaus with patterns of yellow and black paint, the colors of Mestre Pastinha's academy. (*Photo by C. Peçanha*)

they see a possible origin in African languages. In addition, group members say that travelers to the Angolan coast report seeing dances with steps that resemble capoeira techniques.

Practitioners overtly celebrate capoeira's connection to Africa in many ways. Several groups take their names from the n'golo dance or other references to the continent. Zebra-stripe motifs appear in school logos, adorn T-shirts, and decorate instruments in Afrocentric groups. Children participating in a GCAP program composed a ladainha recounting the art's development:

> Iê! Capoeira is an art,
> Capoeira is an art that the black man invented.
> It was from the fight of two zebras that the n'golo was created.
> Arriving here in Brazil, it was called "capoeira."
> Ginga [the basic capoeira step] and dance that had been art were transformed into a weapon
> To liberate the black man from the slave quarters of the master.
> Today I learn this culture to make myself conscious.
> Thanks to Father Ogum [the orixá, or Afro-Brazilian deity of war], the force of the Orixás, comrade. . . . (GCAP 1994)

The song describes the early history of capoeira, explicitly linking it to the children's lives. Learning the art transforms their awareness and joins them to the liberatory struggle.

Members of the Grupo de Capoeira Angola Pelourinho reject the idea that slavery produced capoeira—it is African, they insist—but they suggest that the institution shaped the art. They assume that references to slavery in a host of capoeira songs are evidence that capoeira was a part of slaves' daily life. For example, group members repeatedly singled out the verse "Going to tell my master that the butter spilled." (Another line in the song reminds the listener that "The butter is not mine, the butter is the master's.") Alongside quotidian examples like this one, resistance, escape, and the formation of fugitive communities provide some of the most dramatic narrative elements in the liberatory account of capoeira's history.

In this chapter of liberatory histories, Zumbi, the final ruler of Palmares, serves as the central character. Palmares was a *quilombo*, or community of escaped slaves, that arose in the hinterlands of Brazil in the seventeenth century. GCAP explained the group's dedication to Zumbi in the liner notes to a recording:

> [We] would like to take this opportunity to pay homage to our hero, Zumbi dos Palmares, on the 300th anniversary of his death.[9] Zumbi was

the king of Palmares, the largest *quilombo* in what is the modern state of Pernambuco. Palmares endured repeated attacks over the eighty years of its existence during the seventeenth century. For more than a half-century, the community was led valiantly by Zumbi who fought for freedom for African peoples in Brazil. His assassination was the product of fear, hatred, and a profound lack of understanding. (GCAP 1996: 9)

Palmares and other quilombos play a crucial role in modern memories of the Afro-Brazilian struggle for freedom. These maroon communities refute the once-common portrait of docile Brazilian slaves peacefully acquiescing to servitude. The quilombos demonstrated that Africans could create their own institutions and were capable of self-government. In addition, many admirers consider the quilombos to have been strongholds of African culture in the face of European attack.

Histories and capoeira songs frequently incorporate Palmares and the Revolt of the Malês, a Muslim-led slave rebellion in Bahia in 1835 (see Pereira and Carvalho 1992: 43, 55, 100, 105–107 on Zumbi). Although GCAP's liberatory narratives invariably include mention of both, they scrupulously avoid explicitly claiming that capoeira was practiced by the Malês or in Palmares. In fact, no conclusive evidence confirms that capoeira was used in either setting. But some of the more evocative popular histories are not so fastidious (e.g., Burlamaqui 1928: 11–13). In a children's history written in the United States, for example, the author vividly describes capoeira contests in Palmares and suggests that quilombo leaders such as Zumbi were expert practitioners (Salaam 1983: 15–26).[10] Whether or not capoeira was actually practiced in these prior moments, the liberatory framing of capoeira history makes it logical to include Palmares and the Malês' revolt: they are early examples of struggle against persecution, crucial if one is to understand both capoeira's development and the current condition of black Brazilians.

GCAP members believe that Brazil's dominant groups repressed the art because it was a tool for rebellion and the expression of resistance. The survival of capoeira is testimony to the unbreakable spirit of those who handed down the art. In the words of a GCAP publication, the powerful could not "eradicate the language of discontent or the necessity of struggle" by "cells of the oppressed ethnic group," no matter how viciously they tried (GCAP 1993: 7).[11]

This framing changes the emotional tenor of events also central in the notorious account of capoeira history. For example, references in capoeira songs to "Paraná," the name of the river that forms the border between Brazil and Paraguay, remind many capoeiristas of the war against

Paraguay (cf. Lewis 1992: 181). For those who hear capoeira's history in a notorious key, the survival of *capoeiras* in the war against Paraguay demonstrates their formidability: sent into battle with insufficient firearms, left to win their weapons on the battlefield. Told in a liberatory tone, in contrast, this episode smacks of blatant exploitation: pressed into military service, sent into battle with too few weapons, the *capoeiras* were expendable cannon fodder. Every black Brazilian sent into battle, according to this understanding of the war, was a no-lose proposition. If the soldier killed a Paraguayan, a foreign policy problem was one body closer to being solved; if he died in battle, a future domestic disturbance was eliminated. The notorious reading of this event is neutral or celebratory, dwelling primarily on the valor of the *capoeiras;* the liberatory reading is outraged at how unjustly the state treated black Brazilians.

THE TRAGIC LIFE AND DEATH OF MESTRE PASTINHA

Just as the notorious version of capoeira history has a heroic figure to serve as the primary link between modern practitioners and the past, the liberatory narrative has Mestre Pastinha. To his rare detractors, Mestre Pastinha was merely one of a number of great capoeiristas in his generation, elevated to an exalted position by his influential friends, including novelist Jorge Amado and artist Carybé.[12] To his loyal supporters, Pastinha is a cultural hero: fighter, poet, composer, teacher of teachers, and self-sacrificing guardian of traditional Capoeira Angola. To Mestre Bimba's image as a prizefighting champion, Pastinha plays a complementary role as artist and sage, his wisdom condensed into aphorisms of koan-like complexity. Together, Mestre Pastinha and Mestre Bimba form a vivid contrast that for many capoeiristas embodies the two sides of the art.

Born April 5, 1889, the son of an African mother and Spanish father, Vicente Ferreira Pastinha was introduced to capoeira by a neighbor who saw the slight young boy repeatedly beaten up by a larger rival.[13] Pastinha reported teaching capoeira for decades, but he ascended to public prominence in February 1941, when he inherited from Amorzinho—a legendary *capoeira* of the prior generation—responsibility for directing a recurring roda in the Gengibirra neighborhood of Salvador.[14] Later, in Salvador's historic district, Pastinha opened the *Centro Esportivo de Capoeira Angola*, the first center for teaching Capoeira Angola to be registered with civil authorities.

In the centro, Mestre Pastinha presided over rodas that attracted many spectators, as well as some of Salvador's best capoeiristas. Veteran players described those rodas nostalgically as gatherings of the luminaries of the Bahian art, who played before the eyes of aficionados and naïve

Mestres João Pequeno (left) and João Grande, two of Mestre Pastinha's most renowned students, rest in João Pequeno's academy in the Forte do Santo Antônio Além do Carmo. But even old friends sometimes do not sit close when they are capoeiristas. (Photo by C. Peçanha)

tourists alike. Pastinha served as a cultural representative for Bahia, traveling with four of his students in 1966 as part of the Brazilian delegation to the First International Festival of Black Arts (FESTAC), in Senegal. In addition, Mestre Pastinha trained a generation of apprentices, many of whom, in turn, became some of Salvador's most-respected mestres.

In spite of Pastinha's renown, the municipal government closed the mestre's Centro Esportivo de Capoeira Angola in 1971 to renovate the building that housed it. When the building reopened, the mestre was not allowed to return. Instead, SENAC, a restaurant school for waiters and chefs, took over the building. Ironically, nightly folklore performances are held for tourists at SENAC to this day. Prominent friends and admirers secured for Pastinha a pension from the city, but his academy remained shuttered.[15]

GCAP describes the mestre's final years as unmitigated tragedy:

> Isolated in a tiny apartment near his former academy, practically blind and unable to give classes, he expressed his frustration: "This wooden bench is all that I have. Today I am convinced that I was tricked. I gave it my all, but the truth is that I was used. No matter what, if I were to be born again, I would choose the same life: *capoeira.*"
>
> On November 13, 1981, death took one of the descendants of Zumbi. He died poor, in the company of a few friends and students, forgotten by a society that does not value the living treasures of popular culture. (GCAP 1996: 26–27)

Pastinha's sad end paralleled the demise of Zumbi, Besouro, and Mestre Bimba. As researcher Frederico Abreu puts it, capoeira heroes "tradition-ally" live at "the crossroads of fame and hunger" (*a cruzada de fama e fome*). Mestre Pastinha's descent into poverty, abandonment, and lingering misery—like the treatment of *capoeiras* who served in Paraguay—provides a stinging critique of how Brazil treats its African heritage: taking advantage of it while neglecting those who preserve that legacy.[16]

Capoeiristas invoke Mestre Pastinha's name in the salutations they sing before games—*Iê, viva Pastinh', camará!* They honor him in song dur-ing the course of games, such as in a line I heard frequently: "I play capoeira, [but] Mestre Pastinha is the greatest!" (see J. Oliveira 1989: 125). In the main room of the Grupo de Capoeira Angola Pelourinho's acad-emy, photographs of the late mestre hung above the orchestra bench, his blind eyes unearthly in the high-contrast black and white images. Players often gestured respectfully to these pictures when his name was sung. Mestre Pastinha presided over the roda, in a manner of speaking.

Mestre Pastinha serves many critical roles in GCAP's liberatory narrative: not only did he provide eloquent statements of capoeira principles and demonstrate the moral bankruptcy of Brazil's treatment of black culture, he also anchors the group's genealogy and articulated many critiques of Capoeira Regional. One's teacher is important to establish a capoeirista's legitimacy. For this reason, many modern teachers claim to have trained under Pastinha. In a statement written by GCAP, for example, they link their genealogy and their authenticity explicitly:

> We turned ourselves into disciples of the teachings left by Mestre Pastinha through successive master–disciple relations: Pastinha—João Grande—Moraes—GCAP. In this way, we joined the struggle to main-tain the traditions of Capoeira Angola, today practiced by very few people. (GCAP 1993: 5)

In addition, Mestre Pastinha learned Capoeira Angola from an African, Tio Benedito; at the same time that Pastinha is a source of authority, his historically recent receipt of capoeira from an African strengthens the group's assertion that capoeira originated across the Atlantic.[17] By adher-ing faithfully to the style of capoeira he bequeathed to them, the group believes that it, too, resists the racist erasure of capoeira's African nature. During his lifetime, Pastinha explicitly repudiated Capoeira Regional. GCAP members interpret Pastinha's criticisms as an indictment of the racial politics of Capoeira Regional (cf. Frigerio 1989).

In the dedication of their compact disc, GCAP tied together the four periods of its liberatory history under the subtitle, "Zumbi Lives!":

In many ways, we continue to face the same enemies today. The descendants of Africans living in myriad different places are still aspiring to full citizenship, fighting for the day when the systems built in part through the abduction, violation, torture, and forced labor of African peoples will recognize the rights of all people—including the granddaughters and grandsons of the slaves. To GCAP, Zumbi dos Palmares symbolizes the struggle for those rights. . . . For GCAP, Zumbi lives on, just as do all who have joined in this struggle, like capoeira *mestres* Pastinha, Bimba, Valdemar, Cobrinha Verde, Canjiquinha, Bobó, and others. (GCAP 1996: 9–10)

When group members sing *Eu sou angoleiro* (I am an angoleiro), a swell of pride is palpable. This emotion arises in part from experiencing the connections described in this dedication between contemporary practice and the long struggle for liberation.

ALTERNATIVE HISTORIES

Critics accuse the Grupo de Capoeira Angola Pelourinho and other Afrocentric capoeiristas of themselves being racist or overly "militant," a charge commonly leveled against anyone who draws attention to racism in Brazil. Some versions of the liberatory narrative, instead, downplay race. Mestre Almir das Areias's account of capoeira history, for instance, does not emphasize the racial implications of the art even though he argues that it was born in slavery. Areias, an influential teacher living in São Paulo, asserts that to understand capoeira, the curious must first turn their attention "to the liberatory struggles of Afro-Brazilians and to the suffering, struggles, and aspirations of our people throughout these years, from slavery until our days" (Areias 1983: 8). As he recounts this history, Areias makes a subtle shift; in one sentence capoeira changes from being an expression of the struggles of African slaves to the "aspirations of our people," that is, Brazilians. Areias goes on to explain that black culture under slavery embodied "a necessity that every human has—to struggle and express him- or herself—to be, and to exist as a human being" (ibid.: 8–9). Capoeira may be Afro-Brazilian, but it is the outgrowth of a universal existential need. Because of this existential appeal, adepts like Areias, who see capoeira as universal, often have grand ambitions for the art to spread beyond Brazil's borders. Areias implies that capoeira serves primarily to promote a personal, therapeutic liberation.[18]

Other historical narratives of capoeira's origin abound, some serious and some fanciful. For example, in an effort to disabuse me of the Afrocentric history that I learned at GCAP, a rival mestre insisted that the art originated in the wrestling games of Brazil's indigenous peoples. Other versions of capoeira history suggest that the art's distinctive techniques were learned from watching animals (e.g., Areias 1983; 13–19; Senna 1994). The cabeçada, or head butt, some suggest, was learned from rams; whirling kicks from the stingray or alligator; and back kicks from horses, mules, or zebras. These narratives sometimes link capoeira to ecological thinking. Nestor Capoeira (1985), for example, begins a history of capoeira with the "cosmic ballet," the galaxy, and the appearance of primitive humans, all of which lead inexorably to capoeira and provide its philosophical roots.

Ângelo Decânio relates a "legend of capoeira"—clearly equal parts myth and tall tale—that he heard in the academy of Mestre Bimba (Decânio n.d.a.). In the story, Solomon was walking on the "highway of life." He traveled at dusk, the hour of the trickster orixá Exú, who mediates between humans and the supernatural world. Passing a crossroads, Solomon heard the otherworldly sound of the berimbau and a sad, bewitching voice inviting him to begin a game—"a battle between the conscience and dream! . . . between the Magic and the I!" (ibid.: 26). A *saci*, a malevolent little spirit with a red hat and single leg, attacked Solomon "without tangling up . . . like a snake on the ground . . . to see who was the better fighter [literally, "who could more"] . . ." (ibid.: 26). According to Decânio, that primordial battle between Solomon and the saci continues to this day, as does the call of the trickster, the berimbau, to join the fight.

HOW HISTORIES ARE HEARD

One distinctive characteristic of capoeira memory is that players recall the past in musical performance. When practitioners from different schools come together at public events, players can argue about history through song. A soloist, for example, may initiate a call-and-response verse that forces the audience to assent to an interpretation of capoeira's past with which they don't agree; roda etiquette demands that they enthusiastically sing the response even if they disagree with the lyrics. Several militant angoleiros, for instance, seemed to delight in initiating songs that praised Capoeira Angola at academies of Capoeira Regional.

At the First Regional Seminar of Capoeira and Festival of the Rhythm of Capoeira held in 1981, a watershed event in the reinvigoration of Capoeira Angola, some of Bahia's venerable mestres openly clashed with representatives of the Movimento Negro Unificado (Unified Black Movement or MNU). MNU members argued that abolition in 1888 was a cynical ploy by monarchists to gain black allies, a legal maneuver that did little to change the real condition of Afro-Brazilians. In the midst of the seminar, over the objections of the MNU, Mestre Canjiquinha led the assembly in a traditional song saluting Princesa Isabel:

> Hail! Hail the nation!
> Hail the Brazilian nation!
> Hail Princesa Isabel, oh my God,
> Who delivered me from captivity![19]

The verse asserted that, to borrow from another song, "capoeira loves abolition."[20] By singing this salute, Mestre Canjiquinha invoked popular affection for the princess and the alliance of the maltas with monarchists in the 1880s.

Talking about capoeira memory as narratives, however, can be misleading. Capoeiristas only rarely recall history as a story proceeding from start to finish. A written narrative like this one can ignore the most basic phenomenological facts about the song texts it draws upon, forgetting where they came from when these references are pinned down on a page and arranged into a coherent order. When songs were alive and breathing, they are embedded in instrumental music and sung to accompany games.

In the roda, no chronological progression binds together stories in a meaningful order. References to the past are pulverized and scattered. They emerge in no particular order in the oscillations of call-and-response singing. Stories and names of fallen heroes are shouted out at crucial moments, not in relation to the event sung about before, but to comment upon the game, to instruct, provoke, chastise, or inspire. Discerning historical relations among capoeira song texts is impossible from the performance context alone; the events, names, and places are just too jumbled in fluid improvisation. Sung texts and historical references in the roda do not elaborate a story; they animate a sonic performance space and shape how players experience the art.

5 SINGING THE PAST INTO PLAY

Capoeiristas put the past into play by singing. In addition, teachers use historical analogies to explain movement techniques, old mestres recount capoeira legends, and groups host special events that explore the art's history, or post bulletin boards of old newspaper clippings. Players may seek out more information about capoeira's past in books, articles, or even Salvador's Afro-Brazilian Museum, home to personal effects that once belonged to mestres Bimba and Pastinha. Nevertheless, in capoeira, the past usually arises in the songs that accompany games. Even outside the roda, when capoeiristas talk about the history of the art, they frequently quote from song texts. The habit is acquired by most academics who study the genre, including this one. Songs are frequently said to be the living memory of capoeira, its oral history. But the art's oral history is not sung in isolation; it is recounted as players trade attack and defense in the roda. To understand how the past *feels* to practitioners—that is, to offer a phenomenological analysis of historical memory—one must listen closely to these songs and note how players encounter temporal depth in the art.

A roda is a musical event divided temporally by its song cycle. A soloist opens the roda with a monologue called a "ladainha" before proceeding to two different types of call-and-response song. The first, performed before play can start, is a series of salutations, warnings, prayers, and exhortations. When the call-and-response sequence is over, the leader initiates the *corridos*, songs that accompany play. A number of corridos may follow in succession. The soloist may call for the music to stop at any moment, perhaps because the orchestra has started to lose cohesion, or to allow several musicians to hand off their instruments at once. When the music restarts, the cycle begins anew with a ladainha.

Capoeira songs do not simply accompany the game. Songs can serve as running commentary on the game, or become a medium for verbal play in their own right (see Lewis 1992: 162–187). By adroitly leading the chorus, the soloist directs the two players in the roda, enhances their game, and engages all the participants. A roda without singing, or, worse, with recorded music, is a pale, inadequate substitute for one with a vigorous chorus and orchestra. A clever soloist can goad players to perform their best and moderate the flow of the game, maintaining the taut balance between aggression and cooperation that is a hallmark of the most compelling rodas. In this way, singing animates a sonic space where the best possible capoeira will be played.

Into this dynamic nexus of song, music, and play, capoeiristas sing history. Reminding players of the past produces the ideal experiential environment for the game. History is not recalled as long-ago events to be contemplated. Songs put the past to work, using it actively to excite players' awareness of the sinister implications of the art. How singing contributes to the experiential texture of the roda resembles sung poetry among the Foi of Papua New Guinea, according to anthropologist James Weiner. Weiner explains: "Insofar as poetry can be said to have a 'function,' it is the 'spatial' one of bringing into our present nearness things that have receded into the distance of our historical attention" (1991: 200). When capoeiristas sing past events into nearness, they remind those at a roda that the art arose through violence and struggle. History appears in a poetic mode, calling players to experience the present in new ways.

The rhetorical form in which history is sung—often in the first person, as if the singers themselves were protagonists in past events—encourages capoeiristas to experience the modern art as an echo of the past. Through a form of poetic projection, past events are brought close, and singers are inclined to take up the postures attributed to fallen heroes, who were fearless, aware of danger, mistrustful of authority, and yet playful in the face of violence. At the same time that the violent past looms over the roda in song, players sing their way into the cunning comportments their ancestors used to face these challenges.

THE SONG CYCLE

In the Grupo de Capoeira Angola Pelourinho, once the orchestra established the rhythm, the lead singer initiated the song cycle by bellowing, with a loud chest shout, "Iê!" After the shout—the cue both to begin the roda and to stop the music—followed a long, solo ladainha. To sing the solo litany was a privilege, usually afforded to the senior-most practitioner or delegated to a talented younger player. A soloist might draw from a body of traditional ladainhas or, less frequently, improvise on the spot, often by modifying formulaic verses to suit the current situation.

Mestre João Pequeno (left with hands raised) sings prior to the beginning of a game in the Grupo de Capoeira Angola Pelourinho. Mestre João Grande leads the orchestra (seated between the two players in white pants). (Photo by C. Peçanha)

New students were ordered to listen closely to the ladainha, and play could not start until it ended.

Ladainhas allegedly contain the wisdom and memory of capoeira in condensed form. In addition, veterans told novices that the ladainha was a forum in which a singer could comment on a game or offer players advice tailored to their situation. As the ladainha unfolded, the two capoeiristas who were to begin play crouched to either side of "the foot of the berimbau" (*o pé do berimbau*), listening respectfully. On occasion, a player at the foot of the berimbau offered the ladainha.

Mestre Moraes sings a particularly vivid ladainha to open the recording *Capoeira Angola from Salvador Brazil* (GCAP 1996). The solo invokes the memory of Zumbi of Palmares and argues that the twentieth of November, the "Day of Black Consciousness" on which Zumbi's assassination is commemorated, deserves more attention than the anniversary of abolition on May 13:

History deceives us—it says everything incorrectly,
It even says that abolition happened in the month of May.

The proof of this lie is that I do not escape from misery.
Long live the 20th of November, a moment to be remembered.
I don't see anything about the 13th of May to commemorate.
A long time has passed, and the black man will always struggle.
Zumbi is our hero, Zumbi is our hero, old friend.
　He was the leader of Palmares.
For the cause of the black man, it was he who fought the most.
In spite of all the fighting, my friend, the black man did not liberate himself,
　comrade![1]

After the soloist sings *camará!* (comrade!) to signal the end of the ladainha comes the second part of the song cycle, which members of GCAP call the *chula*. Elsewhere, this part of the song cycle is also referred to as the *canto de entrada* (entry song), the *reza* (prayer), or the *louvação* (eulogy or praising). Soloists spontaneously assemble this call-and-response sequence from familiar elements. The couplets develop a limited number of themes: prayers, salutations of mestres, warnings, and exhortations to play. The soloist chooses the order, usually following a common pattern: praises to God are sung first; invitations to play or warnings last, just before the start of the game. Everyone in the orchestra, waiting to play, and watching nearby forms a chorus that repeats back the soloist's calls, adding "camará!" to the end of each one.

On the GCAP recording, Moraes sings a very brief chula, starting, "It's time, it's time!" Moraes and the chorus continue the call and response:

Ôi iaiá, let's go!
Chorus: Iê, let's go, comrade!

Ôi iá, through the outside!
Chorus: Iê, through the outside, comrade!

Ôi iaiá, Hail to my God!
Chorus: Iê, Hail to my God, comrade!

Ôi iaiá, Hail to my mestre!
Chorus: Iê, Hail to my mestre, comrade!

Ôi iaiá, who taught me
Chorus: Iê, who taught me, comrade!

In some opening salutations, the soloist warns the players that an adversary is especially dangerous—a "head butter," a "sorcerer," or someone who really "knows how to play"—or cautions players by reminding them of the weapons that *capoeiras* once wielded. If a player sings before his or her own game, the chula may assert dramatically that an adversary "wants to kill me" or extravagantly praise an opponent's ability. After these salutations and warnings, the soloist leads the chorus into the corridos. Once the first corrido has begun, the two players who are waiting at the foot of the berimbau can begin their game. Unlike the chula, in which the chorus echoes back the soloist's call, corridos are built around an unchanging choral part. No matter what the caller sings or improvises, unless he or she changes the song, the chorus sings the same line in response. For example, in the recording by the Grupo de Capoeira Angola Pelourinho, Mestre Moraes follows his chula with the call, "*Santa Bárbara que relampuê, é Santa Bárbara que relampuá.*" The chorus recognizes this familiar song, and sings back, "*O Santa Bárbara que relampuê*" (Oh Saint Barbara who brings lightning). They continue to sing this response as Moraes varies his call. During the course of a corrido, a soloist may sing calls that exhort the chorus to respond more energetically, comment on the game, or joke with other players in the roda. At some point, often when the energy of the chorus flags, the soloist breaks into a new corrido over an unchanging instrumental accompaniment.

In other groups the song cycle may proceed straight to the corridos or the roda may be initiated with a brief solo *quadra* and "canto de entrada" sequence, rather than the longer, more solemn ladainha. The formal ladainha–chula structure used by the Grupo de Capoeira Angola Pelourinho mirrors the pacing of the organization's rodas, in which games are given time to develop slowly. The group's advocacy of this song cycle has helped to make this model of capoeira singing widely respected as traditional, even if old recordings of capoeira music do not uniformly evidence the same structure.

SINGING COMMENTARY ON THE GAME

In the roda, the singing should ideally be closely related to the unfolding of the games. Songs should inspire players to engage in spirited, exciting play at the same time that singing moderates the intensity of the action, smothering excessive aggression or stoking competitive fires if a game cools too much. Enthusiastic singing is essential to a good roda. Novice players are encouraged to sing energetically, even if they don't know the response well.

Like the kicks, leg sweeps, and acrobatic dodges used in the roda, singing is a medium for interacting, especially in the hands of a deft song leader. It's not enough to simply sing well and loudly. Aptly choosing which songs to lead is itself a skill, and apprenticeship in capoeira entails acquiring this ability in addition to the physical techniques used in the game. A leader may employ songs to comment upon an event, make a philosophical point or historical argument, or provoke laughter. By choosing songs well, the soloist contributes to the event at the same time that he or she demonstrates a command of the game's dynamics, a sharp aesthetic sense, deep knowledge of the song repertoire, and a quick sense of humor.

For example, if two players become agitated during a game, the song leader may begin a corrido that implores, "*Devagar! Devagar! Capoeira Angola é devagarinho*," telling the pair, "Easy! Easy! Capoeira Angola is [played] slowly." If a game between aggressive players degenerates into a set of ugly, choppy exchanges, a soloist might choose to sing that capoeira is "a beautiful game that I want to see." In one corrido, the chorus responds, "*Nhem, nhem, nhem*," mimicking a child crying—or ridiculing a player who gets upset. Overly violent play may inspire the song "Quebra" which mocks a player: "I'm going to break everything today," and "And tomorrow nothing left to break." Or a singer may plead simply, "Please, my brother, I don't want a brawl here, no." If one player inappropriately holds an adversary, the offending player may be compared to a clinging woman: "Oh, Doralice, don't grab me, no."[2] If the chorus is reluctant to sing, it may be encouraged to do so: "Good heavens, Hail Mary, This roda is mute, and I didn't know!" A song leader is liable to shift abruptly to a new song in response to the action in the roda, winning smiles from the audience for a good choice of verse.

Other songs provoke players. A singer may taunt, telling a capoeirista, "You're not going to get this guy," as the chorus responds, "Give, give, give it to him!" If a player is tripped during a game, a soloist may respond with "My machete struck low" (to which the chorus responds, "The banana tree toppled over"), or "Hail Mary, My God! Never saw a new house fall down!" If the trip occurred in an unevenly matched game, it might be greeted with, "Crab put a fig tree on the ground." A more sympathetic caller might sing, "The *baraúna* tree fell, how much more likely am I [to fall]?" The song consoles the person who has fallen by pointing out that anyone can be caught off guard.

Only the memory and wit of a singer limit how songs might be used to comment on a game. The resources available from the collective artistry of capoeiristas are immense; one well-connected mestre in Rio de Janeiro reported that his group had collected lyrics for over fifteen hundred songs. A virtuoso has a deep well from which to draw. One afternoon, for instance, a player prematurely tried to take a berimbau from a venerable Bahian mestre during a roda. The offending player was greeted with, "This bow is mine, this bow is mine, this bow is mine, it was my father who gave it to me" (cf. Lewis 1992: 170). When a younger capoeirista faced a wizened veteran at the foot of the berimbau, a soloist might initiate, "Protect me God, [and] great St. Benedict." One of the song's calls warns that, "An old hole has a snake inside." At another roda, the arrival of a teacher nicknamed "Shorty" prompted a talented soloist to begin the song, *Salomé, Salomé.* One of the song's calls cautions that "a short man is a wife-stealer" (or that he "steals from women"), which the singer shouted energetically. The warning provoked peels of laughter from the audience, and the visitor emphatically mimed outraged denial of the charge.

Very rarely, what Lowell Lewis (1992) calls "verbal play" may escalate into a full-blown sung duel. Veteran players and archival sources report that, in the past, players engaged in sung duels called *cantigas de sotaque* (ballads of brogue). Instead of a one-sided exchange, in which only the soloist gets to taunt a player ("Look, there's an urchin!"), players sing verses that challenge each other, either improvising lyrics or recalling older couplets (cf. Rego 1968: 55).[3] In these cases, singing resembled capoeira play pursued by other means, displaying the same cunning interactive dynamic found in kicks, head butts, and dodges.

MORTAL SERIOUSNESS AND PRAYER

Capoeira songs frequently suggest that capoeira is a serious, even mortal business. Lowell Lewis suggests that frequent references to death may be a metaphor for a fall in the roda, and that, in addition, "students rehearse the techniques as if their lives depended on them" (1992: 167–168). However, Lewis also points out that claims in songs such as "Capoeira is swift, it's Brazilian, it's for killing," are so blatant that it's hard to construe them as metaphors. In an account of a singing duel, after the players finished trading challenges, the audience applauded and sang a popular corrido to goad the players into action: "Zum, zum, zum, capoeira kills one. Zum, zum, zum, in the yard [only] one remains" (J. Moura 1991: 77). I was told that "zum" is the sound a slashing knife makes.

Capoeiristas frequently discuss the dangers of the roda, referring to the art's violent past and cautioning players about potential perils that still exist. Teachers explained that they encouraged players to recognize the dangers in the roda to prepare them for those rare moments when an adversary actually intends them harm. Warnings about death serve as a reminder to students that they are learning an art of self-defense and need to be careful when they play. Evoking death in song, however, typically does not create an air of caution or somberness in the roda. Rather, mentions of violence generally provoke a swaggering tone, a defiant air of cavalier disregard for danger. Singing about the threat of death, however remote it might be, evokes a mixture of bravado and morbidity around the roda. Every mestre has stories of dire injuries, and teachers repeat them frequently as cautionary tales.

At the same time that their awareness of peril is heightened, players sing prayerlike verses, as if to counteract the danger in the roda. One song, "Saint Anthony Is the Protector" (for which a caller may sing, "Is the protector of capoeira"), has a host of verses that invoke the saint's name for protection.[4] Among the most common songs, one can find prayers to São Bento (Saint Benedict), Santo Antonio, God, Bom Jesus (Good Jesus), Salomão (Solomon), Santa Maria (Holy Mary), and Nossa Senhora (either as "Our Lady," or in specific forms such as "Our Lady of the Immaculate Conception"). Some of these songs overtly resemble pleas for protection, such as: "Protect me God, [and] great St. Benedict," and "Holy Mary, Mother of God, I arrived in the church and confessed." A number of other popular verses make reference to the Afro-Brazilian deities called orixás, caboclos (the spirits of dead Native Americans), ritual actions, and other aspects of Bahian popular religion. In some sense, these songs heighten the seriousness of play; one sings prayers because capoeira could potentially be a grave undertaking.

Practitioners, observers, and scholars alike who have studied capoeira often assert that music restrains the game's violent tendencies. A good leader carefully monitors the intensity of the game and initiates corrective songs to prevent uncontrolled violence from erupting. Paradoxically, while songs can diminish the intensity of play, songs also build tension by continually generating an awareness that potential violence lies just below the surface of the game.

SHIFTING "I" ACROSS TIME

When history is sung in the roda, events from the past reappear in the midst of prayers, taunts, exhortations, and threats. This arrangement primes players to hear continuity between the past and present. Capoeiristas do not isolate the names of fallen heroes, distance themselves from mortal battles, or consign well-worn stories to a remote past. Instead, they apply historical references to the contemporary game, using them, like other song texts, to control, invigorate, and make sense of the ongoing action in the roda. The real nature of capoeira is thought to be revealed in its storied past. Like an evocative metaphor, a historical event, recalled at the right moment in a roda, cracks open the veneer of the obvious, revealing a deeper, more sinister truth lurking beneath the familiar rhythms and athletic steps of the game.

In capoeira songs a grammatical shift in point of reference suggestively encourages players to associate the past and present. Many capoeira songs recount the lives of heroes from a first-person perspective, as if the singer is the protagonist recounting an event from his or her own life. An example of this type of projection occurs in a song heard frequently in GCAP. The soloist begins:

> *When I die, I don't want crying [or "shouting"] or secret rites.*
> *When I die, I don't want crying or secret rites.*
> *I want a berimbau playing, at the gate of the cemetery.*
> *With a yellow ribbon, engraved with her name.*[5]
> *Still, even after death, Besouro Belt of Gold.*
> *What's my name?*

To which the chorus responds

> *It's "Besouro."*

The soloist then continues, "What am I called?" and "Belt of Gold" (one of Besouro's other nicknames), eliciting the response, "It's 'Besouro.'"[6]

Besouro, or "Beetle," was a Bahian thug, a central character in the notorious saga of capoeira discussed in Chapter Four. Capoeiristas know well his reputation as a knife fighter, as well as the treacherous way in which he met his end. As oral history, the song is thin; it provides scant biographical details or narrative development. As an evocative device, however, it possesses a goose-bump-inducing emotional power when juxtaposed to play in the roda.

The text evocatively shifts the perspective of the singer into the position of the fallen hero through projection.[7] For example, a person projects when saying something like, "Amy told me you'd be here. She said, 'If you promise to get there early, I'll be sure he's already there waiting for you.'" For this utterance to make sense, the individuals conversing must recognize that the speaker temporarily speaks from Amy's "position" (Amy, at the place and in the moment where she gave the instruction, is what Karl Bühler called the *origo*, or the "origin" point for speaker of the second sentence). If the listener does not also make this projection, he or she will not understand the shift in verb tenses (in the quotation, Amy used the future tense to refer to the present) or what words like "you" and "there" in the quoted speech signify (they actually designate the same thing the speaker means by "I" and "here" when not quoting). "What's *my* name?" "It's 'Besouro.'" Like any quotation, the song text takes "the vantage point of the source speaker . . . the I, here, and now from which the expressions are chosen" (Clark and Gerrig 1990: 786). Scholars who study deixis—words like "there," "you," or "this," which shift their reference depending on context—have demonstrated that quoting someone may require the speaker and listener to project imaginary space.[8] The song sung with Besouro prepared to die as its origo shows that this imaginary projection can also summon a vivid emotional texture.

This song combines historical reference with the gravity of one heroically facing the possibility of death. Sung references in the first person suggest an immediate relation between the present and a past fraught with intense emotion. The story is not framed with a distancing device, like "Once upon a time" or "Long ago." Instead, the song's ambiguous voicing places pressure on the divide between the commemorator and the person remembered, inviting a participant in the roda to imagine across the gap to an epic, violent past (see also Connerton 1989: 68–69). By poetically deploying the first person pronoun, "I," the song shifts the roda into an indeterminate frame; "I" (which one?) could die.[9] Some songs locate the chorus in paradigmatic historical scenarios. For example, the song "I'm Going to Tell My Master That the Butter Spilled," discussed in the previous chapter, rhetorically projects the chorus into the place of the slave. Epic history is sung in an empathetic voice.

Other capoeira songs tell of impending journeys to places thick with historical significance. By claiming to be "going there," the singer travels not only in space, but also in time to events encased in an epic geography.[10] For example, singing that "tomorrow, I'm going away," bound for Paraná, does not simply report a future journey to southern Brazil. The song shifts the singer into the position of one of the many *capoeiras* pressed into the military and sent to fight against neighboring Paraguay in the bloodiest war in South American history.

AMBIGUOUS TIMES IN SONG

More ambiguous songs create indefinite temporal frames. For example, the following corrido humorously captures the combination of bravado, duplicity, and accommodation that in many ways typifies a capoeirista's malícia, or cunning:

> *We're going to break "little coconuts"*
> *As long as the police don't come.*
> *If the police arrive, we're going to bust them up, too.*

Chorus: We're going to break "little coconuts"
As long as the police don't come.

When the police arrive,
Put water in the coffee and invite the police to join us. . . .[11]

The swaggering tough from whose perspective the song is sung vows to resist police intimidation. He later reconsiders his position—perhaps when the police actually arrive?—and offers them watered-down hospitality.

The song evokes an ambiguous temporal frame. It may be a reference to persecution in the past, such as in Rio de Janeiro in the 1890s, or in Salvador in the 1920s, when a special cadre of mounted police suppressed Afro-Brazilian culture. Or it may be a reference to the present, in which police still harass capoeiristas, especially those who perform in the street, if not for practicing capoeira, simply because many are dark skinned and poor (cf. Mitchell and Wood 1999; Caldeira 2000). The song reinforces lessons learned in the roda: that deception and cunning courtesy toward authority serve well when direct confrontation is too dangerous.

The flexibility of historical reference in capoeira songs is obvious where formulas for evoking the past can be adapted to a range of events. For example, a song that describes a *capoeira* being pressed into military service against Paraguay begins with a versatile couplet: "I was in my home/Without thinking, without imagining. . . ." As the song unfolds, someone summons the singer to fight. Various versions, however, find the singer called to a range of different conflicts. One common variant refers to the Second World War instead of the war against Paraguay, events separated by almost eight decades. That this verse is recycled for a range of historical events—I came across five different "targets" of the projection during my field research—should not strike us as unusual. Classicists, anthropologists, and ethnomusicologists who study vocal performance have long recognized that when composing extemporaneously, performers almost always rely upon a common stock of formulaic expressions, adapting verses to the performance context.[12] In the heat of the moment, singers produce variations on familiar verses, especially when a new composition must conform to a fixed rhythmic structure, melody, or rhyming scheme.

Capoeiristas consistently use the flexibility in the "I was in my home . . ." couplet to project themselves into the same sorts of historical event: pressed into the military, sent to war, braving the dangers of the *capoeiras* of old. The past summoned in the roda is invariably marked by the valor of the singers' predecessors. When mythical imaginings of the past bleed into the present, the strong emotions that accompany these dramatic events saturate the roda.

Songs in capoeira performance are not, from a phenomenological perspective, historical storage. Sung historical references do not primarily preserve information or recount a narrative. In fact, they are usually a meager source of information and too poorly organized to serve as history. The shifts in projection are too disorienting, the detail provided too sparse, and the jumble of the historical sequence during a game too confusing. The most salient experiential dimension of this form of remembering is the affective weight, the violent gravity that these events evoke. Historical references, like coaching, are an evocative form of applied poetry. A capoeirista does not sing in the roda primarily to remember; he or she remembers through song to feel the deeper truth of the game.[13]

PLAYING IN A POETIC PROJECTION

The roda is built, in part, out of singing.[14] Songs produce a lyrical space in which capoeira can be experienced fully, in all its temporal depth. The participants see the present as they hear the echoes of the past. To borrow from Maurice Merleau-Ponty's description of painting, one does not just hear a capoeira song, one hears "according to it, or with it" (1964: 164; cf. Ingold 2000: 265).[15] From a phenomenological perspective, mythic and historical pasts are ingredients that increase the visceral intensity and color the mood of the roda. Song draws to awareness latent traits in the game. By holding fast to images from capoeira's violent past, using them to evoke the latent violence in modern movements that might otherwise appear dancelike, theatrical, or playful, capoeira songs play with practitioners' sense of reality.

Capoeiristas told me repeatedly that these songs affected them deeply. One woman, an instructor, told me that they sometimes brought her close to tears as she imagined the events that the songs described. So powerful were her emotions that she felt this even when she didn't fully understand the lyrics. When I asked Mestre Moraes what to concentrate upon while singing, he told me I should think about my "ancestors." He did not mean my Irish and German forebears who immigrated to the midwestern United States. The capoeiristas who had come before me were now my relevant ancestors; entering the roda makes each capoeirista part of this lineage.

Consistently, when players told me about their favorite songs, they picked songs about history, or songs that they imagined were about capoeira's past. A woman told me that she especially liked a song about playing capoeira by the seaside, for example. She explained that the song reminded her of rodas held on saints' feast days in front of the Nossa Senhora da Imaculada Conceição church in Salvador's port, and of the city's stevedores and sailors, who were once renowned *capoeiras*.

Capoeira songs with historical projections paint a vivid picture of the past, but they also suggest a stance for the listener doing the projecting to complete the song in experience.[16] In these songs, the most crucial dimension of the point of view is typically the protagonist's comportment or emotional state. That is, when capoeiristas project themselves into the past, they do not simply paint a sinister picture; they also implicitly take up a characteristic posture in relation to this ambiance. One sings *of* heroes, persecution, or epic struggle, and one sings *as if one is* a hero, *is* undergoing that persecution, or a party to epic struggle.

From the opening "Iê!" of a song cycle, singing the roda into existence includes taking up the stance implicit in capoeira songs, typically a posture marked by courage and bravado. When one sings the corrido, "Good-bye, Santo Amaro, I'm going off to face Lampião," for example, one is not simply invoking the name of Lampião, a legendary bandit leader and murderer from Brazil's desert backcountry. Is it really possible to pull this song off, to sing it with gusto, without singing one's way toward the mood of someone bidding farewell to his hometown and preparing to face the notorious brigand? The song holds open an experiential door that the chorus can step through when they echo back this lyric; on the other side is space for feeling heroic.

A singer enters—in words Thomas Csordas (1997: 241) uses to describe prophecy—"a paradoxical situation in which the speaker is at the moment of speaking enmeshed in a voice long preceding itself, in which the speaker stands in the path of speech that proceeds from him, and in which . . . the speaking 'I' is not the self." Customary verses allow a singer to project present experience toward a mythical, vibrant past. From a phenomenological perspective, whether history happened exactly as it is described is less important than noticing the position the singer assumes through recounting the past in this heroic style. Singing, in a sense, rehearses characteristic stances toward the world; capoeiristas practice living in the present by singing about a violent past.

PART THREE ✦ PLAYING

6 HEARING THE BERIMBAU

Instrumental music is an essential ingredient in capoeira. Lulls in singing are relatively common, albeit undesirable, during a roda. A disturbance in the rhythm, however, such as a supporting instrument falling out of synch or a broken string on a berimbau, can bring a game to an abrupt halt. For many capoeiristas, movement cannot proceed without music to propel and inspire it.[1]

Instrumental rhythms affect how the game unfolds, control the severity of competition, and set the style of interaction. The roda is a kind of "acoustic space" (Carpenter and McLuhan 1960) made up of distinctive musical textures; good players feel music in their bodies and incorporate it into their movements. In addition, the roda is measured by music, stopped and started, sped up and slowed down by the orchestra. Like song, music shapes the game. Unlike singing, instrumental music influences play constantly, interacting at every moment with the way the players move.

Capoeira music also educates practitioners. Over and over again, teachers told me that an essential step in apprenticeship was learning how to hear the art's distinctive music, especially the sound of the berimbau, the game's signature instrument. When a novice struggled in a game, becoming clumsy, frustrated, or anxious, he or she was exhorted to listen to the berimbau, "the first mestre," as some adepts called it. The rhythms of the berimbau, if one could just learn to hear them, would eventually wash away the novice's awkwardness.

Anthropologist Paul Stoller received similar advice about listening when he studied Songhay magic in West Africa. He describes how a sorcerer chastised him when he failed to "hear" a sick man's spiritual double, separated from him through witchcraft, return to the man's body. Stoller calls it his "first lesson in Songhay hearing" (1989: 113).

He was scolded:

> You look but you do not see. You touch, but you do not feel. You listen,
> but you do not hear. Without sight or touch . . . one can learn a great
> deal. But you must learn how to *hear* or you will learn little about our
> ways. (ibid.: 115)

By implication, for the sorcerer, hearing was not a capacity inherent in
the body; it was a learned skill. In his brief discussion, Stoller relays a
provocative challenge to any ethnographer interested in cultural phenomenology: to understand how culture is lived, one must recognize
that the senses may be trained.

To understand how capoeiristas learn to hear music requires paying
careful attention to the way that players are taught to interact with it.
For example, apprentice capoeiristas must become proficient as musicians and singers. Adepts who do not develop all these skills were said
by my teacher to be *capenga*, "lame." The ability to play the berimbau
shapes how capoeiristas experience music, especially because they are
trained to improvise when playing in the *bateria*, the roda's orchestra.
In addition, players come to associate music with the sensation of moving in the game and interacting with another player. Aesthetic principles build upon this interconnection of hearing with other dimensions
of experience.

Capoeiristas describe diverse, even conflicting, formal arrangements
between particular rhythms and playing styles. Some ethnographers of
capoeira have carefully outlined one or more of these systems. A phenomenological analysis of the unstable, contradictory guidelines capoeiristas
prescribe for the game's musical structure, in contrast, reveals that the
competing "systems" all emerge from and disclose corporeal dimensions
of musical experience. Capoeiristas' apprenticeships in hearing lead them
to perceive the instruments, their own ability to move, even another
player, immediately, in the call of the berimbau.

THE CAPOEIRA ORCHESTRA

Although capoeiristas argue incessantly about the exact configuration of
the orchestra, which supporting instruments it should include, and
which specific rhythms musicians should play, they agree unanimously
that the berimbau is the most important instrument in the ensemble. The
berimbau is a single-stringed, musical bow with a gourd resonator that,
according to Gerhard Kubik (1979) and others who have studied it,
probably originated in Angola or southern Africa but was modified

significantly in Brazil (cf. Lewis 1992: 138–139). To those unfamiliar with it, the instrument looks like the sort of bow used to shoot arrows, except that attached near the bottom is a hollowed-out gourd, which may be as small as a softball, as large as a soccer ball, or any size in between. Brazilians associate the berimbau with capoeira, although it does turn up from time to time in jazz or popular music. The association of the instrument with capoeira is so strong, I was told, that when the art was illegal, just carrying a berimbau in public was grounds for arrest, imprisonment, and even deportation.

The bow of the berimbau is fashioned from the supple trunk of a small *biriba* tree or other hardwood, and ideally strung with a steel belt, or *aço* (iron), torn from the sidewall of a piebald, abandoned tire. A hard-shelled gourd, called a *cabaça*, affixed to one end of the bow, acts as a res-onating chamber. The vibrations from the aço pass through a cord that binds the gourd tightly near one end of the bow. Changing the distance between the hole cut in the cabaça and the musician's belly alters the effective size and shape of the instrument's resonating chamber, modi-fying how the instrument reverberates. The musician strikes the bow with a stick by flicking the wrist, changing the string's tone by pressing against it with a large metal coin, disk, or smooth stone maneuvered by the same hand that holds the instrument. Using this technique, an in-strumentalist can produce three distinct tones: a low open note when the string is "loose" (*solto*), a higher-pitched tone when the coin or stone is pressed hard against the string and "closed" (*fechado*), and a buzzing, intermediate gray tone that one instructor called a "squeak" (*chiado*), made when the coin or stone is held loosely against a vibrating string. A skilled musician can alter these basic tones by shifting the coin or stone while the string is still vibrating, hammering onto the open string, for example, to shift the pitch upward. In addition, the musician holds a small wicker rattle filled with seeds in the same hand as the stick used to strike the bow. This shaker, called a *caxixí*, produces an accent when either striking the string or shaken on its own.

If the berimbau sounds complicated to a reader, it feels even more unwieldy to a novice capoeirista. The musician must balance in one hand the upright bow, about as long as a person is tall to the chest. Worse, the weight of the instrument is borne by the little finger hooked under the cord that binds the gourd to the bow. The same hand must also hold and maneuver the coin or stone, clasping it between the thumb and first knuckle. Controlling the coin, and thus the string's pitch, is extremely dif-ficult to master. When novice players take the whole ensemble in hand—bow, coin, stick, and caxixí—they are hard-pressed just to keep the ungainly bow upright, let alone control the instrument's moving parts or produce clearly differentiated pitches. Capoeira instructors recognize how difficult this is, but they discourage new students from resting a teetering bow against a forehead or shoulder. The instrument's weight slowly chokes off circulation in the little finger and cuts the skin until the student forms a well-earned protective callus. A veteran mestre would hold up his left hand to show his students how his body adapted to decades of playing the instrument: he could dangle his crooked little finger down almost perpendicular to his other fingers.

The reward for mastering this elaborate ensemble of moving parts is that the berimbau meshes with the musician's body to generate a surprisingly diverse range of sound textures. If the musician doesn't muffle the gourd, striking the string generates a drone from the resonator. A skilled berimbau player can use this drone to create a "wah-wah" effect, shifting its tone and volume by changing the gourd's distance from the belly. In addition, various timbres—staccato melodic rhythm and fluctuating drone—are accompanied by the fuzzy, buzzing accents of the caxixí. From a seemingly simple instrument, a skilled musician can produce surprisingly complex, utterly distinctive music.

Berimbau rhythms are built upon recurring basic patterns called *toques*. Players learn to vary these patterns, using the three pitches and inflecting the basic tones to generate countless rhythmic phrases. Even though the most virtuosic musicians depend on the same three tones, improvised performance can become extraordinarily complicated, with staccato delays, syncopation, and subtle shading of the instrument's timbres on a basic toque.

A roda of Capoeira Angola in the Grupo de Capoeira Angola Pelourinho begins with the musician playing the *berimbau gunga*, usually called just the *gunga*—the berimbau with the deepest tone and largest gourd resonator—slowly striking out the toque, or rhythm, to be played. Capoeiristas tune the aço, or string, to complement the gourd; a bow's stiffness and a gourd's size must be properly "married."[2] The first toque played in a roda in GCAP is invariably "Angola," the simplest rhythm. The basic rhythmic motif, played slowly at first, is two short buzzing strokes followed by a deep, then a high tone, and ending with a rest that may be slightly prolonged. The musician with the gunga supposedly should not vary much from this measured rhythm, although some do. Even as the tempo accelerates (as it inevitably does), the gunga sets the pace and signals any changes in the toque, thereby coordinating the orchestra. For this reason, the gunga usually winds up in the hands of a seasoned veteran who is unlikely to accelerate the tempo inadvertently and will, instead, "secure" the rhythm for the whole ensemble.

The bateria, *or capoeira orchestra, at a children's roda in the Grupo de Capoeira Angola Pelourinho. On the left can been seen the* agogô, *the double bell-gong, as well as a child playing a* pandeiro, *much like a tambourine, and three* berimbaus *(the* gunga *with the largest gourd is the leftmost in the hands of the child leading the singing). Another student plays a* pandeiro, *and on the right end of the bench is the tall* atabaque. *(Photo by G. Downey)*

The two other berimbaus in the orchestra follow the gunga's entry; first, the *berimbau médio* with an intermediate pitch, and then the *berimbau viola*, a bow with a small resonator that is tightly strung to produce high tones. In GCAP, the musician with the médio ideally plays the tonal "inverse" of the gunga's rhythm, I was told: generally, high notes when the gunga plays low, and low in place of high. In contrast, the viola provides a variety of rhythmic counterpoint built on the basic toque. The viola is said to "double" the other instruments as these improvised phrases fill the spaces created by the toque and its inverse. Together the three berimbaus create an interlocking, constantly shifting, rhythmic carpet with a steady pulse.

When the three berimbaus have established a deliberate cadence, two musicians join the ensemble playing *pandeiros*. The pandeiro resembles a tambourine with a leather or vinyl face that a musician strikes with the palm, thumb, fingertips, and heal of the hand like a frame drum. Then, the other instrumentalists of the bateria, join: the *atabaque*, a tall, cylindrical drum; the *agogô*, a double bell-gong resembling two cowbells welded together and struck with a stick; and a scraper called a *reco-reco*. In GCAP the musicians with these supporting instruments are discouraged from improvising. Anyone varying the rhythm, especially on the atabaque, was liable to be reprimanded with an angry glare.[3] These instruments all maintain a measured cadence with the toque "Angola," creating a solemn mood for the opening ladainha and chula.

Other capoeira groups employ a variety of rhythms and orchestra configurations that produce different moods. For example, Mestre Bimba, the creator of Capoeira Regional, advocated a small orchestra with a single berimbau and two pandeiros playing a version of the toque "São Bento Grande." Some proponents said that this ensemble was more appropriate for a street roda if the participants suddenly had to flee from the police; an unfortunate capoeirista stuck trying to flee while lugging a bulky atabaque was likely to be captured. The combination of a smaller ensemble with a quicker, dense toque ("São Bento Grande" does not have the rests found in "Angola") produced a much more vigorous, overtly aggressive environment for play. A number of other practitioners suggested that "São Bento Grande" was a "war rhythm." The effect arose not simply from the ensemble playing at an accelerated tempo. The stark sonic space produced by the spare ensemble drove an unornamented style of play in practitioners trained to be sensitive to the music. I found myself growing increasingly tense when playing to this smaller ensemble, for example, deprived of the measured anchor of the atabaque, the lush interplay of three berimbaus, the acoustic thickness of the many subordinate instruments, and the periodic pauses in the toque "Angola," which was more familiar.

MUSICAL INTERACTIONS

The berimbau, especially in the hands of a skilled veteran, moderates capoeira games in several ways. First, the pace of interaction between players follows the musicians' tempo. Novices are easy to recognize because when they become agitated or anxious, they tend to accelerate and play more rapidly than the music. Second, the berimbau regulates the game by cuing particular events with specific rhythmic phrases. For example, a steady stream of beats on the open string suspends play and calls the participants back to the foot of the berimbau. Older mestres suggested that formulaic musical phrases once served as a mnemonic code through which instrumentalists could exchange insults, relay challenges, or even summon a nearby tavern keeper if they needed refreshments, although I didn't see any evidence of the practice during my field research (see J. Moura 1971).

The berimbau moderates the type of game to be played by setting the specific toque (literally, "tolling" or "touch"). A toque is a melodic–rhythmic pattern on the berimbau. Although musicians improvise phrases, the toque serves as a foundation for all variation. When asked, capoeiristas associate each toque with a distinctive style of physical play. A toque resembles a sort of rhythmic mode, possessing kinesthetic and emotional traits. For example, the toque "Angola" designates a slow, reserved game in which players stay close to the ground. Mestre Moraes told us that, as a game progressed, the musicians should shift to play either of the toques "Jogo de Dentro" or "São Bento Grande" when they wanted the players to "open" the game and accelerate their pace. In contrast, another variant of "São Bento Grande," recognizably different from the one played in GCAP, accompanies the quickest and most aggressive games in Capoeira Regional. "Iúna," a toque said to mimic the male and female mating calls of a bird indigenous to Bahia's arid interior, is reserved for games between advanced practitioners (cf. Abreu 1994; Bonates 1999). Another, called either "Santa Maria" or "Apanha Laranja no Chão, Tico-Tico,"[4] often accompanies the rare "money game," in which capoeiristas vie to pick up money with their mouths while playing. Other teachers said that "Santa Maria" should be played to honor a deceased capoeira mestre.

Experiential qualities of the toque motivate the connections drawn to playing styles; capoeiristas believe that the relationship is not arbitrary. For example, some versions of "Iúna" make no use of the high pitch on the berimbau. I was told that the resulting, almost meditative melody helped advanced players remain especially controlled and aided them in performing beautiful movements in harmony. In contrast, another mestre said that the constant alteration between high and low tones, without rests, in "São Bento Grande" of Capoeira Regional generated especially vigorous movement. Although capoeiristas do not agree on the correct forms of the toques or the playing style appropriate for each, these debates reveal a shared assumption that styles of bodily movement and instrumental textures should be intimately related.[5] In fact, capoeiristas made relatively limited use of the toques in most of the rodas I attended. Sometimes a roda of several hours might find them playing only one or two different rhythms. And teachers often lamented that their students were not sufficiently sensitive to changes in toques. Nevertheless, mestres invariably argued that the berimbau's rhythm *should* shape the kinesthetic development of the game, an ideal that suggests how they experience its sound.

THE GRAIN OF THE BERIMBAU

When practitioners talked about the sound of the berimbau, they typically referred to the material qualities of the instrument and the actions that produced the sound, not abstract, purely sonic attributes, like rhythm, tone, or melody. They did not say that they heard a changed pitch, for instance, but that they heard the coin pressing on the string. The sound made present the physical action that produced it. Capoeiristas can readily tell from the sound of the berimbau whether a musician uses a smooth stone rather than a slice of copper ingot to alter the pitch of the bow; if asked, however, they cannot abstract away the qualities of the sound that are distinctive. When players explained the difference in sounds generated by a stone and by a coin, they invariably described the physical qualities of the stone and coin, not objectified qualities of the sound. When the bottom of a caxixí, or shaker, is cut from a plastic milk carton rather than a gourd, adepts say that it does not sound right, that it sounds like plastic. When a bow needs to be restrung, it is not because the pitch is too low; the bow has "grown loose," a description of the instrument rather than the sound.

The palpable presence of the berimbau's material qualities in its music suggests that, for veteran players who use this language, the instrument itself is physically immanent in their experience of its sound. Martin Heidegger argues that the experience of hearing in ordinary life is similar. We do not hear sound, we hear objects through sound—a door slamming, a wind blowing, a coughing child (see Heidegger 1971a: 26). Tim Ingold clarifies this phenomenological insight: it is both the objects and their actions that we sense in noises, for the object itself seldom makes sound until it is put in motion or set to vibrating (Ingold 2000: 245).

Roland Barthes, when writing about vocal music, calls the physical presence of the singer in song, "the grain of the voice." He describes a Russian cantor's voice: "brought to your ears in one and the same movement from deep down in the cavities, the muscles, the membranes, the cartilages, and from deep down in the Slavonic language, as though a single skin lined the inner flesh of the performer and the music he sings" (Barthes 1977: 181–182). The grain of the voice is not an abstract quality of timbre or sound texture. The grain is "the materiality of the body" in the voice, or the sense a listener has of the interaction between the musician's body and an instrument, such as when one can hear the pad of a pianist's fingertips (ibid.: 189). Barthes writes, "The 'grain' is the body in the voice as it sings, the hand as it writes, the limb as it performs" (ibid.: 188).

The berimbau demonstrates that the material presence of the instrument and the musician's action are not universally perceptible qualities of musical sound. Most North Americans, for example, when they first hear the berimbau's distinctive voice, have little idea how the sound was produced. For the "body" of the instrument to be present in its distinctive sound, the listener must have the cultural background, including experience of the berimbau as a sensual whole—visual, auditory, and tactile.

For the adept who knows how to hear it; the grain of the berimbau is the presence in the sound itself of a real aço—a real steel belt rather than the piano wire some contemporary practitioners use. The grain of the berimbau is the bite of a brass coin into the cord (not silver—far too mushy) or the warmer nuzzling against the string of a stone smoothed by a river. The grain is the experiential immediacy of the sound, not a quality of a waveform's attack and decay rates, a pitch frequency, or the harmonics of the bow's resonating chamber. The grain includes the weight of the wood: the solid, tabletop-smooth clarity of a biriba shaft compared with the light, brittle hollowness of the bamboo bows made for tourists. Barthes's use of "grain" is particularly evocative for a phenomenology of capoeira music because the term evokes the veins in a wooden instrument. The trained eye can perceive the inner qualities of wood from the grain's pattern at its surface, just as one can learn to perceive an instrument's material qualities at a distance in its sound.

LISTENING WITH A MUSICIAN'S HANDS

Listening to the berimbau is further complicated for adepts by the way they are trained on the instrument. As part of their apprenticeship, capoeiristas must learn to play in the roda's orchestra, that is, to actively engage their own bodies in producing music. Training to join this ensemble generates a proclivity adepts feel to act in response to the sound. When playing the bow in the ensemble, they do not simply follow along lockstep with the basic toque. Only a novice musician repeatedly plays the unornamented toque or the same sequence of tones. Rather, capoeiristas are encouraged to listen for opportunities to improvise in relation to other instruments. One of the goals of improvising is to create engaging tensions while maintaining the basic pulse of the toque. Musicians vary rhythms and "double" the tempo, or they may drop a beat while another instrument is "securing" the time line, or *marcação*. They hesitate and delay beats or create interlocking phrases with other instruments, sometimes even mischievously attempting to confuse another musician's rhythm.[6]

In other words, just as soon as a student can "secure" the rhythm, he or she is encouraged to depart from it by improvising. As John Chernoff (1979) discovered with the African drummers he studied, capoeiristas listen to other musicians in an ensemble and respond with dynamic, complementary rhythms (cf. Chernoff 1997: 24). Through this active exploration, musicians discover an expanding realm of what is possible and engaging in a rhythm, not merely what is already present. In his study of heavy metal, Robert Walser (1993: xii) describes this facet of musical education as "the ability to recognize, distinguish, and deploy the musical possibilities organized in styles or genres by various communities" (cf. Clifton 1983: 70). An adept instrumentalist does not simply internalize precomposed bits of music. He or she learns to hear musical opportunities in an unfolding performance. Proficiency requires an active, ongoing bodily engagement with music and finely tuned perceptual skills. A musician must know how to hear in order to play; in addition, knowing how to play inexorably affects how music sounds (see Ingold 2000: 352–354).

Developing musical proficiency conditions a practitioner to hear *more than* the rhythm that is actually being played. Alongside the sound of the ensemble, a skilled improviser will "hear," latent in the basic rhythm, different, complementary variations on the berimbau that he or she might potentially play, emerging from his or her own hands. One will sometimes see practitioners "playing along" with capoeira music when they have no instruments, or singing syllabic versions of berimbau improvisations, miming absent, but interconnected, rhythmic variations.

These rhythms are the experiential product of one's own ability to become enmeshed in the orchestra. A "phantom" berimbau arises in the capoeirista's hands, even if they remain still.[7] This absent presence may be a persistent accompaniment or simply a horizon that orients a listener. For example, when a virtuoso player exploded in a flurry of subtle tones, executing difficult syncopations and demonstrating extraordinary control over the instrument, I could hear how fast the musician's fingers had to move the coin, the exquisite control of the string, and the dramatic movements of the bow in relation to my own body's potential. My awe arose, in part, because I could *not* feel my way along with the rhythm or keep up with the actual sound with virtual movements of my own potential hands. My ability—not active in a practical sense—was the experiential horizon that oriented me toward virtuoso performance, playing beyond the envelope of my competency.

Even recordings of capoeira music are generally listened to actively, as if they were teaching materials, rather than received passively. While listening to recordings, novice performers may strive to incorporate the music, translating unfamiliar improvisations that they hear into the movements of the hands and arms that can produce these sounds. The musician's hands form a critical part of the "perceptual system" through which the sound of the instrument is apprehended (see J. Gibson 1966; Ingold 2000: 260–262). The perceptual system for the musician takes in the skilled body, which measures and interacts with another player's performance. The adept's hands, fingers, and belly intertwine with the berimbau—actual or "phantom"—in the presence of music. As Clifford Geertz put it, "Art and the equipment to grasp it are made in the same shop" (1976: 1497).[8]

This experiential meshing of the body and instrument results, in part, from the structure of the berimbau itself. As with virtually all instruments, the body of the musician completes the acoustical dynamics of the musical bow. The musician's stomach and the gourd together form the instrument's resonating chamber. The fingers of the hand that holds the instrument must wind around the cord that connects the gourd to the instrument and control the coin that changes the bow's pitch. At first, the position hurts the thumb or little finger, sometimes leaving them numb or wearing away the skin. Performance slowly reshapes the fingers, stretching and strengthening them until they conform to the berimbau. When I held up a bleeding finger after one long session, an instructor joked, "The capoeira's coming out!" Just as sound flowed out of the union of my body and the instrument, so did the art seep into me through practice and attendant suffering.

HEARING WITH A PLAYER'S BODY

Apprenticeship in the game—the swaying steps, slippery dodges, and stealthy attacks—also conditions a player's experience of hearing capoeira music. Capoeiristas frequently commented on the effect the music has on their bodies, how the berimbau "moves them," "gets in their blood," and, as Mestre Pastinha suggested, gives them "energy" and "swing" (quoted in Freire 1967: 82). Movement is so intimately

linked to sound that Mestre Almir das Areias (1983: 26) called the berimbau the "teacher of every capoeirista," an assertion I heard echoed
frequently. These comments seem less like metaphoric exaggerations
than attempts to communicate the instrument's experiential power.
Although they describe the sound of the berimbau, they also reveal
how the music is apprehended: through a listening player's sense of
potential movement.

The link that capoeiristas assume exists between toques and different
playing styles, for example, indicates that they perceive in experience a
relationship between hearing and playing capoeira. Each toque discloses a distinctive style of being in the game, just as it helps a player
achieve this comportment. That is, the toques, "Angola," "São Bento
Grande," "Iúna," and others reveal ways of being in the roda. As Tom
Clifton suggests in his book on the phenomenology of music, describing
a musical texture as "hollow" or "thin" means that the body of the
listener "adopted an *attitude* of hollowness, thinness, etc." (1983: 68,
emphasis in the original). Describing a toque as "calm," "warlike," or
"traditional" means that in its presence, a sensitive player takes up the
attitude named.

This attitude is not an innate kinesthetic quality of music, nor does it
arise because of a uniform, hard-wired response to sound in the brain. Our
sense of hearing is conditioned by an inextricable tangle of influences—
acoustical physics, human anatomy, cultural context, bodily experience,
childhood development—all linked and feeding back on each other
from our earliest experiences, even prior to birth (see DeCasper and
Spence 1986). Although "evidence of the art of hearing can be historically
shown in all cultures," Max Peter Baumann argues that a "sense of sonic
systems" is not universal (1997: 3; cf. Dowling 2001). Along the same lines,
John Blacking suggests that, as in the case of trance, for music to affect
people viscerally, the individuals must have "acquired certain habits of
assimilating sensory experience" (1985: 64).

The sonic texture of the berimbau is seldom heard outside capoeira.
Practitioners' lived bodies, affected by patterns of acting in relation to
the instrument, respond almost involuntarily to its distinctive sound.
Thomas Csordas (1993: 138) referred to "culturally elaborated ways of
attending to and with one's body" as "somatic modes of attention," an
existential foundation for cultural differences in experience. That is,
before we reflect on music, we are already culturally conditioned to be
attentive to and perceive it through bodily habit and comportment.
In the presence of the berimbau's sound, capoeiristas feel the game's
swaying movements in their bodies, either when they actually play, or,

if they remain still, as an inward quickening, a readiness to move. Likewise, a salsa aficionado may feel dance steps percolate through her body during a Célia Cruz song, or a veteran tango dancer sense her body taking up the spidery-legged stance of tango's close embrace when she hears the forlorn tone of the *bandoneon*. In capoeira, the quickening arises only because players work hard to develop this bodily mode of attention; it is not an inherent quality of the berimbau's sound texture or the listener's body.

Phenomenologist Elizabeth Behnke (1997b) described these sorts of passing sensations as "ghost gestures": movements that are summoned to corporeal awareness even if they are not performed. She writes extensively about how these felt gestures condition our own experiences of our bodies. The twitching of coin movements in the finger, the flicking of stick strokes in the wrist, the internal swaying that is "in the blood" waiting for the berimbau to bring it to life—these are the ghost gestures summoned in a player by capoeira music. Berimbau music creates a soundscape in which capoeiristas feel more acutely the movement abilities they've developed for the game.

Through apprenticeship, the kinesthetic and audible dimensions of musical experience become so tightly intertwined that many capoeiristas come to believe that bodily movement is immanent in the sound of the berimbau itself; they feel that the music *causes* movement. The relationship is so convincing that, after they have learned the techniques, capoeiristas sometimes imagine that one could become proficient in the game just from listening to the music (yet another reason for referring to the instrument as "the mestre of every capoeirista"). I repeatedly heard teachers tell students who made a mistake in the game to listen to the music more closely. Instructors felt the correct movement immanent in the sound and may have assumed that students, too, could find it there. According to a close associate, the late Mestre Bimba was so convinced that students could learn spontaneously from music that he intentionally played the toques with barely perceptible flaws on his first recording (reissued as Machado 1989). Too much fidelity might have made it unnecessary for an aspiring capoeirista to attend his academy and thereby deprive the mestre of his livelihood. Whether or not this story is true, the student's comment reveals the intimate relationship that he perceived between bodily motion and instrumental rhythm.

Without the bodily dispositions developed during apprenticeship, however, the experience of hearing is bereft of its visceral dimensions. Most novices cannot acquire the inward sense of the game's swaying step or the dynamic of interacting in the roda from music alone. To the untrained ear, music may be sound; but it is corporeally incomprehensible, unaccompanied by the bodily skills that an adept listener has attained. To the dancer's ear, part of a whole body trained as a perceptual system, music is a summons to dance.

THE SOCIAL ABILITY OF HEARING

The apprenticeship in hearing in capoeira training also links the player with other people. Hearing not only helps a capoeirista to interact in the roda but also is itself a kind of social ability, a perceptual skill grounded in an awareness of other people's bodies. The game is not a solo expressive dance; it is an agonistic, interactive form of play. Ideally, no capoeira movement exists in isolation, outside the game. Bodily techniques occur only in relation to another person's actions or position, attacks or vulnerabilities. Some teachers insist that to avoid developing bad habits, a student should not rehearse solitary movements to music. Instead, a player should always practice with another player in a musical field, orienting the body to music and to an adversary at the same time.

In his discussion of the grain of the voice, Barthes (1977: 188) asserts that the grain has an "erotic" dimension. He writes that one hears in the grain a relationship with the specific parts of the musician's body that produced the sound. This inclination to perceive another person's body is a form of sociability. The grain of the berimbau has a similar "erotic" quality; the music makes audible an interaction between three bodies: the instrument's wooden and steel flesh, one's own potential to move, and another player in the roda.[9] Because instrumental music—rhythm, tempo, phrasing, toques—moderates the physical relation between players, the trained ear is emphatically intercorporeal; that is, it hears relationships with other people's bodies. The music awakens a hard-won capacity to exploit the opportunities presented by an adversary's movements, the increased responsiveness necessary to avoid being tripped or caught off guard.

Anthropologist and former practitioner Ordep Serra insisted that his teacher, Mestre Pastinha, suggested that when defending himself in the street, a capoeirista should "imagine the rhythms of the berimbau in order to escape harm." The sound of the berimbau would aid in avoiding injury and in quickly dispatching an assailant. Capoeiristas can go so far as to describe hearing a confrontation on the soundscape of the berimbau's rhythms, where the intentions of an adversary become audibly obvious, even predictable. Ideally, if one knew how to listen with one's whole body, an adversary was present and revealed in the sound.

HEARING AS A SKILL

Anthropologist Edmund Carpenter helped pave the way for ethnographic studies of the senses with his elegant portrayal of the perceptual life of the Aivilik Eskimos (Inuit) (e.g., 1973). He wrote: "Any sensory experience is partly a skill and any skill can be cultivated" (1972: 20). As Carpenter suggests, a capoeirista's sense of hearing is a learned ability, an ongoing accomplishment developing during apprenticeship. Carpenter's observation is a warning, as well, that educating the senses is as much an "enskilment" as an "enculturation," more like developing a skill than internalizing a set of ideas or rules. To treat culture as if it just "gave meaning" to raw sensual experience obscures how perception is learned and skill-like.[10]

An acoustical phenomenology of the capoeira roda reveals that practitioners are trained so that they respond viscerally to the sound textures of the berimbau. A novice capoeirista cultivates the ability to hear the music that accompanies play, to move in harmony with it, to hear changes in the rhythms, and to perceive its guidance to avoid being tripped or knocked down. Through arduous physical training a capoeirista links a sense of movement, vision, and sound into an inherently synesthetic perceptual system, where one sense modality is experienced in terms of another. Sound seems to compel action, just as the game seems incomplete without music.

Philosophers who have studied music sometimes note an intimate relationship between musical sound and movement. Phenomenologist Thomas Clifton (1983: 66), for example, characterized perception of music as a "movement of the body." Music is "the outcome of a collaboration between a person, and real or imagined sounds" (ibid.: 74; cf. Ferrara and Behnke 1997: 469). Learning to dance appropriately, coming to live one's way kinesthetically into a distinctive musical world, means "allowing my self to enwrap the object [sound] on condition that it enters me" (Clifton 1983: 68).

Culturally informed listening in the roda is an active mode of taking up a perceptual world and opening oneself to dimensions of it, like song. A musical genre is a style of dwelling in the world, with what Steven Smith (1992: 43) called "its own characteristic way of enthralling." This enthralling in capoeira is a bodily susceptibility to musical sounds, especially the berimbau. Capoeira vividly demonstrates that music can be a medium for educating the senses.

7 PLAY WITH A SINISTER PAST

When students learn capoeira, they prepare for the roda, or capoeira "ring." In my experience, instructors in other martial arts refer constantly to self-defense when they teach. In contrast, capoeiristas usually talk about the "game" of capoeira. Although they may sometimes demonstrate self-defense or theatrical applications of movements, the ideal forum for demonstrating expertise is improvised play in a roda, complete with music and vigorous singing. When practitioners describe capoeira, although they may consider it a martial art, they usually say that they "play" capoeira, not that they "fight."

The roda is both the circular playing space formed by the bodies of those watching and an event in which a series of "games" (*jogos*) takes place. Practitioners, like academics, treat the roda as a historical artifact. They suggest that elements of its rituals survive from bygone days: a hand gesture is a legacy of knife fighting, a song recalls slavery, a strategy was developed by maroons, an instrument came from Africa. When I asked veteran players to explain the musical or ritual dimensions of the roda, they inevitably turned to history. In contrast, practitioners tended to explain attacks and defenses pragmatically; an evasive dodge, for example, was useful to avoid certain sorts of kicks or sweeps.

Modern rodas are, no doubt, the result of historical processes, and songs make specific reference to historical persons and events. From a phenomenological perspective, however, the origins of gestures, songs, or rhythms are less important than the fact that they make modern capoeiristas vividly aware of the past. The roda affects players' experience; the word "traditional" describes how it feels to be in the capoeira ring. That is, the roda is not an inert archive that only a historian could explain; rather, capoeiristas come close to the past and feel history's weight there.[1] Together with music and song, ritual actions in the roda persuade players that they are in direct contact with an epic past. This feeling leads capoeiristas to draw upon their historical imaginations when explaining the roda, even when they admit that they are inventing stories about its origins. In fact, some of the practices considered most "traditional" are all but impossible to explain based on the past that these practices evoke so vividly.

In most cases, capoeiristas feel the art's "sinister" past that they sing about in the roda: fights against slavery and oppression, or epic struggles between gangs of *capoeiras*. The proximity of this past lends gravity and seriousness to capoeira play, revealing that the art was once "a deep and sinister business," to borrow an expression from Ludwig Wittgenstein (1979: 16e). The way capoeiristas evoke history suggests menacingly that the game might still be dangerous.

Historical references to violent events, and the sinister sense of foreboding that they summon, help maintain the delicate balance between creative playfulness and mortal seriousness that makes the game at once so ambiguous and compelling. The roda is suspended in a commemorative frame between ludic and agonistic extremes.[2] The important role served by a sense of the past, with its nuances of implied violence, explains why certain ritual practices are considered so essential to the game's continuity. Veterans' anxieties about lost tradition cluster around the rituals that make the past present because these practices preserve the game's tension. Recalling the past buttresses the roda, making it an environment in which the ambiguity of capoeira might be fully experienced. These rituals generate a shared sense of the game's hidden, sinister side. This chapter specifically describes some of these "traditional" practices and explains how they preserve a delicately balanced sense of play.

REMINDERS OF THE PAST

Like music, the form of the roda, the game's rituals, and the players' dress, are said to be artifacts of capoeira's violent past. For example, the most common explanation for the roda's circular shape, like the presence of instruments, is that the art was once training for unarmed combat, disguised from the eyes of overseers or police. Players suggest that the slaves camouflaged training as a harmless pastime or celebratory dance. They used their bodies to ring the game so that the authorities could not see what happened inside the roda.

Elaborate stories lie just below the game's surface; digging at any point can unearth a relic of capoeira's past. For example, many academies wear white uniforms, allegedly to commemorate the clothes worn

Mestre Cobra Mansa cautiously approaches Cabelo, who does a chamada *with his back turned to the mestre. Mestre João Grande, in the white hat with a white berimbau, presides over the roda.* (*Photo from the collection of C. Peçanha*)

to rodas on saints' feast days. If a player asks about the clothing, he or she will be told that on festival days, capoeiristas played in public plazas, still clad for their religious obligations (Bahian devotees of Candomblé wear white in honor of Oxalá). According to legend, any fall on cobblestones marked a player's white clothes. Those who ended the day pristine left with proof of their skill. Any who fell got to wear the disgrace on their pants.

Adepts also told me not to put my palms on an adversary's clothing; but whereas playing in public plazas would leave a player's hands dirty, this is no longer a concern in diligently swept academies. One veteran mestre told us that he had been able to play capoeira in his youth on the way to pick up a date, wash his hands, and arrive at his destination with no incriminating hand or shoe prints on his clothes. For this reason, we had to do difficult ankle sweeps with the backs of our hands rather than by grasping. We preserved the gentility of the roda while we recalled the past in gesture. Likewise, colored cords used to mark a student's progress in some groups were said to be a reminder for some of the

colored scarves given by Mestre Bimba upon a student's "graduation."
The scarves commemorated similar silk ones worn by turn-of-the-
century *capoeiras* to protect their necks; silk was thought to resist slashing with a razor.

One of the most dramatic, "traditional" sequences in the roda is the
chamada or "call," a formalized challenge enacted through gesture.[3] To
perform a chamada, a player withdraws from the usual give-and-take of
the game. The "caller" steps back, stands upright, and becomes nearly
still. The stationary capoeirista can assume many postures; in the most
common, an adept raises his or her right arm, or holds both arms out
wide. A call is even more provocative and risky if the caller turns away
from an adversary and offers his or her back, casting a wary eye over one
shoulder. While the caller waits, the "called" player typically returns to
the foot of the berimbau. There, crouched low and alert, he or she invokes protection and approaches. The sudden stillness of the chamada
can be abrupt, especially because the call is often issued at the height of
the action, when it seems as though one player is about to fall.

After a brief pause, the player who was called gradually approaches
the stationary caller with a series of movements, often acrobatic *floreios*,
or "flourishes." Both players grow increasingly cautious as the called
player draws near. Finally, the called player maneuvers so that his or her
hands rest lightly on the caller, seemingly at ease, but carefully positioned to deter any attack. A right palm rises deliberately to meet a
raised arm, or arms stretch out to match the caller's posture. In some
cases, an adversary is required to put his or her head against the caller's
belly and remain bent over at the waist, arms crossed before the face to
protect it from a fast-rising knee. In whatever position, the players walk
together, moving about four steps forward and backward while maintaining intimate contact, until the caller stops and offers the floor to his
or her adversary.

At any time, either player may suddenly break the sequence with
a surprise attack; both must remain vigilant even during the most
dramatic floreio. If one player seems vulnerable, the other is likely to
pounce. For example, an instructor demonstrated to a class, using me
as the victim, why callers should never stand with their feet together.
This posture left them especially vulnerable to a sudden *boca de calça*
(cuff of the pants), an attack in which an unsuspecting victim finds his or
her ankles yanked from beneath. (In my case, the demonstration left me
with a fractured wrist.) Although capoeiristas say that players may
prove their fitness to play with an acrobatic approach, an impressive but
ill-advised floreio can also leave a player especially vulnerable.

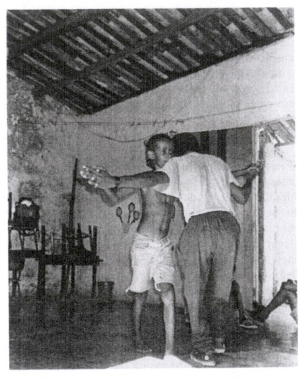

A young student processes back and forth following a chamada with Natinho (Honorato Moraes Trindade) in one of the classes taught in Salvador's poor periphery by the Grupo de Capoeira Angola Pelourinho. (Photo by G. Downey)

At first sight, the chamada is a confusing suspension of play, and it offers no obvious clue to its origin or meaning.[4] Many capoeiristas, especially those not familiar with Bahian styles of Capoeira Angola, do not even know how to respond to the sequence, much to the dismay of traditionalists. Sometimes a player unacquainted with the practice simply attacks a caller. The ritual so dramatically interrupts the flow of a game that first-time observers invariably ask what is going on.

The curious exchange seems to be the antithesis of normal behavior in the roda.

When spectators ask about the chamada, veteran players sometimes offer historical explanations of its origin. One instructor, for instance, suggested that it was a parody of European ballroom dancing. He explained that slaveholders sometimes danced with enslaved women, but also beat them. The chamada satirized this hypocrisy. Although stories like this are intriguing, the fact that even seasoned veterans still occasionally asked renowned mestres to explain the chamada points to a basic irony: one need not be able to describe its origin to be able to do the sequence. Players who cannot offer any historical explanation, however implausible, for the chamada—probably the majority—still assert that it is "traditional."

THE IMPORTANCE OF THE CHAMADA

Although the ritual interrupts the game, practitioners frequently say that the chamada embodies the essence of capoeira. Mestre Curió, for example, insists:

> The chamada is the philosophy of the angoleiro; it is the malícia (cunning) of the angoleiro. Today, people concern themselves very much with becoming strong when doing martial arts, with becoming an athlete to play capoeira. Capoeira does not depend upon this. Capoeira depends upon technique, cunning, and shrewdness. When a comrade is very rough inside the roda, he wants to strike, wants to stomp; I "call" him [do a chamada]. He is going to pay attention in the way that he knows how. Because the violence of the angoleiro is not in giving a leg sweep, or in a kick, or in a punch—the cunning of the angoleiro is really in the chamadas. (quoted in Vieira 1990: 127)

Curió's suggestion may appear counterintuitive: how could the philosophy of capoeira be contained in a sequence that so clearly violates basic principles of interaction? But he is not alone in holding the chamada in high regard. Capoeiristas, especially angoleiros, repeatedly insisted that the game itself was relatively straightforward. The subtle interplay of the chamada, and how one responded to it, posed challenges that demonstrated who truly *knew* the art.

For the chamada to be executed well, a player need not follow a predetermined script. In fact, a chamada is made to be broken, in a manner of speaking, either with a sudden surprise attack or with a breach in conventional patterns. Although we were taught in GCAP how to do a simple chamada, the best, most self-assured players were those that most often confounded an opponent's (and an audience's) expectations, using unusual postures and sudden variations in the sequence to heighten the game's drama. The chamada then really has no "rules"; to suggest this fundamentally misses the point that the players who most faithfully follow the basic model are invariably the least experienced ones. Capoeira instructors offer clearly defined standards only for novices who do not yet have the aesthetic sense and cunning to modify the sequence.

In the case of the chamada, then, learning is not internalizing an orthodox model or a set of instructions by rote (see also Bourdieu 1977, 1990b; Ingold 2000: 357ff.). The more one learns, the more one leaves behind strict dependence upon, and fidelity to, the model. For example, one veteran player sometimes crouched low as an adversary approached his call; the opponent had to figure out how to bend over this unconventional posture without being exposed. I saw other veterans career as if drunk, lean leadenly against another player, "accidentally" place a hand on an adversary's face, and exaggerate their movements. If he had the advantage, Mestre Moraes might rush directly at a caller instead of performing any acrobatic floreios. Doing so implied that the caller was at a disadvantage, and Moraes would not allow his adversary to rest or regroup. Sometimes, a seasoned player slyly danced while calling as a player did floreios, gradually repositioning himself so that the approach grew increasingly difficult. On other occasions, I saw several instructors perform the call suddenly after trapping an adversary at the edge of the roda; moving anywhere for an approach was nearly impossible. In response, one resourceful young adept leapt from the roda and quickly jogged around to the other side, humorously tiptoeing as if by being "stealthy," he might somehow prevent the audience from noticing his obvious breach of the ring. Caller and audience alike smiled at this bold improvisation.

Unusual, innovative variations, performed with flair and confidence, often served as an emotional high point in a game. Creativity—or what some might call "rule bending"—requires that a player have acknowledged expertise (someone might assume a novice's variation was just an error) and be calm enough to execute the variation. Also necessary is the sensitivity to gauge how novel a variation can be before it jeopardizes the game's dynamics. For example, if one's adversary is an agitated rookie or an aggressive master, or if the mestre guiding the roda doesn't want impressionable novices to see too much variety, a player has less latitude to improvise. A dramatic sense of timing and acute sensitivity to the situation are more essential to a convincing chamada than precisely adhering to a proper form. Creative adepts constantly invented new variations on the chamada to take advantage of peculiar circumstances.

THE CHAMADA'S DRAMATIC DYNAMIC

During a game, the chamada provokes or challenges. When capoeira instructors described the paradigmatic situation in which they would do a chamada, they suggested that of a capoeirista who had just gained a decisive advantage. I was told to do a chamada, for example, if I had caused an adversary to fall, befuddled an opponent, or found a vulnerable part of the other person's body wide open. Capoeiristas perform a chamada as if to ask the other player if he or she is fit to continue the game. It might be compared to a "standing eight-count" in boxing, except that no referee judges a player's status. The acrobatic floreios with which the called player responds testify to his or her continued ability to play.

Sometimes a capoeirista humorously inverts the chamada's dynamic. On the verge of falling or rapidly running out of options, one player may suddenly "call" the other; the caller overtly implies that he or she had superior position. Players and spectators alike recognize the inversion and often delight in its incongruity. For example, at one point in a game when Mestre Moraes had thoroughly confounded a student, slowly taking away avenues of retreat until the young man was about to trip over spectators, his adversary suddenly performed a chamada. The capoeiristas watching from the roda laughed. Mestre Moraes stuck his face right up to the student's, as if to challenge him back, while the student struggled to contain a grin at his own brazenness. In other cases, when a player did a chamada immediately after an indecisive exchange, where no clear advantage was gained, the call met with mock incredulity. His opponent made theatrical gestures, as if to say, "You're calling *me* after *that?!* You've got to be *kidding!*" One instructor, after being called, just kept playfully shaking his head as if sad. He stopped during his acrobatic approach repeatedly to size up the chamada, almost disbelieving: "Could this player really think that he was in control? How pathetic."

In other cases, the chamada highlights a strategic move that might be too discreet for a casual observer even to notice. For example, one of Mestre Curió's students described the subtlety of the mestre's game this way: at times, the elusive Curió could slip through an adversary's defenses so quickly that the mestre found vulnerabilities inaccessible to other players. Because his position was already decisive, Curió merely gestured to suggest an attack and then *saiu chamando*, "exited calling."

The mestre's chamada drew attention to the almost imperceptible advantage he had gained, one that a distracted or inexpert spectator might not recognize. The chamada punctuated the game and asserted that, had Curió taken advantage of his position, the victim would be in no condition to continue playing. The chamada called the victim and the audience to imagine how the exchange might have ended differently. Mestre João Grande frequently used the chamada this way. After he had thoroughly outfoxed adversaries, checkmating them hopelessly, the mestre's chamadas offered a reprieve, but also drew attention to an opponent's dire predicament.

When used in this manner, the chamada asserts that an implied attack would have been decisive. The call interrupts play as if to say, "Had I wanted to, I could have ended this game," or "I had you." It places an exclamation point on the violence latent in the game, highlighting moments in which an opportunity for a conclusive attack was available. In this way, the chamada is a challenge that heightens dramatic tension; it calls out an adversary and draws attention to one's own prowess by alluding to potential violence.

At the same time, the chamada also heightens tension in the game by violating basic principles of self-preservation, as Lowell Lewis discusses (1992: 120–127). The sequence requires players to come close together, remain relatively still, and expose themselves. Some teachers even say that the chamada itself is a kind of "opening" or vulnerability offered to the person being called. We should be careful to avoid presenting obvious opportunities, and also be ready to seize them. Throughout the entire sequence, a capoeirista must be extremely cunning, making subtle adjustments in position and balance to forestall surprise attack while preparing for the inevitable end of the temporary truce. The gambit of vulnerability may be especially intriguing and tense after one player has been tripped or knocked down; a player could be calling close an adversary whose pride or body has just been wounded.

Although the chamada underlines latent violence in the game, the sequence simultaneously diminishes overt physical conflict and decreases the intensity of play. The chamada typically ends with a resumption of the *jogo de dentro* (inside game), a restrained testing of form, balance, positioning, and cunning that initiates games in GCAP. Players sometimes use the chamada expressly for this purpose. If play becomes too harried or agitated, a player may issue a chamada to restart the game. In this way, as the chamada increases drama and tension in the game, the sequence reconsolidates the roda. The chamada moderates play while it

also highlights the potential violence latent in it and requires both players to make themselves vulnerable.

PLAY AND IMPLIED VIOLENCE

The chamada helps maintain the ambivalence of capoeira "play." Devoid
of the chamada, one can imagine the game developing in several directions. Without its restraint, a match might become a purely violent struggle. Or without recognition that muzzled attacks could mean mortal
business, the game could resemble a folkloric dance.[5] The ambiguous-
ness of the chamada sequence provides a concentrated forum to play out
the tension between contradictory elements, like conflict and cooperation, that animate the art.

This potent ambivalence explains why most capoeiristas describe the
art as a "game" and say that they "play capoeira" (cf. Lewis 1992: 1–2;
Browning 1995: 88–89). Although they consider it a martial art, players
seldom use the verb *lutar* (to fight) to talk about capoeira; the term is far
too univalent, capturing only one tendency that the game maintains in
a taut, unresolved tension. Older players sometimes employ the verb
brincar when they talk about the game; although it may be translated,
like *jogar*, as "to play," the word connotes even greater levity: "to frolic,"
"to toy," or "to dally." Brazilians say that the spontaneous, fantasy play
of children and the unstructured celebration of *carnaval* are examples of
brincando.

When adepts try to define capoeira, the ambivalence of the art often
poses problems. For example, in his book, *What Capoeira Is*, Mestre
Almir das Areias (1983: 8) writes: "But, after all, what is capoeira? Is it a
form of struggle? A dance? A brawl? Personal defense? Sport? Culture?
Art? Folklore?" Areias answers his own question, "Capoeira is all of this
and much more!" Some capoeiristas tack additional terms onto the list,
but many simply throw in the towel. "Capoeira is capoeira," Mestre
Caiçara reputedly said. The activity is in a category by itself. Or, more
enigmatically, Mestre Pastinha declared that the art is all-encompassing:
"Capoeira is everything that the mouth eats."

Ângelo Decânio deftly sidestepped my question about how to define
capoeira and answered that the art "came before" all the other things
to which it is often compared—dance, fight, game, sport, martial art,
culture, and folklore. He explained this "before-ness" by comparing the
roda to an encounter between animals in the wild: when two animals
meet for the first time, or when young animals are learning how to interact, they play. This play contains the seeds of *all* forms of interaction.

It could just as easily turn into friendship as into fighting with fang and claw. Through play the animals carefully negotiate how they will treat each other and test to see if another is worthy of respect, can be dominated, should be avoided, or, at the very least, might provide some entertainment.

Decânio's definition recalls anthropologist Gregory Bateson's (1972: 177–193) discussion of play. Bateson argues that play, even among animals, is the most elemental way in which an activity is framed as "not real." He observed animals in the zoo and realized that they knew somehow that the bites of play fighting were not real bites. They were implied bites. The resonance between Bateson's observations of play at fighting and the "implied" violence of capoeira appears vividly in a passage by Mestre Squisito (R. Costa 1993: 115):

> Capoeiristas put their lives in the game and stage death in a playful, theatrical form. "Here is a mortal attack," smiles one of the players; to which the other responds: "You struck me fatally . . ." negating the attack. And the game recommences. It is the game of life. It is life and not death that is interesting, that the capoeiristas seek.

Following out the implications of Ângelo Decânio's explanation, however, suggests that the play "bites" in capoeira can grow in intensity until they shatter the game's restraint. Playing at fighting may turn abruptly into just fighting, capoeira teachers often warn (cf. Browning 1995: 90–91). But that danger is one reason why "cunning" or "malice" (malícia) is the most admired trait in a capoeirista.

A malicioso or "cunning" player is exciting to watch because he or she might take advantage of an ill-advised vulnerability with an actual attack. A malicioso player risks the outbreak of violence, pushes an adversary to his or her limits, and threatens to upset the roda's equilibrium, deftly playing at the very edge of fighting. Observers are far more engaged by games in which the boundary with real conflict is periodically approached—what they call "hard" games. Spectators encourage players toward hard games with song and music. At the same time, musicians stand at the ready with the same ritual devices, song and music, to reestablish the balance between violence and cooperation if it is lost. The chamada helps to maintain this ambivalent, even ironic, form of play. The sequence allows players to manipulate the contradictory facets of the art: overt antagonism, exquisite artistry, personal expression, competitive interaction, solemnity, honor, and rough humor. At once a provocation and calming influence, ritual and suggestion of violence, dramatic resource and tactical gambit, we can understand better why Mestre Curió described the chamada as the philosophy of the art.

The ever-present possibility that the game will shift suddenly from one extreme to the other is part of what makes play in the roda so compelling. The chance that a moment of balletlike beauty might arise in the midst of a brawl, that a treacherous blow could get mixed among the implied attacks, or that a pantomimed provocation might actually make an adversary's blood boil—these rivet spectators' attention. Aesthetic performance and violence become, not contradictory forces, but intimately tied together. As Mestre Pastinha insisted:

> Those who have seen the fight understand it better. It looks like a dance, but it isn't, no. Capoeira is a fight, and a violent one. It can kill; it already has killed. Beautiful! In the beauty is contained its violence. The boys are just demonstrating, their attacks pass only grazing each other or are restrained before they reach their opponent. But even like this capoeira is beautiful. (quoted in Freire 1967: 79)

Mestre Pastinha does not suggest that, in spite of violence, capoeira is beautiful. On the contrary, *even restrained*, capoeira remains beautiful to the mestre. The art derives part of its aesthetic appeal from its mortal gravity.

THE SINISTER GRAVITY OF PLAY

By generating a feeling that violence is latent in the art, dimensions of capoeira that are considered to be "traditional"—old songs, the sound of the berimbau, rituals like the chamada—add more than just temporal depth to a player's experience of the roda. Bodily movements and song texts interact with each other and with music, each insinuating greater immediacy or sinister implications for the other.[6] For example, fragments of historical narrative in song texts suggest that, once upon a time, the kick or head butt that a player now restrains was a matter of life and death.

To borrow from Edward Casey's (1987: 216–257) discussion of commemorative rituals, the roda of capoeira makes accessible the past, whether real or imagined. Players can feel history and its relation to the present in an immediate, embodied way, even though they may have no direct personal experience of the events being commemorated, like slavery or a war settled over a century ago. Songs do not simply provide a record of historical facts; they, together with the sound of the berimbau and gestures like the chamada, encourage players to imagine across the gap between the past and present, to experience the resonance of events through time. In commemoration, as Casey writes (ibid.: 251), "representation cedes place to participation," participation in the endurance of the past.

In the interview just quoted, Mestre Pastinha went on to describe how historical violence was experientially close to the game, and the sense of danger that it created:

> But what serves for self-defense may also serve for attack. Capoeira is as aggressive as it is dangerous. He who doesn't know how to fight is always taken unprepared. Rogues and unhappy people discovered in these techniques a way to assault others, take revenge upon their enemies, and confront the police. It was a sad time for capoeira. I was familiar [with it]. I saw. In the gangs of the docks . . . Violent struggle, no one was able to contain it. (quoted in Freire 1967: 80, ellipsis in the original)

As he continued, the nearly blind mestre described a shift in experience brought about by the accelerating rhythm of a roda or class being held nearby. The music led him from recollecting to a more intimate imaginary transportation:

> Now that the rhythm is faster, I feel the agility of these two men, and I imagine each one of their blows striking the target with full force. I imagine rage, fear, spite, despair, propelling these feet . . . One time I saw a capoeirista put to flight an entire police patrol. Another time: in a dark place, a woman [waits]; a guy wanting something arrives—a man wanting a woman is always unprepared. Then, suddenly, he is struck, only once and falls injured, knocked-out, or dead. Yes sir, there were rogue capoeiristas that dressed themselves as women to rob the Don Juans. (ibid., ellipsis in the original)

The changing rhythm of the roda encourages Mestre Pastinha to sense parallels, to feel violent events loom up around the implied, restrained attacks of the game.

Players make dramatic use of the past that hovers over the roda. For instance, after performing a chamada, Mestre Curió sometimes cocked his wrist sideways and downward, and drew his index finger across an adversary's throat. The awkward positioning of his wrist was identical to that allegedly used by *capoeiras* when holding a straight razor to fight. On one occasion, the mestre playing against Curió recoiled from the hand position in exaggerated horror, avoiding the imagined razor as it slashed at his throat. The violence implied by the gesture, a projection to a time and place when *capoeiras* fought with blade and club, conditioned the experience of the game.

Ironically, implied violence is held outside the frame of play and pre-
vented from erupting by some of the same musical, aesthetic, and ritual
devices that also summon memories of past hostility. Insinuated and
ambiguous, this violence can be experienced as the echo of diverse
ancestral conflicts: struggle for liberation, fighting against racism, heroic
personal combat, vicious urban survivalism, even mythological or
divine battles. Like other commemorative practices, the roda "thrives
on indirection; it lives from unresolved, unimaged remainders"
(Casey 1987: 220). All the various narratives of capoeira, imagined
origins and epic histories, are mobilized in song, music, and gesture to
produce the roda as an experiential space. The roda allows players
to duck contradictions between the various histories and derives greater
commemorative vitality from the many layers of potential violence that
a player may sense in it.

The reverberation of violent histories lends the roda an ominous emotional gravity similar to the "sinister" sense that Ludwig Wittgenstein
identified in commemorative ritual. In his discussion of Sir James
Frazer's *Golden Bough*, Wittgenstein (1979) describes the sensation generated by a rite in which participants drew bits of cake like lots. Frazer
argued that the custom was once a method to choose a human sacrifice.
Wittgenstein suggests, instead, that the custom merely "looks like the
ruins of casting lots. And through this aspect it suddenly gains depth"
(ibid.: 15). The "thought of that ancestry" lent great affective weight to its
"reenactment," whether or not the rite was originally "a deep and sinister
business" ending in human sacrifice (ibid.: 16). Similarly, the restrained
attacks of capoeira gain greater depth when players are repeatedly
reminded that lives were once in the balance. For example, Mestre
Squisito (R. Costa 1993: 26) claims that the roda was transformed over
time into a "sinister pastime" (his term) in the absence of real conflict.[7]
Although Squisito comes out strongly against violence in contemporary
rodas, he also insists that capoeiristas inherently feel that they are
"potential urban warriors."

This sense that violence is still possible distinguishes capoeira from
some commemorative rituals. Teachers explicitly prepare their students
for uncontrolled fighting in the roda. They tell stories of violence and
capoeiristas averting treachery as cautionary tales. In GCAP, our instructors constantly warned us about the perils of rodas outside our
academy, showed us "mortal" variants of playful techniques, and chastised us for leaving ourselves vulnerable to potential malevolence.
These warnings encouraged caution. But repeatedly calling attention
to every imaginable danger in the roda also imparted sinister gravity to

each moment of play. The roda is an unclosed commemoration, a space where it appears that history might repeat itself.

A SENSE OF TRADITION

Although capoeiristas typically claim that their game is a modern relic of a violent past, ironically, when fighting does break out in a roda, a loss of tradition is often blamed. Mestre João Pequeno, for example, complained that "forgetting" led capoeira to become "more violent," as it paradoxically grew "less dangerous." Capoeira was less dangerous because capoeiristas did not learn malícia, a trait they could not develop if the game was merely an overt physical struggle, even if more people now got hurt in violent games. Overwhelmingly, when critics complained that traditions were being forgotten, their anxieties concentrated on singing, instrumental rhythms, the relation of music to play, and rituals like the chamada.

Capoeiristas do not long for bygone days of persecution or feel nostalgia for harrowing brawls in the roda. Nevertheless, the subtle discrepancy between what capoeiristas consider to be "traditional" about practice and the events from capoeira's history that capture their imagination focuses our attention on the complex phenomenology of commemoration. Commemorative rituals seldom physically reenact past events faithfully, as Edward Casey discusses (1987: 216–257). The chamada, for example, considered to be a hallmark of "traditional" games, does not simply repeat an event from the art's epic history. Songs that bring players into contact with the art's fallen heroes were not actually sung by the people from whose perspective they were composed. And capoeiristas of yore did not go into battle to the sound of the berimbau, the instrument that now causes a capoeirista's pulse to race with anticipation.[8]

The experiential presence of the past cannot be accounted for simply by the persistence of a practice over time.[9] Everything that is old does not make the past vividly evident to us. Rather, in the roda, the past is intentionally summoned through ritual, music, and song, all done to the spontaneous unfolding of the game, so that this past will affect how the game is lived. When practitioners fear a loss of tradition, they do not worry *only* that the art's history will be forgotten or that certain dimensions of the game will disappear. In fact, some argue that capoeira inevitably changes anew with each generation, and that every capoeirista should develop an individual style. Instead, veteran practitioners focus their concerns about lost tradition on exactly those dimensions of play that make the past a visceral presence.

Practitioners frequently say that the difference between traditional capoeira and other martial arts is that violence is "implied" in traditional games, while it is "actual" in other styles. Capoeiristas do not typically attack with full force in the roda. In contrast, in some regulated forms of capoeira as a sport, as in other fighting sports, a player must make forceful contact with an opponent to score any points. Ironically, restraint, coupled with the commemorative dynamics of the roda, allows capoeiristas in the roda to *imply* a much greater level of violence than could ever be permitted in a more straightforward sport. In a musical and ritual space where capoeira's brutal history of gang warfare seems to hang in the air, Mestre Curió can recall a treacherous knifing with a subtle gesture. Without the violent past folding in upon the present, the awkward movements of his wrist that evoke a razor blade become experientially shallow and tactically meaningless. An "implied" attack, if one's adversary has no awareness of what is implied, is simply ineffectual.

When practitioners say that the roda is "traditional," they do not mean *only* that it is old and that they'd like to preserve it. They also describe how it feels. The roda, as Ferrara and Behnke (1997: 472) write about music, holds open "the historical–cultural world it presupposes so that this world can endure." The danger of lost "tradition" that veterans fear is that the opportunity to experience the past in the roda will be lost. If a player cannot feel the palpable presence of danger and history, he or she cannot understand what the game implies, and it may turn into a mere display of physical dexterity. The roda, a commemorative frame generating the sense that capoeira was once a deep and sinister business, makes it compelling to engage in an unresolved, ambiguous form of play.

8 THE ROGUE'S SWAGGER

In the roda, capoeiristas are in almost constant motion. Swaying and bobbing, back and forth, they appear to dance as they fight. In some sports, the demands of competition determine entirely a contestant's motions. In contrast, capoeira practitioners appear to engage in movement for its own sake, with aesthetic impulses shaping their steps as much as pragmatic concerns. Whereas some athletes clearly reveal their strain and effort, capoeiristas' gangly looseness suggests that they are not even exerting themselves. Players often assert that this kinesthetic, the overall quality of movement, defines capoeira. Practitioners invariably say that the *ginga*, the "sway," capoeira's basic step, makes the art's movement texture distinctive among martial arts.

Practitioners believe that the character of the first capoeiristas shapes this kinesthetic: Africans, escaped slaves, gang members, tough guys, sailors, dockworkers, and poor farmers all allegedly left their mark on the ginga. Its texture allegedly reflects both how these earlier practitioners comported themselves and their outlook on life. Above all else, the kinesthetic of capoeira closely allies adepts with the *malandro*, the "rogue" of Brazilian popular imagination (see Dias 2001: 110, 159–178).

Roberto DaMatta (1991) describes the malandro, an urbane hustler who figures prominently in Brazilian samba, soccer, literature, and even sociological analyses. DaMatta considers the malandro to be one of three archetypes that generate the primary Brazilian "social drama," a struggle between order and disorder (the other two types being the conservative *caixas*, or "dim-witted straight," and the revolutionary "renouncer" [ibid.: 207–211]). The stereotypical malandro dwells outside respectable society, without morals, forming no lasting alliances and taking up no long-term causes.[1] Not a revolutionary, he lives emphatically in the present and exhibits little interest in changing the institutions and inequalities that he confronts in everyday life. Instead, he is content to carve out a small space of opportunity through deception, quick wits, and his consummate survivalist skills, reveling in the constant challenge of *malandragem*, or sly "roguery."

Brazilians consider a talent for malandragem to be a national trait. Malandragem is allegedly evident in the national team's distinctive style of soccer (Rowe and Schelling 1991: 138–142; A. Soares 1994), celebrated in samba lyrics (Matos 1982; Oliven 1984), and manifest in the steps of the best samba dancers (Guillermoprieto 1990). Samba composers are the bards of the malandro's universe, and the World Cup the international stage on which Brazil's bodily cunning is tested. Capoeira, however, has long been considered to be the malandro science, a technology to cultivate a person's cunning (cf. Moura 1980b; Vieira 1990; Barbieri 1993).

Malícia guides both the malandro and the capoeirista. No doubt, the link was reinforced by historical propaganda against the gangs of *capoeiras*, much maligned as "malandros," as well as by the self-presentation of some contemporary capoeiristas, who play up the rakish image of the nattily dressed hustler. But the link is also visceral. The texture of capoeira movement itself, like the virtuoso dribbling of Brazilian soccer stars, embodies malandragem, and allegedly cunning can be "caught" from doing the art. One can become a rogue by doing capoeira.

The connection between posture and character, between learning capoeira and a growing propensity for malandragem, arises from habits and styles of moving. Images of the malandro in Brazilian popular culture are invariably portraits of a comportment, rendered in gait, gesture, and clothing (see A. Soares 1994: 18). For example, in Wilson Batista's samba *"Lenço no Pescoço"* ("Scarf on the Neck"), we find, as in most depictions, that styles of walking and dress flesh out the malandro's character:

> My hat to the side, / Shoes dragging,
> Scarf about my neck, / Razor in my pocket,
> I pass swaying. / I provoke and challenge.
> I am proud / Of being such a vagrant.
> I know that they talk / About my behavior.
> I see those who work / Walking in misery.
> I am a vagabond / Because I had the inclination. . . .
> (quoted in Oliven 1984: 78)

The swaying vagabond, hat cocked to the side, feet dragging as he walks, armed and well dressed, friendly and dangerous, disdainful of hard work—romanticized though the image may be, the malandro condenses a relation Brazilians perceive between personality and habitual comportment. Treating the malandro not as a cultural symbol but rather as a mode of carrying oneself requires examining how it might feel to swagger when one walks, and what swaying could do to a person's body. According to capoeiristas, one learns to sway in the ginga. Whereas songs and rituals invite imaginary projection, movement techniques and skills, like the ginga, shape a practitioner's bearing, disposition, outlook, and behavior. As Ordep Serra (1988) suggested in his account of enrolling in Mestre Pastinha's school, a novice ideally comes to incorporate the ginga into everyday movements. The swaggering walk undergirds a style of being-in-the-world.[2]

THE GINGA

The distinctive movement texture of capoeira arises from the ginga. New students learn it in their first capoeira lessons, trying to synchronize the shifts in balance with the arm and leg movements that make up the step. Neither strictly an attack nor a defense (Lewis 1992: 98–99), the sinewy, evasive ginga is, Mestre Itapoan writes, the "point of departure for all future acquisitions [of capoeira techniques]. It is the 'fundamental' position of the Capoeirista, taken in a figurative sense, the key to his agility and evasiveness" (R. Almeida 1994a: 80). Or, as Lowell Lewis writes, "The *ginga* turns out to be the *alpha* and *omega* of capoeira, the first thing learned and the ultimate signature of the expert" (1992: 98). Novices train so that they become habituated to "ginga-ing" and do not stop moving when in the roda. The formal rules of Mestre Bimba's academy, for example, included the guideline: "Try *always* to do the ginga" (Machado 1989). The step produces constant momentum, like coiling and uncoiling a spring, ideally heightening a player's readiness and concealing a player's intentions.

A novice student first learns a basic ginga in which the body moves from side to side through a wide-legged stance. When the player's weight shifts onto one leg, the inside foot drops back behind it so that the player moves slightly backward. The arms move to counterbalance the body, alternately crossing in front of a player so that they are in position to guard against a sudden attack to the head or chest. The ginga is stable but dynamic, sometimes hesitating momentarily when a player rocks back at the end of each pass. In spite of erratic movements and elusive swaying, which usually grow more extreme as a player becomes

Visiting students at the Grupo de Capoeira Angola Pelourinho practice a low, broken ginga.   *(Photo by C. Peçanha)*

more proficient, capoeiristas maintain a surprisingly careful control over their bodies when they ginga (it is both noun and verb).

Some instructors, whether inadvertently or intentionally, lead students to develop a regular, rhythmic ginga. Others, like my teachers, encourage students to depart from the basic step in elaborate, unpredictable variations, just as a musician improvises on the basic toque. Mestre Squisito warns his reader that improvising is necessary to prevent a player, even a whole group, from becoming predictable:

> Ginga—a capoeirista knows, just as the mathematician is able to calculate, that the ginga has a practically infinite number of possible combinations. To combine consciously these possibilities, so as to be as unpredictable as possible, is to have the best technical command of the ginga. Ultimately there is a tendency to develop a standardized ginga, regular in timing and in its logic of combination [or sequence]. The result: the capoeirista becomes predictable [literally, "is revealed"]; a whole group becomes predictable. Technically, this approach, that is, standardizing the ginga, does not appear to be very efficient. (R. Costa 1993: 68–69)

Experienced capoeiristas can use the ginga to confound adversaries. Virtuosos anticipate an opponent's moves and shift to await an unfolding of vulnerability, already in place to seize any advantage. Incessant repositioning through the ginga alone can stymie an adversary from attacking.

Adepts claim that the ginga clearly distinguishes the art from other combat sports. Unlike practitioners of some Asian fighting styles, for example, who develop powerful, stable stances from which to generate force and deflect an opponent's blows, capoeiristas move constantly to disorient an adversary and avoid attacks. In contrast to wrestlers or practitioners of fighting styles like judo, who attempt to grapple or throw an opponent to the ground, capoeiristas avoid any entangling contact. They work hard to perfect the evasive potential inherent in the ginga. For this reason, even though players may be close together, they often seem to flow together in the roda, stepping, spinning, ducking, and dodging, with little contact.

Capoeiristas argue that, although the ginga is the art's fundamental technique and an aesthetic that saturates every movement, "two identical gingas do not exist" (R. Almeida 1994b: 80). Differences in a player's teacher, personality, social class, race, and even place of origin allegedly inflect his or her kinesthetic (cf. Wilson 2001: 22–23). Styles range from introspective to explosive, careful to careening, subtle to brutal, straightforward to slippery, hyperkinetic to minimalist. For example, some practitioners step solidly when performing the ginga in a firmly rooted, almost plodding stride. Other practitioners ginga in an elastic fashion; they rebound from the ground without resting for a moment. Some players hold their arms stiffly, clenching their fists and locking their muscles as if braced for impact. In contrast, others move their arms in flowing, liquid arcs with their hands open and relaxed. Still others gesture in a restrained, minimalist fashion. Just as some practitioners execute the ginga in an extremely regular, metronome-like rhythm, others create baroque combinations of syncopated steps and ornamental movements with little perceivable regularity, or, for that matter, any resemblance to the basic ginga. Ideally, several old mestres told me, all students should develop their own individual styles.

Capoeiristas agree, even if they do not practice the ginga in the same form, that the movement is the foundation of cunning. Practitioner and scholar Cesar Barbieri (1993: 59) states this unequivocally:

Capoeiras are unanimous in affirming that the ginga is the first principle of capoeira. The constant action of uninterrupted movement of one's body—to ginga—is the principle that permits the creation of the snares of deception, of trickery, in which the adversary will be taken unawares. Ginga and counterattack, counterattack and ginga—they are the inseparable elements that allow one to take a person by surprise.

As Barbieri suggests, the ginga's importance is not merely aesthetic. The step's kinesthetic produces opportunities for trickery, surprise, and malícia.

FUNDAMENTALS OF CUNNING

Malícia is said to be the "fundamental" or secret of capoeira play.[3] In contrast to its English cousin, "malice," the Brazilian term, especially among capoeira adepts, denotes positive aspects of character. The term, translated here as "cunning," in fact denotes a constellation of qualities: a combination of wariness, quick wit, savvy, unpredictability, playfulness, viciousness, aesthetic flare, and a talent for deception. Although malicioso traits are morally ambivalent, they are widely admired and intentionally cultivated by capoeiristas (cf. Lewis 1992: 49; Wilson 2001: 26–29).[4] The antonym of "malícia" is "naïveté," rather than the Portuguese equivalents of "benevolence" or "good will." The cardinal character flaw, from a capoeirista's perspective, is to be too easily duped. Through apprenticeship, a student should discover how to avoid being a sucker or rube (otário). Malícia, earned in the roda as in a hard life, is the antidote to naïveté; it is an essential skill for surviving in the "street."[5]

Capoeiristas and scholars who study the game often argue that the art's emphasis on cunning indicates that it developed as a "weapon of the weak," to borrow a phrase from James Scott (1985). Experience in the roda teaches a player that the game—like life, I was told repeatedly—is an unequal struggle. Capoeira is best suited to help the weaker party in a lopsided conflict, allegedly like guerrilla warfare, with which it is often compared (e.g., Sodré 1983: 213). Using malícia, a frail, disadvantaged individual might overcome a more powerful adversary. Along these lines, the development of capoeira is often recounted as a series of asymmetrical conflicts in which malícia helped defeat superior forces. Cunning was the great equalizer.[6]

With malícia as a "fundamental" in capoeira, no presumption of fair play motivates the creation of a "level playing field," as in many sports. The roda does not match players by weight, experience, age, or sex; one finds green novices playing against grizzled veterans, men against women, and small children against much larger seniors. Amateur sports around the globe, in contrast, often exhaustively classify participants to match them as evenly as possible. Olympic sporting ideals hold that producing an impartial, clearly regulated playing space should allow a pure form of competition, in which superior ability alone determines the outcome. According to many capoeiristas, this artificial leveling actually benefits the competitor with better conditioning or preparation, advantages often gained as a result of social status. They believe that enforcing "fair play" deprives disadvantaged participants of resources like surprise, trickery, secret techniques, and the bending of rules.

One essential dimension of malícia that the English word "cunning" does not capture is playfulness. Capoeiristas use humor in spite of—or as a defense against—the inherent perils of the world. Unlike a malicious individual, a person who is malicioso is a sly trickster, ever vigilant for a chance to enjoy a good laugh as well as to exploit an adversary's vulnerabilities: "Life is a struggle? Life is a fight? The player perceives that capoeira is teaching him to *dance* within the fight!" (Capoeira 1992: 125, emphasis in the original). Mestre Nestor Capoeira asserts that through a playful spirit, an adept derives amusement from hardship, counteracting the long-term effects of constant wariness. The mestre writes that this ludic dimension of malícia helps a capoeirista avoid such pitfalls as cynicism, an "arid" disposition, and egotism (ibid.: 128). Capoeira teaches a practitioner to take advantage of opportunities to play, even in dire circumstances.

Nestor Capoeira suggests that malícia is capoeira's philosophy, but he qualifies his use of the word "philosophy" significantly: "It is not something that can be rationalized. It is not something that can be understood with the use of the mind—in spite of the fact that it is, itself, a form of understanding" (ibid.: 121–122). Searching for a way to talk about malícia, he offers a range of descriptions; malícia is "the perspective of the capoeirista, his way of facing life, the world, and other people . . . this specific type of vision of things, this type of perception of the universe . . . this type of wisdom." Although malícia might be described as a "philosophy," it does not, in fact, translate well into an articulate form. Researcher Frederico Abreu admitted that, when he actually convinced mestres to talk about capoeira "philosophy," he typically was left asking, incredulously, *"That's it?!"* (*Só isso?!*). When spelled out, malícia appeared to be superficial or simplistically pragmatic; or it was frustratingly contradictory when taken outside the context of play.

Instead of a set of principles, malícia—the "fundamento" of capoeira—is better described as a comportment taken up in relation to the world, a posture developed over time. Nestor Capoeira describes how a player cultivates this stance: "It is realized by playing the game with different players, inside the roda to the sound of the berimbau, over the years. . . . It is, yes, a living, experiencing, absorbing, digesting, incarnating" (ibid.). Malícia need not be explicitly described for a student to learn it, nor must it be the goal of practice for it to serve as its fundamento.

> In the meantime—and it's important that this remains clear—although malícia is the basis from which [capoeira] arises and to which it refers . . . no player practices capoeira with the initial intention of obtaining this knowledge. Capoeira is played out of love, enrapture, passion, and vice. Malícia, the central point of practice, comes indirectly and by dirtying one's hands. (Capoeira 1992: 122)

Rather than an ideology or an overt motive for taking up the practice, the term "malícia" is an attempt to make explicit an emphatically embodied understanding, or more accurately, a style of being-in-the-world, learned "indirectly and by dirtying one's hands." Understanding malícia, then, requires careful attention to the habits that capoeira training develops in a student, starting with the ginga.

THE DESPISED WAIST

To do the ginga—and eventually to develop the art's more extreme acrobatic techniques—a novice must learn to control the torso and increase its flexibility. Ângelo Decânio writes in free verse: "it is fundamental/to insist from the very beginning of instruction that/the ginga is born of the waist/spreading itself through the trunk and the spinal column/to reach the head/and the members in a harmonious way" (n.d.a.: 45). Born of the waist, trickling out through the torso, pervading the limbs, eventually touching the head: the ginga demands a complete commitment of the body to movement starting at the waist, which capoeiristas are taught to experience as the source of both balance and mobility.

How capoeira training treats the torso contrasts vividly with other bodily disciplines and sports. For example, in many forms of dance and martial arts, novices are encouraged to develop a sense of the body's "center" or "center of gravity" below the navel, and to perceive that bodily core as rooted to the ground energetically.[7] Some East Asian arts have developed very sophisticated, quasi-mystical understandings of the role of the body's center in the generation and channeling of chi (also ki), or "life force." Teachers of these arts encourage students to generate greater force and stability by actively imagining a connection to the ground through the "center." The efficacy of these theories of "center" arises less from convincing students intellectually of their "truth" than from providing new ways to act, perceive, and enmesh the body in the world.

In contrast, although capoeiristas must also increase awareness of how the torso is aligned, at the Grupo de Capoeira Angola Pelourinho, the ginga set the student's trunk in motion, swaying, bending, and shifting suddenly to make the practitioner more elusive and unpredictable. These exercises lead a player to experiment with articulating the waist and using movement to maintain equilibrium in the midst of a dynamic, even erratic, ginga. Most every person can bend at the waist. But, as James Morley (2001: 76) writes about breathing techniques in yoga, training can lead a person to "occupy or inhabit corporeal space" that might otherwise be habitually neglected. The capoeira ginga leads a student to use a greater range of flexibility. Whereas other bodily disciplines condition the torso to become a stable proprioceptive root or energetic font, capoeira training sets it loose to twist and feint erratically, even to tumble inverted through cartwheels or headstands. A contrast could be drawn between techniques of the "center" and those of the "waist," like capoeira: "centering" exercises encourage a heightened awareness and tight control of the trunk. Training with a vigorous ginga, in contrast, encourages a player to experience the "waist," the torso's ability to generate force through twisting and torsion, and to bend far beyond what is normal in everyday life.

Mestre Bimba, the creator of Capoeira Regional, designed a series of choreographed attacks, escapes, and counterattacks that he called the *cintura desprezada*, literally the "despised" or "disdained waist." These advanced pedagogical sequences include *balões*, techniques in which an adept throws or propels his adversary through the air. The exercises demand that a player remain relaxed even when being picked up, thrown, or flipped upside down. Júlio Tavares (1984: 71) suggested that the goal of the "despised waist" exercises was "the dismantling of the rules of rigidity of the body." In interviews with Mestre Bimba's students, Cesar Barbieri (1993: 65) found that the cintura desprezada taught adepts "how to get out of situations" like being grabbed. In the cintura desprezada, players were supposed to learn to "fall well." The sequences suggested to students that they need not violently resist being grabbed or thrown in a fight; instead, they should flow with an attack, to be able to regain balance and bodily control quickly.

Instructors at GCAP also discouraged rigidity with constant exhortations to "relax!" Even during handstands, we were told to keep our waists flexible; that way, we could easily move, kick downward, or pike our knees to defend if attacked while upside down. During a kick like the

Mestre João Grande, doing a meia-lua de frente, *or front half-moon
kick, and leaning back, teaches students to avoid it by doing a* negativa.
(Photo by C. Peçanha)

"front half-moon" (*meia-lua de frente*), Mestre Moraes encouraged us to
lean backward as far as possible and stretch out the kicking leg, counterbalancing the momentum of the leg with the torso's weight. This motion
developed flexibility and strength in the abdomen and a tendency to stay
upright by vigorous counterbalancing movements as in the arm movements of the ginga. In contrast, students of other martial arts frequently
hold the body upright and firm during similar kicks to "keep their
balance" and block an adversary's counterattack. Not simply a transitional holding pattern between attacks, the ginga is a distinctive kinesthetic that inflects all movements. Some Brazilian authors even use the
(Brazilianized) English word *suingue* (swing), suggesting that the ginga is
akin to the rhythmic feel of jazz (e.g., Lopes 1994).

A SWAYING STRIDE

The swaying movement of the ginga and the loosening of the torso are
said to transform one's comportment, even outside the roda. For example, some practitioners insist that capoeira instills a characteristic rolling

gait—an *andar gingando*, or "swaying stride"—that is easy to recognize (cf. Freyre 1986b: 41–42; L. Reis 1993: 219–220). Jair Moura (1991: 13–14) cites a popular verse, sung from an urbane ruffian's perspective, in his description of this comportment:

> The trickery or evasion of *capoeiragem*, and the flexibility that its constant exercise produced in practitioners' bodies, gave them a distinctive walk. This swaying stride . . . is described in the lyrics of a song, formerly very popular in Salvador, that portrays the *capoeira* in a few words:

> *Swaying in the street,*
> *Brim of [my] hat turned down,*
> *Scarf about my neck,*
> *A club in hand,*
> *Everyone respects me*
> *As a ruffian.*

In fact, Brazilians widely consider an "andar gingando" to be characteristic of an individual who is *esperto*. Although the word literally means "shrewd," "esperto" is used popularly, like "malícia," to describe the sense that a person is both devious and not easily fooled, opportunistic and observant. They assume that no clear boundary exists between psychological character and bodily comportment.

Brazilian slang also associates the waist with savvy in the popular expression *jogo de cintura*. Lowell Lewis writes that "jogo de cintura," or "game of·the waist," "refers to the creation of facades or smoke screens behind which to hide shady activities" (1992: 190). Although "jogo" in the idiomatic expression is usually taken to mean "game," the word also signifies "play" in the sense of "looseness" or "flexibility," as in the "play" of a tight rope or wire secured at both ends.

Like the multivalent term "ginga," the expression "jogo de cintura" implies a relation between corporeal malleability—specifically in the trunk or waist—and shrewdness, deceptiveness, and the ability to finesse situations to one's advantage (cf. Tavares 1984: 113). A panelist from GCAP discussing the history of capoeira through decades of persecution, for example, suggested that only "a great deal of ginga and jogo de cintura" kept capoeiristas from being captured by the police (cf. Butler 1998a). Although the use may be metaphoric, the term suggestively confounds corporeality and character.

Similarly, Brazilians frequently say that national soccer players, like malandros and capoeiristas, have "good jogo de cintura" with which they can deceive, outwit, and overcome an adversary. The expression captures both psychological and athletic tendencies in a single phrase. In contrast, European soccer players, like novice capoeiristas, are said to suffer from a *cintura dura*, a "hard waist," and thus are likely to be "unnerved" by Brazilian "jogo de cintura" (A. Soares 1994: 78). Hardness in the waist leaves people more susceptible to being deceived and less able to squirm out of adverse conditions. A person's adaptability and responsiveness appear to be located in the torso. Those who "despise" this part of the body, who do not loosen a "hard waist," are too rigid to respond with the cunning of the swaying malandro.

In the volume *O Universo do Futebol*, Roberto DaMatta and his collaborators describe the "jogo de cintura" in soccer and Brazilian social life in terms that could be pulled directly from capoeiristas' discussions. The jogo de cintura, they write, is "an authentically Brazilian mode of defense that consists in letting the adverse force pass and liberating the self from it by means of a simple, but precise, movement of the body" (DaMatta et al. 1982: 28; cited in A. Soares 1994: 81). The authors write that both "the good soccer player and the astute politician" know how to use the jogo de cintura: "In place of confronting an adversary face-to-face, directly, it is always preferable to free oneself from him with a deft movement of the body in an irrefutable way" (ibid.). Physical skills are equated to political strategies, and both are aspects of the same paradigmatically Brazilian comportment.

DaMatta (1993) elsewhere credits patterns of activity, specifically the necessity that one play with one's feet in soccer, with creating a dexterous body and malicioso character in Brazilians. He suggests a link with capoeira:

> Use of the foot, in contrast to the use of the hands, obligates the inclusion of the whole body. It especially accentuates the use of the legs, hips, and waist, parts of the human anatomy that are the subjects of elaborate symbolism in Brazilian society. Thus, we speak of a shrewd Brazilian and "malandro"—that one who knows how to live and "to take part of everything"—as a person who has a "good game of the waist." The expression is applied as often to populist politicians as to excellent soccer players, and to the distinctive style of practicing the sport in Brazil. . . . Could there be, on the other side, in this exclusive use of the feet that characterized club soccer, an unconscious relationship with the game of capoeira that the African slaves practiced in Brazil? (ibid.: 16–17)[8]

People in a range of cultural contexts perceive links between character and posture. Kathryn Linn Geurts, for example, found that Anlo speakers in southern Ghana were convinced that, "there is a clear connection, or association, between bodily sensations and who you are or who you become: your character, your moral fortitude is embodied in the way you move, and the way you move embodies an essence of your nature" (2002a: 76). Geurts discusses a mother who worried that her sons' *lugu-lugu* ways—dawdling around on the way to fetch water, walking aimlessly, slouching, swaying, even staggering about, playing as if they might fall—might make them develop a *lugulugu* character—aimless, irresponsible, and lazy. As Geurts put it, the Anlo were convinced that "bodily movement both shaped character and revealed demeanor" (ibid.: 83; cf. Geurts 2002b: 12–13).

Bodily flexibility and rigidity are often linked to character. Pierre Bourdieu found that among the Kabyle in Algeria, the opposition between masculinity and femininity, honor and virtue,

> is realized in posture, in the gestures and movements of the body, in the form of the opposition between the straight and the bent, between firmness, uprightness and directness (a man faces forward, looking and striking directly at his adversary), and restraint, reserve and flexibility. As is shown by the fact that most of the words that refer to bodily postures evoke virtues and states of mind, these two relations to the body are charged with two relations to other people, time and the world, and through these to two systems of value. (1990b: 70)

Similarly, bodily uprightness, and a corresponding stately rigidity of the spine, has for centuries been associated in many European societies with a dignified, properly cultivated individual (Vigarello 1989; cf. Elias 1978). Geurts (2002a: 76–77) points out that the intertwining of "bodily habits and psychological outlook" that she found among the Anlo has analogues in Western "folk epistemology." Links between bodily straightness and social virtues such as dignity, honesty, forthrightness, pride, and courage are surprisingly pervasive.

POSTURE AND SELF-TRANSFORMATION

It is not as if there were a universal "physiological substrate" to personality, as if swaying *invariably* led to the erosion of moral character, deceptiveness, and cunning. Rather, the physical demands placed on us by the aesthetic standards we strive to attain with our bodies affect our character through our experiences of self-making disciplines. In his discussion of "techniques of the body," Marcel Mauss (1973: 86) suggests that the "education in composure" characteristic of each society is often corporeal. Mauss writes that the "great tests of stoicism" are usually bodily and, "for the majority of mankind, have as their aim to teach composure, resistance, seriousness, presence of mind, dignity, etc." The discipline demanded by self-mortification or voluntary starvation, the resoluteness to confront tests of courage, the placidity to endure physical humiliation, even the appetite for pleasures in hedonism—desirable character traits are often instilled through bodily practice. Even ambitious programs of self-transformation, such as elite military training, entry into monastic orders, mystical disciplines, and total institutions of all sorts, fixate on bodily minutiae. They shape devotees' character and influence how they see the world by seizing on seemingly insignificant details of behavior and comportment, details that may have no apparent relation to a project's express rationale.

Theorists often explain that regimens of self-transformation seize upon the minutiae of everyday conduct because changed habits are a subtle, covert channel by which to smuggle new ideas or symbolic structures into a person's mind. A phenomenological analysis of bodily transformation reveals that changing habits and everyday actions, although possible, is actually very difficult; embodiment is no easy path of access to a person. Modifying our styles of self-comportment, unconscious patterns of action, deep-seated proclivities, and personal dispositions, even for a limited activity like capoeira or boxing (see Wacquant 1995b), can be a colossal undertaking, demanding constant vigilance, extensive social support, and extraordinary sacrifice. Changing one's mind may be far simpler than shaping one's body. A better explanation for physical discipline's role in transformation is that taking one's own body on as a project brings about change, in part, because the "project" always accompanies a person, incessantly demanding that one modify everyday actions to successfully reform. In other words, one does not develop a desired "virtue" because a technique successfully shapes a person's body, like a stylus inscribing symbols on soft clay. Rather, one can change one's body only by transforming one's character at the same time, behaving consistently in new ways. In these projects, people slowly bend and prune the tendencies of their recalcitrant bodies.

To return to the ginga, to saturate all their movements with its texture, students must learn to carry their bodies in a new manner. One becomes malicioso by doing the ginga because to do the ginga correctly, one must become more cunning, treacherous, playful, supple, artistic, quick witted, and aware of the body. The skill is both the means for bringing about change and the measure of one's progress. Specifically, teachers report that the greatest challenge to developing a truly malicioso ginga is to relax during the game: the player must keep his or her body loose even though the action may grow heated. A novice who tenses up during a confrontation, grows nervous or aggressive, or becomes rigid when excited—all very common tendencies—cannot bend quickly enough to evade sudden attacks or launch an unexpected counterattack. The flawed ginga makes a student's emotional state obvious. If a student can manage to keep the torso loose, the other parts of the body tend to take care of themselves.

To maintain flexibility and relaxation while moving means learning to exert oneself without strain, generate force without tension, use minimum effort to accomplish each action, and tighten only when absolutely necessary, for as little time as possible. The resulting style of exertion brings to mind that capoeira was once referred to as *vadiação* (idleness or

Students of Mestre João Grande in New York City laugh as a player bends over backward to escape a malicioso "blessing," a benção *kick. (Photo by C. Peçanha)*

vagrancy). Although the term was, no doubt, used ironically, it also captures this approach to physical effort. Players give the impression that their movements are effortless, distracted, lackadaisical, or even lazy. In spite of the extraordinary athletic demands of the game, the loose, gangly state of the participants makes the word "idleness" seem strangely apropos.

Holding the body in novel comportments—like learning to stay relaxed, loose, and playful in the midst of physical confrontation—offers players opportunities to learn about (and from) their bodies. For example, by relaxing in the ginga, a player might notice that a tense posture demands much more energy than a loose-limbed ginga. At first, I marveled that veterans could play back-to-back games for more than a half-hour; I heard incredulously that two mestres played a heated game that lasted almost an hour in our academy. In contrast, novices who kept their muscles tense became winded almost instantly, virtually collapsing after mere minutes. Relaxation was the key to stamina in the roda, instructors tried to tell students. This dawning realization led to months of experiments and self-coaching (reminding myself, "Relax! Relax!" whenever I grew tense), all dedicated to instilling a new bodily tendency in place of the old disposition to become too easily excited.[9]

As students take up and experiment with new comportment, they may find that similar styles of engaging the world make sense outside the roda. For example, one student told me that the indeterminacy of capoeira play taught him not to define social relations too early. He reported that he began to understand the unfolding of relationships, even their "cunning" negotiation, as akin to ambiguous play in the roda. But perhaps the most well-elaborated extension of the ginga to comportment outside the roda that I encountered was found in tales of "courage" in capoeira.

CRYING AT AN ADVERSARY'S FEET

The capoeira ginga is distinctive in that practitioners strive to avoid contact when an adversary attacks. Unlike other martial arts in which students learn defensive blocks, capoeiristas are taught "escapes" (saidas), "dodges" or "sidesteps" (esquivas), and even "flights" (fugas). From these defenses, capoeiristas understand a "courageous" comportment in ways that might surprise an outsider. Although Mestre Bimba is reputed to have said, "Only those who have courage can play [like children]," proverbs, stories about capoeira heroes, and mestres' advice all encourage the adept to avoid fights.

In stories about their lives, famous capoeiristas, even some of the most formidable, flee from conflict and use trickery rather than fight against unfavorable odds. They demonstrate little concern for honor or pride, as these concepts are typically understood.[10] Ângelo Decânio (n.d.c.: 28), for instance, recounted with unconcealed admiration a story about Mestre Bentinho. When approached during a crowded festival by an assailant armed with a machete, a moment before the angry man reached him, Bentinho fell to the ground screaming that the man had struck him. "It was him! He hit me!" the capoeirista allegedly shrieked, writhing as if already grievously injured. Gleefully, Decânio reports that the furious, frightened crowd descended upon the startled would-be assailant, followed closely by the police, and Bentinho escaped in the confusion.

In capoeira stories, one finds few heroic stands against impossible odds, no tales akin to the Seven Samurai or the Alamo. Far from it. One veteran capoeirista told me a legend she had heard about Besouro Mangangá that, for her, captured the lesson of malícia. She recounted how, when surrounded by a squadron of police, Besouro fell to the ground and cried like a baby. She added emphatically: "Like a woman!" The police were stupefied upon finding the notorious thug curled up on the ground sobbing shamelessly, begging them not to hurt him. She related this story to a proverb Mestre João Grande had once told her that "the first weapon of a capoeirista is to disarm" an adversary. Or, as Mestre Pastinha reportedly said: "A capoeirista has an obligation to cry at the foot of his adversary." This aphorism was discussed at a seminar in GCAP where a student explained it as "deception" (tapeação), a way to trick an adversary into letting down his or her guard. Mestre Moraes added that capoeira taught one to use whatever trick was necessary to gain an advantage, regardless of one's pride or moral reservations. In addition to skills, a lack of concern for social norms or honor, according to Moraes, made a capoeirista especially dangerous and unpredictable.

The ginga and dodging defenses in the roda offer concrete, sensual examples of a comportment that, transposed into other situations, encourages capoeiristas to avoid taking a stand if at a disadvantage. Players are offered firsthand experiences of what it feels like to take up a flexible, evasive posture in the roda. Having learned this way of being, a practitioner may experiment with a similar approach to confrontations outside the game. The transformation in everyday strategies, however, is far from automatic. Teachers frequently lamented that some students never got it, either the ginga or the malicioso comportment it is supposed to instill. But exploring opportunities to use a malicioso comportment in everyday life may start to affect how one lives one's corporeality and carries oneself outside the roda.

Can doing the ginga and bending at the waist really *produce* cunning? At the risk of being misunderstood, this chapter suggests that, yes, they *may*. To really do the ginga well—which not every student will do—and to imbue all movements in the roda with its swaying kinesthetic, a player must hold his or her body in new ways. Not surprisingly, how a person experiences and carries his or her torso is a crucial sensual underpinning to the bodily sense of self. As Iris Young suggests, "The chest, the house of the heart, is an important center of a person's being. I may locate my consciousness in my head, but my self, my existence as a solid person in the world, starts from my chest, from which I feel myself rise and radiate" (1990: 189). Although she states her point in culturally specific terms, such as "heart,"[11] my Brazilian colleagues share Young's sense that the self arises from the body, especially the trunk. Capoeira focuses attention on the simple experience of having a flexible body—a sensation common to us all—increasing the trait and experimenting with the perceptions that greater flexibility might generate.

As a capoeirista gingas in the roda, he or she encounters opportunities to experience an ability to adapt, to shift suddenly and unpredictably, to refuse to be stationary, to avoid confrontation, and to play with indeterminacy, traits typical of a cunning comportment. Language may register the qualities, but they are fashioned by habits and skills that leave their trace on the person who lives through them. Learning the swaying walk of a capoeirista is not a cosmetic change to a person's "jeito" or kinesthetic style, nor is it merely a social marker of an identity. More profoundly, the swaggering step is a symptom that a person is experimenting with a gingando comportment, trying it on, or even committing to it more seriously, as a way of being-in-the-world. Some will never achieve this comportment—they may even actively try to avoid it—but cultivating the ginga as a bodily skill, this peculiar constellation of flexibility, relaxation, and cunning, offers opportunities to feel what it might be like to walk with a malandro's swaggering stride.

9 CLOSING THE BODY

New students joining the Grupo de Capoeira Angola Pelourinho, after they had spent a little while practicing the ginga and learning a few techniques—the "half-moon" and "stingray's tail" kicks, the evasive "negativa," perhaps the aú (cartwheel) or rolê (side roll)—were almost immediately thrown into a game. The results were predictable. No matter how slowly the orchestra played, hapless rookies would lean the wrong way into oncoming kicks. Or they would leave themselves wide open for sweeps or trips. In even the most basic exercises, they would stumble, turn the wrong way, lose sight of their partner, fall to the ground, or put themselves into awkward, indefensible positions. Easily befuddled, they left themselves exposed in the most obvious ways.

Sometimes novices were so vulnerable—and yet unpredictable—that they were dangerous to themselves and others; avoiding their wild techniques, gently knocking them down, and picking apart their flimsy defenses was a job for an experienced, surgically precise veteran. In my first classes, far from feeling my competence grow, I had the sense that I was just learning new ways to be taken advantage of, yet another chain of techniques that wound up with me on the floor, one more trick I could fall for, and myriad postures that left me exposed. If novices like me were practicing anything, it seemed that it was to be victimized.

To counteract this sense of incompetence and to begin building the skills that a player needs in the game, most instructors choreograph sequences of movements—some very brief or repetitive, others long and complicated—so that students become inclined to respond appropriately inside the roda. They learn to lean *away* from an oncoming kick, to adjust their techniques to avoid crashing into a spectator, to balance so that they don't lose control of a kick, and to make smooth transitions from one movement to the next. Teachers start to point out details in bodily posture: how to carry oneself to prevent exposure, where to probe in an adversary's technique for a chance to strike decisively, what to look for in an opponent's defenses. Slowly, a student's awareness of vulnerability and how to decrease (or exploit) it grows.

As Nicholai Bernstein (1996: 204) points out, the idea that beginners learning skills are somehow "beating a trail or imprinting a certain trace onto the central nervous system" runs up against an obvious fact:

> A human starts learning a movement because he cannot do it. Therefore, at the very beginning of skill development, there is nothing to be beaten, or the only thing available for imprinting is wrong, clumsy movements that he is able to perform at the very beginning of skill acquisition.

If the first passes of capoeira were merely about imprinting or rehearsing, then the diligence with which veterans hunt out a novice's vulnerabilities could only be described as sadism, and the clumsiness of the novice as a lifetime sentence.

Rather, this sort of exercise might be understood less as a rehearsal of a foreordained script for interacting than as a technique for shifting a player's perceptions. The steady stream of physical feedback sensitizes players to their vulnerabilities. The trips, kicks, head butts, sweeps, and falls slowly shape an awareness in apprentices of how they are susceptible—when they are *aberto* (open), as capoeiristas say—as well as an ability to perceive when a counterattack might be successful. Learning how to remain *fechado* (closed), as unexposed as possible, requires a meshing of one's perception of an adversary's position with a sense of how one's own body is vulnerable during a movement. Psychologists and other scholars have referred to the awareness of one's own body as "proprioception"; exercises sensitizing players to vulnerability shift this awareness. Capoeira training must instill a vivid, visceral sense of how and where one is "open" if a player is to avoid being "closed on" in the roda. And initiates learn how they are at risk, primarily, by having their vulnerabilities exploited.

Through experience, example, and instruction, capoeiristas respond to the impossibility of being absolutely closed and permanently safe from attack by manipulating the ways that they are open. That is, capoeira training encourages adepts to use feints and false openings to lure adversaries into traps. Because the perceptual systems through which capoeiristas perceive openings are composed of dispositions to act as well as the skill to perceive, players find that they can use their own body's vulnerability tactically. They can use their own weakness as a weapon. Doing so requires that they perceive immediately the tendencies, intentions, and responses of an adversary so that they can anticipate and manipulate them. In other words, the dynamic sense capoeiristas have of their own bodies' opening and closing requires an acute sensitivity of their relationship with other people's bodies in terms of posture and potential for action.

Although the awareness of being exposed is forged in training for the game, the players' shifting sense of their own vulnerability often affects their conduct outside the roda. Many analysts of capoeira, noticing that the art shares an interest in "closing the body" with the Afro-Brazilian religion Candomblé, have suggested that the *idea* of bodily closure links the two practices. Some suggest that a concept of an "open body" originated in African religion or magic and helped to generate closure practices in both capoeira and Candomblé, making the two part of a single cultural complex. Whether or not this is the case historically, careful ethnographic study of capoeiristas' magical and religious practices suggests that felt links between capoeira and forms of supernormal power seem to arise, instead, from this immediate sense of the body's openness. In a piecemeal fashion, the dawning awareness of how they are exposed inspires capoeiristas to use magic, just as it motivates shifts in posture in the roda.

BECOMING AWARE OF ONE'S OPENNESS

In capoeira, vulnerability is described as "being open." In a discussion of play, Mestre Squisito demonstrates how central this way of experiencing the body is to the art, referring repeatedly to "opening" and "closing":

> We have to be humbled when we fall victim to a well-done entry by an adversary in the game! Humbled to recognize that we vacillated, or in other words, we *opened* our guard without wanting to and *our adversary found us.*
>
> An efficient *capoeirista*, whether an Angoleiro or Regional player, knows how to *close* his game, when he wants. . . . But this is very different from playing *outside* of (distant from) the adversary. To play *closed* is to be very close, but at the same time not to permit our adversary to get us (encounter us). This is without letting the game become tangled, without grabbing each other, without losing [literally "exiting"] the rhythm of the berimbau and the *roda;* and principally without opening our defenses. To play *closed* is to maintain your guard at all times and not to let yourself be captured by an opponent. (R. Costa 1993: 58, emphasis in the original)

Mestre Squisito continually describes the objectives of the game in terms of "entering" another player when he or she "opens," or "finding" a vulnerability left unconcealed. In classes, students expect to hear *Abriu!*—"You opened!"—after being swept or head-butted abruptly to the ground. In much of capoeira training, the game is talked about this way: as entry and exit, opening and closing, concealing and finding. Capoeiristas suggest that their bodies are porous, penetrable, "findable"; and that it is possible to close, seal up, and hide them.

The body, of course, is not so porous; nor is there anyplace, really, to hide in the roda. Kicks and head butts do not enter a person's body in any literal way, no matter how much they might hurt or startle. Even getting struck, tripped, or knocked down, worst-case scenarios in a game played within normal levels of violence, does not typically break the skin. And the best defenses cannot conceal a player's body. How and why, then, do practitioners use the metaphors of being entered or found?

In a typical closed movement, a player folds the limbs in to cover the face, neck, and torso—areas that *capoeiras* are trained to experience as vulnerable—just as the fingers cover the palm when a hand makes a fist, a gesture players frequently used to demonstrate closure. In an open movement, in contrast, the limbs are extended straight, just as the fingers of an open hand extend from the palm. In an open aú, or cartwheel, for example, the legs splay out from the trunk, and the arms are fully extended to support the player's weight. The closed variant of the aú, in contrast, is done with the waist doubled, the hips and knees bent so far that a player's legs are in front of his or her chest as protection.

When a movement is not successfully closed, a player offers an adversary an "opening," a moment of vulnerability. The "vital" parts of the body, according to capoeiristas, are the face, neck, chest, belly, and sides. Parts of the body not considered to be open, such as the top of the head, the arms, the buttocks, and the legs, are used to guard those that are vulnerable. That is, allegedly nonessential parts are moved to obstruct an adversary's access to vital regions, as if parts like limbs were themselves invulnerable to striking. Only a poorly trained or ill-mannered player strikes the "nonvital" parts of the body. For example, when a player at the Grupo de Capoeira Angola Pelourinho kicked another in the leg—a target felt to offer little vulnerability—the victim might step back and theatrically dust off the point of contact with an exaggerated look of disgust. Ideally, an adept waits patiently during a game until a decisive attack is possible, instead of prematurely forcing attacks on poorly chosen closed positions. The aesthetic sensibility that capoeira instructors seek to develop in students includes a preference for elegant and crisp attacks over frequent, unconvincing ones.

An awareness of the body's vulnerability develops in particular, cultural contexts and through life experiences. The bodily vulnerabilities that capoeiristas exploit, for example, are not all of those actually offered by an adversary's anatomy. Although capoeiristas consider a kick to the knee or shin to be inelegant and avoid the movement, fighters in many traditions, such as Thai boxing, use kicks to the legs to wear down an adversary, stop an advancing fighter, or damage an opponent's leg. An exposed knee offers opportunities for a Thai boxer, but not for a capoeirista, unless he or she perceives it *in spite of* training to avoid such an "inelegant" attack.[1] Although capoeira instructors often use a language of pragmatism and self-defense, they work from their own felt sense of vulnerability, schooled to perceive certain postures and body parts as imperiled. In contrast to the sense of invulnerability developed at the leg or knee, repeatedly being kicked and struck brusquely in the belly during apprenticeship develops a sensitivity of the body's availability to an attacker there; it creates a lived sense of an opening.

This awareness of vulnerability must be more dynamic than a simple anatomical map and, if a player is to avoid being caught in the unfolding of capoeira movement, it must extend into the surrounding space. For example, one instructor demonstrated that, during a rolê, a kind of sideways roll, a player could "enter" the movement to counteract it at a specific moment, jamming a shin against the inside of the other player's knee so that the rolê could not be finished. In this position, our teacher explained, the attacker was "inside" the rolê, already past a felt boundary at which defense might have been possible. Similarly, during a spinning kick called an *armada*, we were taught to recognize that, because the technique required a player to turn his or her back for a moment, an adversary could stay close and duck away from the kick, possibly sweeping the kicker's pivot leg. We had to anticipate the sweep and be prepared to escape if necessary into a cartwheel. The inchoate awareness of our own vulnerability had to take into account an adversary's body, predicting how one's own shifting position could generate opportunities for another player to attack, depending on that adversary's position. Vulnerability did not simply cling to particular body parts; it arose from the conjunction of an adversary's movements with one's own.

THE IMPOSSIBILITY OF CLOSING

One great challenge of capoeira, according to practitioners, is that every action, especially an attack, inevitably makes a person vulnerable. To accomplish anything, therefore, a player must open him- or herself.

Anthropologist Iria d'Aquino (1983: 47–48), in her discussion of counterattacks, describes this dilemma:

> Every golpe [strike], regardless of its power and efficacy, has a moment which leaves the fighter vulnerable. It may be just a fraction of a second, either immediately before or immediately after the contact point of the golpe, in which the fighter is lifting his foot or facing away from his opponent.

A great deal of instruction focuses on coaching students to perceive these ideal opportunities to counterattack as adversaries invariably leave themselves open.

Mestre Curió, one of Bahia's "old guard" angoleiros, showed a class how even the jab, the simplest punch, left an attacker vulnerable. The mestre demonstrated that the front elbow, when held normally in a fighting stance, shielded the ribs on the side turned toward the target. When a fighter started to punch off the front foot, however, the arm had to extend and draw the elbow away from that side, creating an opening. At the moment of impact, with the arm fully extended, a vital area was open for any player patient enough to wait and dexterous enough to sidestep the straight jab. Even a split second early or late, however, and the elbow of the jabbing arm, then bent, would deflect the counterattack. Thus to exploit the opening, a capoeirista had to develop an acute sense of timing to anticipate the opening and seize it.

The ideal response to any attack is its *negaça*, according to capoeiristas, a complementary counterattack timed and placed perfectly to hit its opening. The negaça combines escape and counterattack into a single efficient motion. In the case of Mestre Curió's punch, the negaça required a player to duck outside the punch at the last possible moment (so that the unsuspecting victim would not be able to stop the attack), and transfer the combined force of the attacker's lunge and the counterattack to the exposed ribs. To accomplish a negaça of any sort, a capoeirista must become acutely aware of another person's body, anticipate its movements, and respond instantly. As Nicholai Bernstein (1996: 181) writes about skills more generally, a capoeirista must not learn "a permanent cliché," but rather

> a peculiar, specific *maneuverability*. The brain sensory systems gradually learn to be more and more skillful in making an instantaneous translation from the language of incoming sensations and perceptions reflecting the movement process into the language of corrective motor impulses that need to be sent to one or another muscle. (emphasis in the original)

Convinced that no posture can remain secure for long against an able adversary, capoeiristas refuse to defend any fixed place or remain long in any single posture. In fact, training exercises and teachers' comments suggest to the novice that the safest place to be during a game is actually "inside" another player, that is, moving into an opponent's space, staying close, and finding the negaça within attacks. Retreating was ill advised; it allowed an adversary to simply advance and continue attacking. Getting "inside" other players put them on the defensive and forced them to contend with counterattacks against their own vulnerabilities. I often felt that another player, especially a good, aggressive one, had no interest in being anywhere in the roda except in whatever little corner of it I occupied at the moment. Some virtuoso players seemed to inhabit the space surrounding an adversary, staying so close that they passed over or under their quarry. The very best crowded in, anticipating every movement and arriving there first, until they "closed" on a target, leaving him or her *parado*, "stopped" or immobilized. This strategy puts constant pressure on an opponent, not allowing him or her to rest.

Boca do Rio (Marcelo Conceicão dos Santos, left) and Cizinho (Tarcisio Sales Trinidade) play a very "closed" jogo de dentro, or inside game. (Photo by G. Downey)

This approach to capoeira was said to be best learned in the *jogo de dentro*, the inside game, a type of play that usually begins matches of Capoeira Angola. The pace of play in the jogo de dentro is slow—sometimes excruciatingly so—and players stay close to each other. Some training exercises exaggerate this to an extreme. In one drill, students of Mestre Jogo de Dentro, named for his mastery of this portion of play, stood in a ring no more than six feet in diameter. Two students at a time played in the tight confines marked by their classmates' bodies, pushed back in if they threatened to fall out of the circle and chastised if they stood up straight. Players could barely extend a kicking leg fully, and retreat was impossible. To play this close, students had to accommodate an adversary's attacks in an almost cooperative fashion, staying inside the axes of kicks, for example, conforming to them to be able to escape, cartwheeling over sweeps, and deftly sliding under head butts.[2] Players turned their elbows outward and let their knees protrude as they rolled and turned close to the ground, shifting joints and less vital parts of the body constantly to keep any potential head butt or kick at bay in such close quarters. This style of play, in spite of its leisurely pace, is an exhausting physical chess game of shifts in contortionist postures held low. It demands precise escapes, exquisitely timed counterattacks, and constant adjustments. The jogo de dentro heightens a player's bodily control and the malleability of techniques to the numberless circumstances that can arise in the game.

Conditioned by being tripped, knocked down, and struck countless times in the belly, dogged by instructors to perceive one's own position—"*Stop right there!* Do you see how *easy* you are to sweep?"—a capoeirista starts to anticipate attacks and "closes" openings before an adversary can exploit them. As was the case for Loïc Wacquant when he learned to box, one learns how well one is doing in strategic exchanges immediately, by the success of counterattacks one suffers (2004: 59). Players learn to calmly turn, twist, or roll a vulnerable area out of the path of an oncoming attack, and they probe for openings to counterattack. When one first learns to play, all these perceptions and techniques are a disarticulated mess; by the time a novice sees an opening and recalls the technique used to exploit it, an adversary has already found a glaring opening in the rookie's halting moves.[3]

To do the jogo de dentro or "inside game" well—smoothly, with the body relaxed, close to the ground, and closed—a player must become aware of another person's body as a field of opportunities in relation to the tools the player has at his or her own disposal. This requires more than simply "techniques of the body," as Marcel Mauss (1973) described them,

Natinho (Honorato Moraes Trinidade), preparing to do a cartwheel, plays a jogo de dentro *with a young student.* (Photo by G. Downey)

with which to attack or defend. Tim Ingold argues that skillful action requires a tuning of perception and action, an ability to deploy one's trained body in relation to relevant information from the environment. Skill is not simply "an isolated ability in a person's body, but is better understood as a meshing of a person's intentions, through their abilities, with the environment (including other people), already interrogated by a skillful person for significant information" (2000: 353 ff.). In other words, the ability to play requires what James Gibson (1966) called "perceptual systems" that integrate actions with astute perceptions. An expert capoeirista develops instincts for the roda so that sensing an opening seems to trigger an almost automatic response.

At the same time, keeping closed requires that a player sense how his or her own body presents a changing set of vulnerabilities for an adversary. Capoeira proficiency assumes that skill is reciprocal. To remain closed, players must become immediately aware that they, too, are the target of skillful action, the same sort that they are trying to use. A cunning player is aware of these interlocking perceptual systems—an opponent's sense of shifting vulnerabilities and his or her own. The play back and forth of perception multiplies opportunities for deception.

OPENING AN ADVERSARY

When they recognize their own vulnerability, players also learn that openness is itself a tool to use in the game. After falling victim to countless ruses, novices realize that not all apparent openings are real. Feints can lure an opponent into a compromised position. The reflexes that they develop to integrate perceiving an opening and automatically attacking it can be tricked. Skills can be their own sort of vulnerability. When I began to teach a few friends some basic capoeira techniques, I found that they were initially immune to feints of any sort because they could not perceive that I had made myself vulnerable or they responded too slowly. True novices do not fall into traps because they cannot yet skillfully perceive the capoeira bait.

Feints in capoeira are typically described as openings that players intentionally create. Mestre Nestor Capoeira (1985: 90), for example, describes the ideal feint: "He 'opened' his game to call the attack of the other and, already anticipating what the attack would be, he had the counterattack ready." The cunning capoeirista lies in wait to transform a false opening into a counterattack as soon as an adversary responds to the feigned attack. For a virtuoso, passive perception of opportunity cedes to active manipulation, as veterans use a fine-tuned awareness of an opponent's learned instincts against him or her. For example, a savvy capoeirista may recognize that an opponent likes a particular attack, say a rasteira, or leg sweep, against spinning kicks. The veteran then feigns a slow or careless step into a precarious "armada," or back spinning kick. When the overeager adversary, excited by the vulnerability, attempts to seize the advantage with his favorite rasteira, the "victim" already has a counterstrike prepared (see U. Almeida 1986: 163–164). During a game, a lazy cartwheel that appears sloppy and ill timed can be transformed abruptly into a cunning attack on a player trying to do a head butt into the available opening.

Because all techniques leave the attacker open to some degree, a player must not commit fully to an opportunity until certain that it is not a ruse. Every movement is suspect, as capoeiristas fake constantly at each other to provoke counterattacks and their inherent openings. The game can become a battle of feint and counterfeint, a constant search for a decisive opening in a continuing exchange of provocations: "We win by falsehood," Jair Moura explains (1991: 9). Technical expertise is of secondary importance:

> There could be a player of capoeira without any physical preparation, who was only familiar with a half-dozen strikes and falls, who had very

little mobility, few flourishes, and at the same time if he has "malícia" he is a true capoeirista. He is even more so than another player who has all the technical qualities, who plays beautifully, who is effective, but at the same time is not malicioso. (Capoeira 1985: 109)

In summary, capoeira training conditions players to experience their own bodies as perpetually vulnerable. Aware that no strategy can make them permanently invulnerable, capoeiristas have to adjust constantly to decrease their exposure, recognizing how their own bodies and others' hold out both opportunities and dangers as they move.[4] Perceiving vulnerability, in one's self and in others, generates a heightened awareness of one's position in the world, and new patterns of deploying one's body.

CLOSING THE BODY IN CANDOMBLÉ

Like capoeiristas, other Brazilians worry about vulnerability and seek to protect themselves against hostile elements in the world. Many analysts of capoeira draw attention to the fact that practitioners of Candomblé, a set of Afro-Brazilian religious practices prominent in Bahia,[5] also talk about the body being "open." Particularly because of their shared ethnic roots, many scholars in African diaspora studies suggest that bodily closure provides a foundation for both Candomblé and capoeira (e.g., Browning 1995; Dawson 1994b). Some suggest that the concern with keeping oneself closed arose first in West African religion and magic and was later applied to capoeira (cf. Lewis 1992: 111).[6]

According to practitioners of Candomblé, a person is "open" when he or she is vulnerable to supernatural attack or contamination. Devotees understand the world to be full of beneficial and harmful energies, sometimes resembling fluids, as Ruy do Campo Póvoas (1989: 170) suggests. An "open" body is porous and cannot resist incursions by sickness, misfortune, unwelcome entities, or the malevolence of enemies. Diverse practices, such as herbal bathing, ritual scarring, amulet wearing, and initiation, seek to maintain the body's integrity, closing it against harmful forces. In addition, a porous body can leak magical energy or life force, what Candomblé practitioners refer to as axé. According to Paul Johnson (2002: 126):

> A closed body, however, is sealed against such risks, both the risks of losing axé and the risks of deadly intrusions. From the perspective of the religious system, this is the primary motivation for undergoing initiation, to learn how to compensate or elude Death and so to live in luck, health, and prosperity.

As Johnson describes, "moments when the integrity of the body is breached"—menstruation, sexual intercourse, before ritual incisions heal, even cutting the hair or clipping fingernails—are "moments of potential risk" (ibid.: 120).

Candomblé devotees ritually close key points on the body, for example, the top of the head and spine, shoulders, and stomach, to diminish an initiate's vulnerability to external magical influences.[7] Tiny incisions are made at vulnerable points and treated with ritual preparations so that they heal back more securely. Small scars left over from ritual incision, under the hair or on the shoulders, are what Barbara Browning (1995: 176, n. 7) calls evidence of "the very wounding which . . . offers protection."

Numerous similarities exist between "closing the body" in Candomblé and what capoeiristas hope to accomplish: in both cases practitioners fear an atmosphere rife with dangers, believe the body is porous, and even see "wounding" (or learning by falling) as a way to close the body. But for all the similarities, differences are marked. Candomblé devotees, for example, believe that rituals can permanently close the body and thus bring increased protection. They are far more optimistic than most capoeiristas, who respond to the body's openness with constant diligence, without hope that any single act or posture might make the body less permeable. If anything, capoeira training makes adepts increasingly aware of their own vulnerability. Although both groups talk about "openness," they employ profoundly different strategies to counteract the dangers in the world.[8] When capoeiristas turn to Candomblé—as many do—they often draw on religious resources out of the physical sense of danger instilled by capoeira, rather than any logic internal to Candomblé. They sample Candomblé as one in a diverse repertoire of defensive maneuvers, using ritual, religious practice, and magic as they would capoeira techniques.[9]

SIGNING THE CROSS

An unabashedly autobiographical anecdote might offer a good way to tease out the subtle differences between closing the body in the roda and in Candomblé. At some point during my capoeira apprenticeship in Salvador, I inadvertently began to sign the cross and kiss my thumb, a popular Catholic custom in Bahia (cf. Cascudo 1976: 75). I was raised a Roman Catholic and had spent a dozen years in Catholic schools, so the gesture was familiar. But before living in Salvador, I had not been accustomed to performing it regularly, nor in this distinctive fashion—that is, kissing the tip of my thumb at the end. Without thinking, however, the gesture became part of my capoeira game. I blessed myself before a match and then for dramatic effect if an opponent's kick passed too close for comfort, or I narrowly escaped from some fast-closing trap. I soon found myself doing the gesture outside the roda, using it in everyday life to punctuate storytelling.

When I returned to the United States, my friends were struck by my odd new habit. The gesture was not explicitly intentional, nor had I taken much notice of acquiring it. I picked it up as part of a constellation of little quirks, along with a singsong Baiano accent, distinctive slang from Salvador, and other mannerisms, souvenirs of my time there. The gesture had insinuated itself into my habitual comportment as I lived my way into harmonious interaction with my friends in the capoeira world.

But simple emulation did not explain how, in certain moments, signing the cross made sense to me, or even felt necessary in an unreflective, visceral way. When I scarcely dodged a technique in the roda, when I prepared for an anxiety-causing encounter, or when I recounted a particularly harrowing adventure, the gesture emerged from my body in response to danger, present or remembered. The sign of the cross had become a kind of warding practice in my everyday repertoire of actions, like knocking on wood, part of the posture I took up when I perceived risk.

A similar dynamic seems to be captured in a collection of manuscripts by the late Daniel Noronha, a legendary practitioner of capoeira. The texts were published posthumously in facsimile form to preserve the visual aesthetic of his pages, sprinkled with symbols, sketches, and his distinctive handwriting. On one page in particular, where Noronha recounts how he frequented dangerous rodas in the hilly outskirts of Salvador, his prose brims with symbols and formulaic phrases:

> I, Mestre Noronha, give this statement because I frequented this roda of toughs because they always treated me very well, thanks to the divine Holy Spirit, Amen. †.†.†. *. J. M. J. *. I, Mestre Noronha, always went to the rodas of capoeira there in the hills with my body closed, with my orixá in God and my prayer. Amen. Xango [an orixá] my father in God. . . . * J. M. J. * . . . P. D. N. S. J. Christ is who cares for me in the hour of my affliction. Amen. †.†.†. * (Coutinho 1993: 28; NB: stars [*] in text represent pentacles topped with small crosses in the original.)

Noronha's testimony is shot through with written "gestures," much as the sign of the cross arises in capoeira games. When I first read this passage, the pacing, rhythm, and phrasing vividly summoned to mind the way other old mestres told stories, interspersing them with gestures of gratitude and caution. Phrases, such as "Thanks to the divine Holy Spirit, Amen" and "Christ is who cares for me in the hour of my afflic-tion," recur frequently throughout Noronha's writings. Abbreviations like "J.M.J." (*Jesus, Maria, José*) and "P. D. N. S. J. Cristo" (probably *Pai de Nosso Senhor Jesus Cristo*, or "Father of Our Lord Jesus Christ"), sit along-side magical symbols—crosses and five-pointed stars topped with small crosses, the *Cinco Salomão* ("Five of Solomon").[10] Noronha evokes both Christian figures and orixás, the divine spirits that possess the "children" in Candomblé houses. But he also resorts to magical symbols from other sources: Islam? Judaism? European mysticism?

A historian could attempt to trace the trajectories that produced this treasure trove of symbols. The challenges posed by this religious mangle might give even the most diligent pause, however. The tangle of elements from West and North Africa, Arabia, Portugal, and France—possibly from Jewish or even Romany traditions—was already weaving together for centuries on the Iberian Peninsula, even before they were brought into the fierce dynamic of New World slavery. For an anthro-pologist committed to ethnographic methods, the thought of trying to unravel this mixture makes the head swim, especially because these symbols may evoke so many different meanings.

A phenomenological analysis of these practices, both signing the cross and scrawling initials pregnant with magic, focuses instead on how they are deployed and to what experiential effect. In Noronha's writing, their use suggests his awareness of the supernatural and some of the techniques he might use to combat danger. For example, when recounting his biography, Noronha may have been concerned that, if he did not demonstrate sufficient gratitude for the aid that he had received—from the Holy Spirit, from his father Xango, from J. Cristo—he might provoke misfortune. His phrases of thanks and gestures of protection seem to arise from an awareness of vulnerability, like shifts in posture to guard against openness in the roda.

I started signing the cross after throwing myself into capoeira apprenticeship, when I was striving to learn the physical techniques of the art as completely as possible. For many dimensions of capoeira, learning involved consciously performing exercises and struggling to extend physical skills. The sign of the cross, however, slipped into my habitual comportment largely without my awareness, under cover of so much intentional training. It was part of a way a capoeirista held him- or herself emotionally and corporeally in response to perceived danger.

Someone in the United States asked me if I thought that the gesture actually worked. The question would never have occurred to me because it was not done after calculating its effect. The gesture became part of the way I actively related to the world around me. When anxious, the gesture emerged as part of a wary comportment, sometimes drawing up genuine, even automatic protective maneuvers. But the posture was also available for comedic effect when I used it to mock another player's ineffectual attack. I did not perceive the gesture; I engaged the world *through* it.

Although other practitioners no doubt had experiences very different from mine, my manner of acquiring this protective habit suggests one way we might understand bodily openness and closure. Other theorists have analyzed the sign of the cross in Brazil as a symbol, suggesting that it brings together African concepts—the crossroads, the line between the world of the living and the dead—with Christian iconography. The gesture's origins, however, do not compel people to do it. I suspect that, like me, many take it up and continue to use it because it generates a distinctive emotional, perceptual, and muscular preparedness in relation to risk. Although it may "mean" many things as a symbol, the gesture exists experientially at a crossroads between tension and readiness, as a capoeirista takes up a defensive stance in a perilous world.

GESTURE, POSTURE, AND VULNERABILITY

Gestures like the sign of the cross suggest that capoeiristas live in a shifting topography of felt risk. Whether signing the cross or whispering formulaic prayers, practitioners respond to danger by taking up postures of preparedness and closure. Gestures key shifts in comportment, changes in the way *capoeiras* hold themselves and interrogate the world, depending on how they perceive the environment. Just before a game starts, they may motion to the sky, trace symbols on the ground, touch the earth ("for protection," I was told), sign the cross, or take a St. Christopher medal dangling from a necklace into their mouths (that way it also doesn't bang into their faces during cartwheels and headstands). Throughout the game, when they want to collect themselves after losing their composure, practitioners return to these gestures, using them to recuperate their cunning stance toward the world. Mestre Moraes suggested that players should pray in their own way at the foot of the berimbau before a games starts, whether to the orixás or Jesus Christ or anything else—"even the Buddha!" he advised. Although the gestures have symbolic connections to supernatural forces, the posture of heightened awareness—of one's own vulnerability and of potential attacks—provides the experiential basis for their use.[11]

One could argue, then, that for capoeiristas the connection between Candomblé and capoeira is not that the two are cut from the same symbolic cloth or historically tied, but that adepts piece together their own protective clothing from any patches of fabric that seem promising. Ethnographer Waldeloir Rego seems to concur. Although capoeira was practitioners' primary point of reference, he found that adepts strove with every technique at their disposal to protect themselves and attack their enemies. Rego writes: "At every instant a capoeirista 'is burning' another, that is, doing ebó (witchcraft) to his companion, having always in sight the competition and quarrels arising from this" (1968: 38). In that sense, capoeiristas will likely add new gestures, symbols, and prayers to their repertoire to sit alongside or replace the current amalgamation, as the vulnerability that they feel constantly prods them to improve their defensive postures.

Closely examining this dynamic posture suggests that being a person in the world is not simply a material fact. Rather, we have an experiential sense of how we are available to others and to forces around us. Training in capoeira—like an assault, a serious illness, or an unexpected fall—may cause a person's sense of his or her availability to the world to shift, transforming experience of the environment and such things as slippery steps, a coughing colleague, a darkened street, or a moving adversary.

An awareness of other people's bodies and actions seems very much to be a part of everyone's existential situation, not just capoeiristas'.[12] Capoeira training, especially that concerning being open and closed, poses as a problem the placement of the novice's body in fields of other people's potential action. The adept's immediate sense of physical self is molded through training until he or she experiences the environment as dangerous and the body as penetrable in distinctive ways (e.g., at the belly, but not at the knee). Given that one cannot avoid being open in some way, capoeira coaches students to manipulate their vulnerability in a cunning fashion to deceive others.

We all feel our bodies as available to the world—to danger, to pleasure, to accidents, to interaction, to being seen, and so on—just as we feel that the world offers us particular opportunities based on our needs, abilities, skills, and perceptual tendencies. Capoeira training molds the experiential body as a nexus of perception, opportunity, and availability. Exercises teach novices to perceive opportunities of which they had been unaware, both in their own person and in those around them. Being embodied does not make capoeira distinctive; particular styles of deploying the body and modes of perceiving the world developed in the art do. Learning to feel how one is vulnerable is as important to proficiency as mastering the art's other facets, perhaps more so in the artful transformation of an adept's everyday comportment.

10 Walking in Evil

According to instructors, a capoeira student ideally does not just learn a game for the roda. He or she also begins to act differently outside it—to sense danger, move more carefully, conceal abilities, and think strategically in everyday life. As the two preceding chapters suggest, doing the ginga and learning how one is vulnerable affect a student's self-awareness, perceptions, and habits. Capoeira provides additional guidance about how to live this new way of being and offers many strategies for contending with the dangers a player comes to perceive. A whole series of stories, disjointed bits of advice, exercises, and experiences in the roda provide a repertoire of skills for living a cunning life. Although not every student will learn each bit of wisdom, these many resources may transform one's awareness and behavior, crafting a capoeirista in a piecemeal and idiosyncratic fashion.

The ideal capoeirista develops a pervasive wariness and distrust of the world. Legendary mestre Daniel Noronha describes the constant state of vigilance for which capoeiristas strive as "walking in evil" and discusses how it saturates their everyday comportment:

> The capoeirista walks thinking in evil, not because he is a bully. It is a question of self-defense because a person can be assaulted at any moment. Life is difficult for those who work, while for a scoundrel it is easy. When the scoundrel encounters a sucker, he comes out well; but when he encounters a capoeirista, he gets a razor across his face. . . . And this is the reason that a capoeirista walks in evil; it is for this reason and not because he is a ruffian. All capoeiristas are workers and not vagabonds. (Coutinho 1993: 42)

Noronha insists that a capoeirista is a productive worker, not a bully, ruffian, or vagabond. A practitioner "walks in evil" or "walks thinking in evil" only because the world is a treacherous place. An appropriate response is to become wary, learn to anticipate trouble, avoid danger, and fend off treachery when it inevitably comes. Walking in evil, however, does not result from merely convincing a person intellectually that the world is a dangerous place.[1] Capoeira as a form of physical education offers detailed practical lessons to a student about how to respond to dangers outside the roda.

Capoeira instructors tell students where to look, how to walk, places in which to be particularly careful, strategies to deal with specific dilemmas, over and over, until students begin to actively search out potential dangers in the environment and develop novel tactics to avoid them in everyday life. Capoeiristas do not shrink from a violent world but instead "walk in evil." Players learn to conceal their abilities in the roda and are then told that they must do the same outside the academy's doors. If others are unable to recognize that they study capoeira, they can both guard against prejudice and make their skills all the more effective when they prove necessary. As new skills affect fundamentally students' everyday habits—such as how they stand or walk—they ideally camouflage these fundamental changes. A capoeirista "walks in evil" but feigns a carefree stroll; he or she remains ever vigilant but pretends to be cheerfully oblivious.

This chapter offers a careful analysis of how capoeiristas learn to look in order to show the life-shaping effects of skills and habits. Training to see takes hold of behaviors directly in explicit, practical instruction, while it also affects experience indirectly, as a student, following this guidance, starts to perceive the world through new behaviors. Doing a practice means living, perceiving, and understanding through it. If one learns to look in a specific way, the world will appear differently than it might through another style of seeing. Just as musical proficiency in capoeira shapes how an adept hears the berimbau, so too do techniques that some adepts call the "sideways glance" affect how practitioners see, what they see, and how they appear to other people. Since vision is a whole perceptual system, as James Gibson (1979) describes, learning to move one's head differently or shifting one's habitual scanning pattern can profoundly affect how one sees. Behavior and experience are directly related in skills.[2]

Capoeira apprenticeship presents players with the chance to learn diverse skills and change their perceptual habits. Trained adepts accumulate an array of dispositions, habits, and sensitivities that make up their way of being-in-the-world, or at least *one* of the ways that they might be in the world. Some elements, like a well-told cautionary tale, may circulate widely in the community; but even these may influence a capoeirista's habits and imagination in diverse ways. To "walk in evil" is not a single principle but an assemblage of tricks and techniques to get by in a hazardous environment, different for each practitioner. And seen through stories of betrayal, tactics to avoid ambush, and the sideways glance, the world looks shadowy and treacherous, indeed.

HARD JOKES AND CAUTIONARY TALES

At a reception in Salvador to inaugurate the Fundação Mestre Bimba, an organization dedicated to the teachings left by the legendary mestre, Dr. Ângelo Decânio was the keynote speaker. Decânio, a retired surgeon, author, and former official in the Bahian Boxing Federation, was one of only a handful of capoeiristas awarded a white silk scarf by Mestre Bimba and the title "contramestre," to honor his devotion to the art. With innumerable hours spent as close to Bimba as an adopted son—he lived in the mestre's house for some time—Decânio was eminently qualified to talk about his teacher's legacy.

As tears welled in his eyes and the crowd of several hundred hung on every word, Decânio offered a meandering, disconnected speech: no warm story of good times or camaraderie, no summary of Mestre Bimba's impressive accomplishments, no moral about determination or hard work. Instead, Decânio presented a series of anecdotes and expressions, all cautionary tales about how dangerous life was. In a manuscript Decânio shared with me, he offers page after page of similar stories. In a section entitled, "Dangers at corners, doorways, and overhangs," he writes:

> Practicing capoeira habituated us to watch the environment constantly, evaluating: where could the next danger await us?! In a poorly-calculated movement, in a traitorous invitation, in a feigned friendly gesture, or under the guise of an apparently innocent movement?! If we made a mistake analyzing what we saw and heard, that is to say, in the evaluation of the hidden danger of a corner—what might be behind a door left open or the thick trunk of a tree? Especially at night?!
>
> Mestre Bimba's jovial stories, accompanied by his wide and expressive gestures, left no doubt about the dangers! ... The defensive reflexes remained with us for the rest of our lives: "a Pavlovian response," Professor Novis would say. "In the blood!" our Mestre would say, put there by the infinite repetition of the dangers of every moment of guile or cunning, characteristics of capoeira. The practical

jokes necessitated a constant state of vigilance! Pulling down one's pants to change into clothes for training created the possibility that one would fall victim to a rasteira [a leg sweep] while the legs were caught in the cuffs of the pants. Distracted? [Someone might give you] a *galopante* [open-handed slap to the head] as a present!

Be careful when someone approaches! An absent-minded walk might slyly conceal evil intentions? Perhaps a *banda-traçada* [a capoeira throw] or a "vengeance" [an attack to upend an opponent]? God only knows what else.

Remember Jesus, our verbose colleague who studied Aeronautics. One night, when turning a street corner, he was unexpectedly stabbed with a knife that punctured the book that he carried slung over his shoulder! It was an example always cited by the Mestre! (Decânio n.d.a.: 55–56)[3]

Although Decânio might be more long-winded and relentless than most commentators, this presentation was far from unusual. Disjointed and only loosely related to each other, the lessons prescribed a perpetual state of wariness verging on paranoia. If there was any moral to the rambling list, it had to be: "Trust no one."

When capoeiristas reminisced about their teachers' most important lessons, they frequently described what seemed to be minor tactics for self-preservation. Older men, some of whom had not played capoeira regularly in decades, would wax nostalgic about a mestre instructing them never to sit in public with their backs to the street.[4] Gildo Alfinete, a student of Mestre Pastinha, enthusiastically showed me how his teacher had taught him to cross his arms or to put his hand on his head when arguing. That way he took up a fighting posture without a potential adversary noticing. Frede Abreu reported that one of his favorite aphorisms was, "In capoeira, the best friend of Waldemar was Traitor." In fact, one of Bahia's most famous capoeiristas was Traíra, or "Traitor," a colleague of Waldemar, a member of Bahia's old guard.[5] The proverb reiterates a theme that one hears repeatedly in capoeira; even one's closest ally is capable of betrayal. As a whole, these bits of advice and stories implied that everyday life was thinly veiled conflict and that no amount of suspicion was too much.

One practice that helps to heighten a student's wariness, alluded to in Decânio's comments, is *brincadeira dura* (hard joking), rough practical jokes that capoeiristas play on each other inside and outside the academy.[6] "Hard jokes" provide ample incentive for a student to remain vigilant. Just as Decânio describes, on many occasions I saw a student changing clothes, who had his pants around his ankles, pushed over and sent tumbling to the dressing room floor. The joke was considered especially funny if the perpetrator could execute a gentle push so that it was almost imperceptible, as though the result of accidental jostling. Once the victim was sent sprawling, the perpetrator could feign innocence, sometimes slyly winking at the same time.

Students played a host of similar pranks on each other. For example, during an academy renovation project, a group member who was carrying a long piece of wood and had asked where to put it unexpectedly wheeled around, "inadvertently" swinging the board at the head of the person giving directions. Many who saw the joke, and the intended victim's last-second duck, laughed uproariously. Other times, my fellow practitioners would suddenly stretch their legs, "accidentally" tripping a colleague trying to step over them. And consistently, when players lost a hat or a hair tie while playing in the roda, opponents tossed them back to the owner and attacked the distracted recipient at the same moment.

These sorts of jokes affect players' emotional states, how they move, where they stand, and how they survey their surroundings. Similarly, stories and lessons induce students to alter the habits that they specifically address and stimulate changes in a person's overall comportment. To "walk thinking in evil" requires not merely following the letter of a mestre's admonition. A novice must become more savvy and suspicious, actively searching out fresh sources of potential danger in his or her surroundings.

DISSEMBLING IN A TREACHEROUS WORLD

Capoeiristas respond to the treacherous state of the world by maintaining secrecy. Subtle elisions, subterfuges, half-lies, and sleights-of-hand become increasingly important in everyday life as capoeiristas employ deception extensively both in and out of the roda. Mestre Pastinha advised:

> No one can show everything that he or she has. The treacheries and revelations have to be offered only to few. This [approach] serves one in capoeira, in the family, and in life. There are secrets that cannot be revealed to everyone. There are moments that cannot be shared with anyone. (quoted in GCAP/Rio n.d.)

Habitual secrecy becomes the counterpart to the pervasive distrust that capoeiristas learn through hard jokes and cautionary tales. To close oneself off in this way requires that capoeiristas also actively conceal that they have any secrets, offering misleading information to mask the absence of real disclosures for both defensive and aggressive reasons.

"Defensive secrecy" occurs when "stigmatized persons keep secrets to protect themselves from economic, legal and social punishments" (Karl Scheibe, cited in Tefft 1980: 14). Defensive secrecy figures prominently in capoeiristas' way of recalling history. Prior to the 1930s, being a *capoeira* was a status crime punishable under law, like being a "vagrant" I was told, and those who knew the art were persecuted. Although the art is no longer illegal, some capoeiristas claim that they still encounter widespread prejudice. These adepts may strive to conceal their knowledge of capoeira as a defense against social stigma.

Some celebrated cases of dissembling in capoeira history are now institutionalized in the game. Slaves originally did capoeira to music, for example, so that slaveholders might think their slaves were just dancing rather than training to fight, according to practitioners. This historical ruse allegedly explains the art's hybrid "dance–fight" nature. The widespread use of nicknames, (*apelidos*) or "war names" (*nomes de guerra*), once concealed *capoeiras'* identities from the police (cf. R. Almeida 1994b: 63).[7] Even the name "Capoeira Regional" was alleged to be the product of dissembling. According to some historians, because "capoeira" was still expressly prohibited by law, when Mestre Bimba opened the first legally recognized academy, he called the activity he taught "the Bahian regional fighting style" (*a luta regional baiana*).

According to some contemporary practitioners, when capoeira was illegal, adepts went to great lengths to conceal that they knew the art, and these old habits die hard. One colleague told me of an older player who, outside the academy, still carried his berimbau wrapped in newspaper. Another veteran laughed at the irony that some contemporary capoeiristas got pictures of berimbaus tattooed on their bodies, signs of a status he had once carefully concealed. Mestre Moraes, likewise, frequently admonished his students not to carry instruments in the street or perform capoeira in public. He prohibited group members from wearing their uniforms outside the academy; we had to arrive at and leave from the academy in street clothes, being especially careful to conceal T-shirts with the group's insignia. He explained that secrecy shielded students from members of rival academies, as well as stigma. He criticized capoeiristas who appeared in public in white pants and shirts silk-screened with academy logos—the most common capoeira uniform—likening them to spies who openly declared their occupations.

Concealing one's knowledge of the art also served as an "aggressive" form of secrecy, creating its own tactical advantages. In the regulations for Mestre Bimba's Centro de Cultura Física Regional, for example, students were told to conceal what they were learning: "Avoid demonstrating to your friends from outside the roda of capoeira your progress. Remember that surprise is the best ally in a fight." Ângelo Decânio (n.d.a.: 61–62) recounted that on one occasion Mestre Bimba and his students were giving a demonstration after a weight-lifting competition. The iron bar lifted by the winner—weighing 80 kilograms—had been left in the center of the space. Mestre Bimba asked his student Rosendo to move it. Wanting to show off, Rosendo grabbed the bar in one hand and, swaying, carried it from the floor. When Bimba saw, he shouted, "You fool! You should have grabbed it with another person, and still sweated while lifting it!" (ibid.: 62). Decânio explains that capoeiristas should always affect being weaker than they are, so that, if challenged, they prove stronger than anyone might suspect. Similarly, in the roda players frequently feign injuries, complain dramatically about the pains of "old age," protest that they are too tired or sick to play, and even pretend to grow excessively fatigued during games. All are ways of dissembling the true extent of a player's ability. The fact that these ruses are sometimes transparent or even comic does not prevent players from practicing deception as a habitual way of engaging the world.

For similar reasons, observers sometimes criticize players who do elaborate acrobatics when a game starts or during a chamada. This practice is widespread in folklore shows and public demonstrations and is one reason that capoeira teachers criticize training regimes that teach students theatrical styles of the art. Mestre Acordeon (U. Almeida 1986: 157), for example, advises against opening acrobatics: "Don't let your opponent know how stupid you are, naively showing strength and weakness before the game begins."

The cultivation of secrecy as part of a cunning comportment affects practitioners in concrete, corporeal ways that shape how they interact in the roda. Players mask their intentions through feints, conceal the extent of their abilities, and otherwise use dissimulation of all sorts. At the same time, they struggle to uncover each other's secrets—to discern the skills, to learn the tendencies, and to anticipate the actions of an adversary. Outside the roda, capoeiristas try to conceal what they know, both to avoid stigma and as a tactic to make their skills all the more effective through surprise. The struggle for concealed knowledge shapes practitioners' visual behaviors and starts to affect how they look at the world.

THE SIDEWAYS GLANCE

Boca do Rio, one of my instructors, was a lesson in studied disinterest when he played capoeira. At times, his eyes wandered as he gazed off into space, or he seemed to stare vacantly past an adversary. He often appeared to be distracted during a game. The appearance was false, of course, part of a repertoire of cunning artifice he had developed by training his eyes.

Perhaps his most dependable trick, one that I fell for several times before learning to mistrust him sufficiently, was to cock his ear during a game and turn suddenly toward the orchestra, seeming to focus his attention on the musicians, acting as if he had heard a musical signal calling for a break in the action. Although his posture and movement alone might have been sufficient to take in an inexperienced player—he sometimes gestured toward the musicians with open, up-turned palms—his eyes were the most distracting part of the ruse. When he suddenly turned, he fixed his gaze on the orchestra's lead berimbau. An inexperienced adversary's attention almost inevitably followed along with Boca's, looking for whatever had caught his eye. Realizing at the last moment that there was, in fact, nothing to see, the novice player quickly turned back, too late. Boca do Rio had already started a kick or sweep. Now his eyes told a different story. He arched his brows and looked sideways, disapproving, as he stepped back to do a chamada.

Boca do Rio was a virtuoso, adeptly manipulating the social dynamics of vision to confound his opponents; at one time or another, however, almost all capoeira novices, have to train themselves in different techniques for looking. The most basic, as Ângelo Decânio (n.d.a.: 218) writes in his "Commandments of the *Capoeira*," is: "Always watch everyone . . . and pay attention to your surroundings. Do not lose sight of the movements of your partner." A capoeirista learns that even during spinning movements and acrobatics that upend the body, one should never lose sight of an opponent, not for an instant (cf. Lewis 1992: 102). This was hammered home to me in one of my very first classes when I performed a cartwheel looking at the floor. An instructor politely head butted me in the chest, sending me tumbling onto my back. As I rushed to return to my feet, he paused and, wordlessly, pointed to his eye: "Pay attention," the gesture communicated.

The admonishment holds outside of play, and capoeiristas will break the game's frame to demonstrate the necessity of constant vigilance. For example, if a student sitting outside a roda does not pay close attention, a teacher may suddenly launch a surprise attack at the negligent spectator, even if it requires reaching out of the playing area. Students learn that they must watch warily, even when at rest. If we saw each other in the street, members of the Grupo de Capoeira Angola Pelourinho would sometimes stalk each other, sneaking up on our friends outside the academy. Students who were approached might claim to have noticed the stalker much earlier, concealing countersurveillance just as the approaching capoeirista tried to use the urban terrain and other pedestrians to hide pursuit. Frame breaks like this insinuate the cunning logic of play outside the game so that students begin to scan their surroundings more attentively.

In spite of the necessity to watch constantly, a player ideally should not focus his or her eyes directly on an adversary. Capoeiristas like Boca do Rio cultivate an apparent disinterest during games. Lowell Lewis confirms that "many master players avoid looking one directly in the eye; in fact, they almost always use peripheral vision so that they can appear not to be watching!" (1992: 102). These practitioners often seem to be only dimly aware of each other while playing, staring off into space vacantly or suddenly fixing their gaze on points outside the roda.

A capoeirista learns to avoid fixing his or her sight during play because one's gaze, facial expression, or posture can forewarn a perceptive adversary of upcoming actions. Frederico Abreu suggested that to conceal their intentions, capoeiristas frequently use peripheral vision or the "sideways glance" (olhar de soslaio). As Jair Moura (1991: 12) explains:

> The peripheral vision possessed by every capable capoeirista permitted him to control all the movements of his adversary.
>
> During a counterattack, a capoeirista should strive to follow the movements of his opponent's eyes closely. By watching, he can know what an aggressor is looking at, and in this way, before [the aggressor] is able to make the attack, the capoeirista can see the vulnerable point to be struck.
>
> To avoid being discovered in this way, capoeiristas . . . sought to train and possess the "cunning look" or the sideways glance, avoiding, in this way, that an adversary fix their eyes. [A capoeirista] kept his eyes lowered or looked at different places, watching the other contender out of the "corner of the eyes," or by means of quick glances.

Techniques like the "sideways glance" described by Moura were pervasive.

Players' efforts to conceal their attention suggests that capoeira raises their awareness of the social physics of vision and treats the act of looking as itself an object in the world capable of revealing one's intentions. Regardless of whether players are consciously aware of the techniques of glancing sideways, or talk about them explicitly as Abreu and Moura did, they use the fact that vision is simultaneously a "channel" for collecting information and a "signal," as Argyle and Cook describe (1976: 167). Players who do not control their facial expressions—especially their eyes—discover that astute opponents can anticipate their actions. Once a capoeirista recognizes that looking is itself palpable to others, he or she can deploy looking tactically, with cunning, rather than guilelessly as merely a means for gathering information. Gaze manipulation takes different forms, from concealment—gaze aversion—to actively mis- leading an adversary, what some capoeiristas call the "strike of sight" (*golpe de visto*).

These visual techniques attempt to escape from the reciprocity that Georg Simmel (1969: 358) claimed is inherent in sight: "By the glance which reveals the other, one discloses himself. By the same act in which the observer seeks to know the observed, he surrenders himself to be understood by the observed" (cf. Berger 1972: 9). A visual duel can arise in capoeira when both players simultaneously try to conceal the object of their gaze and discern what an adversary is focusing on through furtive glances.

SEEING THROUGH SHIFTY EYES

Although the sideways glance is used defensively to keep an adept's intentions secret, Jair Moura (1991: 12) also makes a stronger claim for this technique: that it allows a capoeirista to "control" another's move- ments. Rereading Moura's assertion reminded me of an event that stuck out in my field notes. During a roda at the Grupo de Capoeira Angola Pelourinho one Sunday afternoon, a group of capoeira students I knew from another academy showed up to watch us play. That night, the roda was well attended; the visitors joined forty or more spectators seated on benches and castoff plastic chairs. More than two dozen adult members of GCAP played along with some of the young students in the group's classes for Projeto Axé, a program dedicated to helping Salvador's "street children" (*meninos da rua*). The crowd made for a lively night. Unlike in most academies, visitors were seldom invited to play in GCAP. These students had simply come to watch, traveling a great distance to do so; at least they had chanced upon a particularly good night.

During a game between Mestre Moraes and one of his students, a bare-chested spectator entered our school, his shirt dangling from the waist of his pants, violating an academy rule. He was obviously a local resident wandering in to watch, and he probably meant no disrespect on a steamy evening. Before anyone else could react, even the assistant instructor who was supposedly watching the door, Moraes interrupted his game in midkick, stepped away from his adversary, and told the visitor that if he wanted to stay, he would have to put on his shirt. The man apologized as the mestre dove back into action. The moment was over so quickly that I doubt everyone in the room even noticed the interruption.

The incident found its way into my field notes, but I thought little about it at the time; it was pretty typical of Mestre Moraes. Several weeks later, however, another student from the visitors' academy asked me if Moraes really noticed people entering our school without shirts while he was playing. This student hadn't been there to see it for himself. I realized that the story was circulating as proof of Moraes's mastery of the game. A visitor must have felt that our teacher's impressive proficiency was demonstrated, not merely by his prowess in the roda, but also by his sensitivity to what happened outside it.

Mestre Moraes possessed an awareness of the restricted space of the roda that bordered on the preternatural. Although he careened around the roda at high speed while playing heated games, spinning and bounding over and around an opponent as if totally out of control, he managed to survey constantly the entire academy. His erratic movements left players sitting on the edge of the roda with white knuckles; the same stunningly fast pirouettes and leaps could also paralyze an adversary. I sometimes marveled that he was aware of his adversary's position and movements as well as the music (he noticed instantly if someone fell out of rhythm or a berimbau string broke), the players seated inches from where he would alight before counterattacking, and even visitors who entered the academy. And he could keep track of it all while staring off into space, appearing so distant and unengaged that I feared he might crash into me when we played.

During a class, Mestre Moraes insisted that the staggering, spinning ginga that he favored allowed him to observe the entire roda. His stumbling, erratic steps appeared careless and without purpose, but they permitted his distantly focused eyes to scan the space around him. He explained that a capoeirista's "swaggering walk" when strolling through city streets allowed the same sort of head and body movements to expand an adept's field of vision. Other capoeiristas agreed that capoeira can affect a practitioner's perceptions. "If developed properly," Mestre Squisito (R. Costa 1993: 82) writes,

... the capoeirista becomes able to discern more and more along with what is seen directly in front of the eyes, developing the ability to perceive things outside the front angle of vision. In this way, the capoeirista can even become able to see behind himself!

Mestre Moraes's coaching suggests that students should use whole-body motion to enhance vision, a discussion that makes sense theoretically only if we recognize that sight is part of an integrated perceptual system.

Psychologist James Gibson (1979) has noted that vision is not the passive function of an isolated organ. Sight is an active ability to engage with the world that deploys, not merely the eyes, but other parts of the body: orienting muscles that turn and focus the eyes, a rotating head, a guiding ear, a swiveling neck, a trained brain, and a mobile body. Seeing is the result of scanning, looking, focusing, and visually searching (cf. Ingold 2000). With Gibson's broad understanding of vision as an active perceptual system, dependent on behavior as well as trainable abilities, it becomes much easier to understand how the sideways glance and the swaying stride might shift how one sees.[8]

Players also encourage a sideways glance as part of their habitual comportment to prevent attention from becoming overly focused. Mestre Moraes's ability to notice a shirtless visitor while playing demonstrates an ideal sensory state for the game: the practitioner's attention disperses and covers the space both inside and outside the roda.[9] Whenever a player focuses his or her vision, this concentration can become a liability. To see an object, "to respond to [its] summons by actually concentrating upon it," is to become "anchored in it," capoeiristas' actions imply, borrowing language from Merleau-Ponty (1962: 67).

A capoeirista divining that an adversary has focused his or her attention should ideally be able to exploit this. The part of the body on which attention is focused, the anchor for the attention, can be used to feint. Capoeiristas will even attempt to draw each other into fixing their gaze, suddenly motioning with a hand, for example, "showing" (*mostrando*) to incite an opponent to watch the hand rather than a kick that it conceals. Not fixing one's gaze safeguards against any control that an object of attention could exert over the one observing it.

The act of looking itself may be used to ensnare an adversary's attention. If one player watches the eyes of another, the person watched can use those eyes to feint. A player may appear suddenly to have his or her

Cizinho (Tarcisio Sales Trindade) and Boca do Rio (Marcelo Conceição dos Santos, with his back to the camera) shake hands and prepare to play, always wary of what the other might do. (*Photo by G. Downey*)

attention caught by the berimbau, for example, or look as if preparing to attack from a particular direction. When an opponent turns to attend to the same object or reacts to the "preparation" for an attack, the trap is sprung, and the player who initiated the shared looking springs into action. Corporeally aware of the properties of seeing, capoeiristas transform looking itself into a tool for dissimulation. Layers of manipulation and artifice pile up on looking until players intentionally reconstitute the social physics of vision with an eye toward tactical advantage.

A practitioner must pay careful attention all at once to the whole body of his or her adversary because some capoeiristas practice disjointed movements that permit attacks to be thrown from unforeseen angles. Rather than being grounded in the cooperative action of the entire body, movements involve only a single part in isolation, making it very hard to anticipate what's happening from observing other body parts. In addition, to be safe, a practitioner's field of attention should include the spectators who may "buy into" an ongoing game, replacing an opponent. Novices hear cautionary stories about capoeiristas who, while playing, perceived an adversary's allies preparing an ambush outside the space or getting ready to slip a weapon into it. In these stories the protagonist typically does not defeat an armed opponent; instead, he or she perceives an attack before it can be made.

The only way to watch everything at once, I was told, was to look at nothing in particular. Jair Moura, in his comments on the sideways glance, suggests that peripheral vision is more sensitive to sudden movements, and by not focusing intensely on any one thing, a player could allow the whole field of vision to be as sensitive as possible. When I first received similar advice from an instructor, I found it hard to believe. The recommendation indicated that capoeiristas perceived the visual field as complex, with different areas of sensitivity, not just a transparent window on the world. The most observant among them were studying how the senses worked from the inside, trying to make the most out of the opportunities that their bodies and movements afforded.

Although I cannot be certain, players employing the sideways glance seemed to be noticing characteristics of the visual field that arise, in part, from the neural anatomy of the eye and, perhaps, were even working to change them. For example, the foveation of the retina in many primates causes the center of their visual field to be most sensitive to detail. In contrast, some researchers believe that the periphery of the visual field is more attuned to sudden movements (Hardin 1988: 8–12, 101). Refusing to focus the eyes directly on an adversary could manipulate the visual field to increase a person's responsiveness to sudden surprise attacks. Recent research also suggests that separate neural–optical systems may exist, one for explicitly recognizing objects and another for orienting action. Goodale and Humphrey (2001: 333–334) observe that unlike the object perception system, the action system may lack concentrated focus in the center of the visual field.[10] This allegedly allows us to pick up objects, step over obstacles, grasp doorknobs, and turn off lights in the course of everyday life without refocusing our sight for each activity. If so, this might help us to understand capoeiristas' convictions that peripheral vision is sensitive to movement and can be used to direct action.

The intriguing ethnographic insight is not that ongoing neurological research can or cannot prove what capoeiristas tell us, or that capoeiristas have somehow already ascertained facts only recently discovered by neuroscientists. Rather, the sideways glance and capoeiristas' techniques for looking demonstrate that adepts are exploring the experiential characteristics of the visual field, manipulating their own perceptual systems, perhaps even training themselves to increase their sensitivity to specific sorts of stimuli.[11] Although few recent discoveries in neurosciences are without debate, researchers are finding abundant evidence that human bodies and brains are surprisingly plastic, responding to patterns of activity by changing physiology. Different physical disciplines like capoeira might have profound effects on how our bodies develop physically, effacing the division sometimes drawn between biology and culture. Capoeira training takes hold of the entire perceptual system of sight, including not only the eyes, but also the head that holds them, the neck that swivels to keep sight of things, the body the forms its foundation, and perhaps even the neural pathways that parse light into useful information.

A CUNNING COMPORTMENT

Capoeiristas insist that the roda is not an isolated game, and mestres exhort their students to apply what they have learned in the game to everyday life. Mestre Moraes, for example, tells his students that everything they learn in the "smaller roda," the roda of capoeira, is applicable to the "greater roda," life (cf. GCAP 1993). Moraes and other mestres do not mean that cartwheels, head butts, and "half-moon" kicks should be used to deflect the slings and arrows of everyday misfortune (although one should always hold these resources in reserve, hidden, just in case). Instead, they suggest that the senses, strategies, and comportment that students develop in the art should be used to get by in a dangerous world by warily "walking in evil," as Mestre Noronha put it.

The transfer from the smaller roda to the larger one, however, is not a simple matter, nor does it happen automatically. A person can become convinced that life is treacherous without mastering the techniques available to decrease the risks. Even after students are quite good at the game, their everyday comportment may not change, I heard their teachers lament frequently. Instructors have to work very hard to convince students—through coaching, hard jokes, explicit instruction, and cautionary stories—to apply these techniques in everyday life. Only patient ethnographic research reveals the paths that these skills might take as they expand beyond the forum in which they are learned, the roda, into other spheres of life.

Nor do all the disparate, sometimes contradictory, tendencies that a student might learn resolve themselves neatly into a consistent set of principles. For example, when one learns to swagger in order to increase one's field of vision and, at the same time, that swaggering is a hallmark of capoeiristas that one should conceal, no "logic" can resolve the practical contradiction. The lessons and anecdotes that older capoeiristas share—a teacher telling them how to stand when arguing, how to cross a street or round a corner, how to sit in a corner bar, tales of treachery, and rough practical jokes—are as fragmented as they sound. For the most part, however, capoeira instructors are not concerned with explaining the world consistently. They are trying to train their students to engage it with cunning, to shift strategies quickly when necessary. The myriad instructions and pragmatic details forge a new type of actor, a capoeirista, by modifying a person's habitual comportments. Being in the world like a capoeirista does not come easily, in part, because it has to be built up piece by piece, one skill at a time, and practitioners must experiment with using their hard-won skills in new contexts outside the roda. Even if training is successful, nothing guarantees that every student will learn to comport him- or herself in the same way. As they come to live through these habits, first in the roda and then, maybe, in everyday life, capoeiristas learn to walk in evil, perceiving and preparing for it when others see nothing so sinister.

11 THE LIMITS OF WHITENING

Although young men of Brazil's ruling families—and even an occasional federal minister or police chief—may have learned how to deliver a head butt or throw a "half-moon" kick, practitioners argue that the creation of the first academy brought about a whole new way of doing capoeira. In particular, a new "style," Capoeira Regional (capoeira from the *region* of Bahia), became popular. For the first time, large numbers of middle-class, light-skinned students took up the art. Observers noticed that something new was afoot. In the words of journalist Admon Ganem (1948: 16):

> [Capoeira] Regional is the modern capoeira, felicitous creation of "Mestre Bimba," who has been transmitting it for a long time to many young sportsmen. Capoeira Regional is in the body of students, doctors, of engineers, lawyers, businessmen, members of our police force, officials, and members of the armed forces. . . .

Discovered by these new adepts, the Bahian art encountered different sorts of bodies: people unaccustomed to samba, to Afro-Brazilian religious dance, to manual labor, or to street fights, perhaps a bit quicker to feel shame, and seeking a feeling of power or competence that made sense to them.

Proponents claimed that stripped of folklore and superstition, and proven in the ring in Mestre Bimba's prizefights, Capoeira Regional was more effective for self-defense. Traditional capoeira, they said, was a pastime, suitable only for playing at festivals, undignified and impractical for anyone serious about fighting. Detractors of Capoeira Regional, in contrast, saw the form as a bastardization of authentic capoeira, "bleached" of its ethnic character, packaged for middle-class adoption, and diluted to make it palatable to naïve consumers. Historians credit Mestre Bimba with inventing Capoeira Regional, but many observers argue that its distinct kinesthetics arose from the dispositions brought to his academy by new groups of students—university educated, white or light skinned, well-to-do. Social traits are allegedly visible in movement. Some critics go so far as to argue that the ways in which practitioners of Capoeira Regional move demonstrates "whitened" or "bourgeois" tendencies.

The link between a way of moving and a social class or ethnic group is not obvious. Assuming that black-skinned people move in a particular way, whites in another, begs important questions about the reasons. Moreover, the assertion does not bear up well under scrutiny. There are many exceptions, too many to ignore; even the contrast between the black Mestre Bimba, creator of an allegedly "white" style, and mulatto Mestre Pastinha, defender of "African" Capoeira Angola, belies the assertion. In fact, more black Brazilians in Salvador play "whitened" forms of capoeira than styles that radical activists claim better reflect their racial identity. To assume that all these practitioners are exceptions, so that the "rule" that style corresponds to race still holds, is not empirically sound. In general, one's movement or habits do not automatically grow out of one's social positioning; all children tend to be ill mannered, uncultured, and in need of training, no matter the group to which they're born.

A closer examination of how capoeira changed when middle-class students took up the art reveals a more subtle interplay between bodily training and self-comportment. The fact that a way of moving can be considered to be "white" or "middle class"—or, for that matter, "black" or "working class"—offers a chance to ask how it feels to wear a particular status in the flesh. Careful attention to the "whitening" of capoeira does not reveal an essential racial identity manifested in movement. Instead, discussions of "whitening" highlight the challenges that cultivating new habits and unfamiliar styles of moving pose for the novice. "Whitened" capoeira appears to be a solution to movement problems, not merely a dilution of the art's "African" nature, a solution that demonstrates what an accomplishment learning capoeira is.

THE EMERGENCE OF CAPOEIRA REGIONAL

Beginning in the 1930s, the populist government of President Getúlio Vargas promoted popular culture, including samba, soccer, and carnival, to consolidate political support and as symbols of Brazil's distinctive character. Police efforts had already broken the urban maltas, although persecution of *capoeiras* continued. As historian Kim Butler (1998b: 187) writes, ironically, new legislation was passed against capoeira practice in public in the very year, 1932, that the first capoeira school was legally opened in Salvador (cf. Rego 1968: 282–283). Carefully constrained and practiced by the right sorts of people, capoeira might become acceptable, even valuable.

Mestre Bimba benefited from the more hospitable environment for capoeira practice, and, at the same time, was one of the preeminent reasons for the change in climate. Through his fighting prowess, charisma, and ability to attract skillful collaborators, Bimba was able to achieve for capoeira the same respect given to imported combat sports. He and his dedicated students eventually won a place for the art in university physical education departments, limited support from the state, and widespread public acceptance. When President Vargas, in 1953, enthusiastically asserted that capoeira was "the only truly national sport," this public endorsement was the result both of capoeiristas' struggles to gain respect and of ongoing efforts to mobilize popular culture as a rallying point for the Brazilian "New State."

The founding of the first legally recognized academy laid the groundwork for the division of contemporary capoeira into two principal "styles": Capoeira Regional and Capoeira Angola.[1] From very early in his public career in the 1920s, Mestre Bimba declared that he practiced his own variant of capoeira, "Capoeira Regional." He and his students insisted that Bimba had improved upon traditional capoeira, an art that he felt "left a lot to be desired in terms of a fighting style" (R. Almeida 1982: 14). As Bimba himself explained: "Capoeira Angola can serve merely for rhythmic public demonstrations and not for a fight characterized by violent force and decided by agility."[2] In the prizefighting ring, he sought to prove the pugilistic efficiency of Capoeira Regional and issued challenges to any fighter willing to meet him there. These challenges, and Bimba's insistence that he had invented many capoeira techniques—whereas Capoeira Angola allegedly had only 9 attacks, Regional included as many as 120 (R. Almeida 1994b: 17)[3]—did little to endear him with fellow capoeiristas. They did, however, attract many new students to his school. Capoeira Regional became so popular that when Bahian capoeira spread throughout Brazil and abroad, practitioners typically claimed to teach some version of it, whether or not they actually had learned the art from Mestre Bimba.

When Mestre Pastinha founded the second formally recognized academy in Salvador, he ardently asserted that the style of capoeira practiced there was "Capoeira Angola," or "Capoeira *from* Angola" (*Capoeira de Angola*). Contemporary practitioners widely consider Capoeira Angola to be the "traditional" form of the Bahian art, allegedly ancestral to Capoeira Regional, although it is now far less widespread than the Regional style.

Players typically say that they play one of the two styles, or a combination of both. Hybrids are probably more common than forms hewing faithfully to either Pastinha's or Bimba's standards, especially outside Salvador. Some modern capoeiristas assert that they practice "capoeira, without a last name" (*capoeira, sem sobrenome*)—neither Angola nor Regional—alluding to the art prior to the division, or to a style learned from a teacher outside the two dominant lineages (there are many in Salvador). Lowell Lewis (1992: 62, 103–115) found that many practitioners were doing what one referred to as *capoeira atual*, "contemporary capoeira," implying that they had successfully integrated both styles and superseded the split.

In spite of this mixing, even those who claimed that their capoeira was "without a last name" were quite capable of distinguishing the two schools and used the distinction often to describe play. Aficionados could pick out markers in a player's style, even going so far as to identify which elements in a mixture originated in either form. In some contemporary rodas, time is set aside for both styles; players are first allowed to play "Capoeira Angola," and then the music accelerates for games of "Capoeira Regional." Purists of both stripes reject these hybrid rodas. The Grupo de Capoeira Angola Pelourinho's chapter in Rio de Janeiro, for example, published a pamphlet quoting Mestre Pastinha: "A man can speak two languages, but one of them is false" (cited in GCAP/Rio n.d.).

During Capoeira Regional's early development, the distinction between it and other forms of the art was obvious: practitioners of Capoeira Regional were the students of Mestre Bimba. Over time, a growing number of teachers, less clearly defined, claimed to teach "Capoeira Regional." Under strict definitions, a fair number of capoeiristas seemed to fall outside the two schools, neither devout traditionalists like Mestre Pastinha, nor following precisely in Mestre Bimba's model. The designation "Capoeira Regional" became an aesthetic judgment, applied broadly. Practitioners of "Capoeira Regional" were said to be more overtly aggressive in play, to move in a distinctive style, and to be wealthier, whiter, and with greater formal education than other practitioners, no matter whether they did or did not follow Mestre Bimba's teachings.

Mestres Nenel (left) and the late Dermeval, two of the sons of Mestre Bimba, play Capoeira Regional.   (Photo by G. Downey)

CRITIQUES OF CAPOEIRA REGIONAL

From his first moment in the public eye, Mestre Bimba faced criticism for introducing innovations into capoeira. His opponents in prizefights objected to his tactics, complaining that he fought unfairly even though they had agreed to fight according to *vale tudo*, or "anything goes," rules (J. Moura 1991: 23; cf. Abreu 1999; R. Almeida 1994b: 27). When he founded his school for capoeira, fellow masters criticized the academy structure itself, especially his school's exclusiveness: only novices possessing student identification or proof of employment and able to pay monthly fees were allowed to practice there (L. Costa 1962: 20; cf. Areias 1983: 69). Outsiders criticized the commercial nature of the academy, saying it broke long-standing norms of hospitality and customs governing mestre–apprentice relations. Others disapproved of the way the founder systematized the art (e.g., Mestre Cobrinha Verde, quoted in M. Santos 1991: 20). Some critics reportedly found the martial tone of the mestre's instruction disagreeable, insisting that it exacerbated violence and eroded the playful, musical, or artistic dimensions of capoeira.

When some of his students, striving to prove themselves, intentionally disrupted the rodas at popular festivals and other meeting places, the criticisms only grew louder.

But perhaps the most enduring criticism of Mestre Bimba asserts that the innovations of Capoeira Regional fundamentally undermined the nature of the art, diluting its essential character with alien elements. Novelist Jorge Amado, for example, accused Mestre Bimba of copying techniques from jujitsu, boxing, and a North American wrestling style, "catch-as-can-catch":

> It happened that Mestre Bimba went to Rio de Janeiro to demonstrate to the inhabitants of the Lapa neighborhood how it is that one plays capoeira. And there he learned techniques of *catch-as-can-catch*, jujitsu, and boxing. He mixed all of this with the capoeira of Angola, that which was born of an Afro-Brazilians' dance, and returned to his city talking about a new capoeira, a "regional capoeira." (Amado 1961, cited in Vieira 1990: 20)

Concerned about the changes, Amado allegedly convened a council of masters to pass judgment on Capoeira Regional:

> Ten of the most frequently consulted capoeiristas affirmed to me, in a lengthy and democratic debate that we engaged about the new school of Mestre Bimba, that "regional" did not deserve confidence and is an adulteration of the old capoeira "angola," the only true capoeira. (ibid.)

Amado assumed that Mestre Bimba's innovations were the result of encounters with foreign fighting styles in Rio de Janeiro; other observers believe, in contrast, that these elements originated among his students, some of whom were proficient in Asian martial arts and "imported" combat sports.[4] In either case, critics worried that any changes necessarily endangered the art's authenticity.

Similar concerns about authenticity crop up in academic discussions of Mestre Bimba's teachings. Waldeloir Rego (1968: 33) and folklorist Edison Carneiro (1957: 206), for example, describe Capoeira Regional as a form of capoeira essentially "polluted" or "adulterated," or even no longer fundamentally "capoeira."[5] The same romanticism that inspires some academics to embrace capoeira as "folklore," an authentic expression of the Brazilian national genius, also seems to produce in them an extreme cultural conservativism, fueling their ire at Mestre Bimba (cf. Ortiz 1985: 69–72; J. Santos 1998).

Assertions that Capoeira Regional is a corrupted variant of traditional capoeira continue. Practitioners of Capoeira Angola, especially, rail against the changes wrought in Capoeira Regional, even though many of the innovations are now widely accepted. For example, contemporary Capoeira Angola is unimaginable without academies, student fees, group uniforms, "workshops," and large classes, all pioneered in Capoeira Regional classes. Some angoleiros even incorporate such widely criticized additions as the *martelo*, or "hammer" kick, and colored belts to mark students' achievements. Far from rejecting entirely the example offered by Mestre Bimba, many contemporary practitioners adopt certain practices from his school, including some that past mestres condemned strenuously, but try to hold the line against changes in the way students move.

Afrocentric practitioners frequently assert that Capoeira Regional removed capoeira's most African characteristics to make it more enticing to middle-class, light-skinned, and well-educated students. This charge resonates with long-standing debates about Brazilian culture and racism, raising the specter of racist cultural appropriation or "theft." By most accounts, however, the style's creator was thoroughly immersed in Afro-Bahian popular practices, even more so than Mestre Pastinha. Mestre Bimba was an adherent of Candomblé, for example, drumming for possession ceremonies in a house supervised by one of his wives. He was also allegedly an expert in preparing traditional Afro-Brazilian medicines and had learned capoeira directly from an African. For many critics, the crucial change happened not in Mestre Bimba's own playing style, but in its transmission, when his style ran up against his students' characters, habits, and desires.

BIMBA'S STUDENTS AND "WHITENING"

Around 1936 or 1937, José Sisnando Lima, then a medical student, started to learn capoeira from Mestre Bimba. The redoubtable master already had a circle of comrades-in-arms and disciples about him, but Sisnando was his first university-educated student. A charismatic figure and formidable fighter himself, Sisnando recruited numerous colleagues to his mestre's classes from Salvador's schools of medicine, dentistry, and engineering. In addition, Mestre Bimba occasionally was hired by wealthy families to teach their young boys capoeira, presumably as physical education and self-defense (Decânio 2001: 14). Fascinated with the renowned champion, sons of the elite began to learn an art that their parents' and grandparents' generations had disparaged (cf. Decânio n.d.a.: 99–100).

Mestre Itapoan, a former student, sees the confluence of the mestre's art with his students' talents as critical to the success of Capoeira Regional: "This mixture of popular culture with the organization of the students gave to the Academy of the Mestre the structure to become the Temple of Capoeira" (R. Almeida 1994b: 18). Students also brought access to patronage and a desire to see capoeira respected by their peers. With their greater access to publicity vehicles such as the state's tourism agency and traveling folklore troupes, Mestre Bimba's students spread Capoeira Regional throughout Brazil. They created fixed training procedures, navigated local bureaucracies, and established ties with other institutions. As they grew older, many of Bimba's students assumed positions in the government, sports clubs, and the press, from which they promoted their former teacher.[6] This conjunction of forces allowed Capoeira Regional to achieve widespread social acceptance, prestige, and technical development.

According to proponents and detractors alike, elite students exerted subtle pressure on Mestre Bimba to adapt capoeira or, at the very least, to teach the dimensions of the art that most intrigued them. As former student Ângelo Decânio (2001: 14) explained, "Bimba always adjusted himself to the setting, adapting his teachings to his students and the historic moment, like the true mestre that he was." His students were more interested in self-defense than in participating in traditional rodas, for example, so together with their mestre, they explored the art's potential as a tool for self-defense instead of dwelling upon musical dimensions of the practice. Critics suggest that the prospect of increased income induced Mestre Bimba to modify capoeira to conform to middle-class physical predilections, habits, prejudices, concepts of strength, and their allegedly exaggerated aggressiveness (e.g., R. Costa 1993: 101).[7] Observers allege that the art grew more and more to reflect the expectations of elite adepts, especially as Mestre Bimba's teachings inspired further innovation outside his academy and outside his control.

Anthropologist Alejandro Frigerio (1989: 85), for example, asserts that capoeira changed from a "black art" into a "white sport":

> To be legitimated and integrated into the system, it was necessary that [Afro-Brazilian practices] lose various of the characteristics that were proper to them because of their ethnic origin, [in order] to acquire other traits that made them more acceptable in the eyes of the dominant classes.

Like many of the groups with whom both Frigerio and I conducted our research,[8] my colleague argues that "we can interpret the appearance of

Capoeira Regional as an *embranquecimento* [whitening] of traditional Capoeira (Angola)" (ibid.).[9]

For Frigerio, "embranquecimento" went beyond the enrollment of white students, the entry of capoeira into sports clubs, or the addition of "white" forms of organizing. "Whitening" entailed a shift in the bodily practice itself, a change in the way players *do* capoeira that allegedly made it more agreeable to elite practitioners. Other critics have labeled this transformation "bourgeois-ification," suggesting that it was a change in class, or "rationalization," and pointing to structural and pedagogical changes as the source of the modified kinesthetic. All these designations suggest that the social ascension of capoeira produced, and was facilitated by, an essential change in the nature of practice. By calling it "whitening," Frigerio and others evoke an intense debate in Brazil, conjuring up a long history of racist policies and ideas.

WHITENING IN BRAZIL

Since the nineteenth century, Brazilians have discussed widely the racial concept of "embranquecimento," "whitening" or "bleaching," adopting it to label a confusing range of phenomena. Originally, the European-descended elite of Brazil relied on the concept to counter the pessimistic predictions of "scientific" racists, like Count Gobineau, that race mixing would inevitably produce a degenerate population in the tropical country.[10] Optimistic Brazilian elites, drawing on the very same racist ideas that they were disputing, "discarded two of that theory's principal assumptions—the innateness of racial differences and the degeneracy of mixed bloods—in order to formulate their own solution to the 'Negro problem'" (Skidmore 1993b: 77). They believed that through intermarriage, the Brazilian population would "whiten," and thereby improve. They assumed both that "white blood" was clearly superior and that, because it was superior, it would naturally dominate in any mix. The faith in whitening allowed Brazilians simultaneously to congratulate themselves for not being racist, because mixed-race children demonstrated their tolerance, and still rest assured that the "Negro problem" would eventually solve itself. Although intended to combat the racist view of Brazil by European theorists, this whitening ideology was obviously founded on racist assumptions of white superiority.

Along with being a national ideology, according to many observers, whitening also came to be a strategy to ascend the "pigmentocracy," to borrow a term from Chilean anthropologist Alejandro Lipschutz (cited in Stam 1997: 47). Individuals allegedly tried to "marry lighter" so that their children might have higher social status. Ironically, although romantic desire allegedly dissolved barriers between the races, researchers such as France Twine (1998) have found that Brazilian ideals of beauty evidence a clear racist preference for European features, partly because of their dominance in Brazil's powerful media (cf. Kottak 1990; Simpson 1993). Brazilians also "whiten" the color terms that they apply to others as a form of politeness, offering a symbolic "upgrade" in status to anyone occupying a prestigious role, dressing well, or bearing outward signs of education (Harris 1970; Sanjek 1971). Of course, this assumes that a person would want to be as lightly colored as possible. The stigma attached to African cultural practices means that many Brazilians expect those who are upwardly mobile to shed any outward signs of Afro-Brazilian ancestry as their new social peers consent to elevate their color status (Bastide 1978: 158; Ortiz 1978: 30).

Beginning with the work of Gilberto Freyre, in *Casa-Grande e Senzala* (translated as *The Masters and the Slaves* [1986a]), "embranquecimento" acquired other cultural meanings. Using ideas similar to Freyre's, capoeiristas suggest that their art might "whiten" in at least two senses: demographically, more white people might play, or, aesthetically, the practice could demonstrate "bleached" values or style (see Bastide 1978: 281). Often the two seem to go together. Cultural practices could be altered if they are subjected to a "white aesthetic" by new groups of middle-class practitioners (Ortiz 1978: 22). A way of moving could be "white" just as a person might be so described on the basis of skin color, hair, or nose.

CHANGES IN MOVEMENT STYLE

Pierre Bourdieu, in his survey of research issues in the sociology of sport, observes that consistency in the name of sports conceals the nonuniformity in people's styles of playing:

> One of the difficulties of the analysis of sporting practices resides in the fact that the nominal unity (tennis, skiing, football) registered by statistics (including the best and most recent of them) masks a dispersal, greater or less depending on the sports, of the ways of playing them, and this dispersal increases when the increase in the number of players . . . is accompanied by a social diversification of those who play. (1990a: 158)

Bourdieu implies that the ways of playing are as important as which sports a group chooses to practice (cf. Desmond 1997 on dance). With no official rules, no standardized forms, no regulating body, and no widely agreed-upon standard for evaluating performance, capoeira has generated myriad stylistic splinters and ways of playing. Bahian forms of the art have spread from a small and clearly defined social group to a diverse, even international, public, which brings a host of different kinesthetics to the roda.

Although Mestre Bimba is sometimes vilified for whitening capoeira, critics reserve their greatest venom for groups that emerged out of Rio de Janeiro and São Paulo. For example, some observers single out for criticsm the *Grupo Senzala*, named for "slavequarters," one of the most influential capoeira organizations. After the Grupo Senzala won the first three *Berimbau de Ouro* (Golden Berimbau) tournaments in Rio in 1967, 1968, and 1969, journalist Marina Lemle (n.d.) explained the group's appeal:

> With the contacts and cultural background that the group had, it did not take long for Senzala to achieve success. The bourgeois public applauded their presentations because the youths knew what the public wanted: a clean aesthetic, organized, standardized. And this they were not lacking, for they were methodical in the extreme. Their capoeira reflected the "system," and perhaps precisely because of this, it was so pleasing.

Mestre Squisito, like many people I talked to, suggests that the group's distinctive aesthetic spread: "Later, many groups came to adopt the characteristics of this 'style.' If one is familiar enough with its features, watching a few of an adept's movements is enough to recognize, immediately, that the player belongs to Grupo Senzala" (R. Costa 1993: 41; cf. Capoeira 1992: 93). The "Senzala style," what Marina Lemle described as the "clean aesthetic" and "organized, standardized" form, became the archetype for the popular understanding of the kinesthetic of Capoeira Regional despite marked differences from the teachings of Mestre Bimba.[11]

Whereas Mestre Bimba once told his students to keep one limb on the floor at all times, for instance, the popular version of "Capoeira Regional" developed spectacular flips, flying kicks, and other leaping acrobatics. When one opens a capoeira magazine or attends a tourist show, one is likely to see flashy aerial maneuvers and feats of balance featured as a capoeirista's crowning accomplishment. The emerging form, in Marina Lemle's words, became "distinguished by rapid rhythm and the plasticity and efficiency of the movements" (ibid.).

Members of the Grupo Senzala and its emulators trained to maximize their speed and flexibility, and to perform techniques with an elegant fluidity and extension. Their bodily postures tended to be relatively "open" in comparison to other practitioners of capoeira, even Bimba's students. That is, their limbs and torsos were more fully extended, in part to increase the movements' efficiency, I was told. Whereas capoeira had often been referred to as "idleness" or "vagrancy," possibly because of players' loose swaying, the kinesthetic of the "whitened" styles became much more vigorous, muscularly taut, and obviously athletic. Players threw themselves into the movements with great energy. As a result, the typical game shortened because the more demanding movements left players fatigued faster than the relaxed, uneven pacing of other forms of play.

The word "clean" comes up repeatedly in descriptions of whitened capoeira, connoting a range of meanings: flowing movements, spiffy uniforms, high-visibility acrobatics, clear articulation of techniques, and abiding by accepted rules—no "dirty" fighting (see J. Santos 1998: 127). Mestre Cobrinha Mansa explained to Kenneth Dossar (1994: 81), for example, that "middle class white people did not want to put their hands on the floor, to get them dirty, or to perform the animal like movements of *capoeira angola.*" Players were supposed to have "clean" interactions— orderly and well synchronized so that attack and escape interweave instantaneously, even if they are formulaic. Carlos Senna (1980: 58), in the regulations he wrote for competitions, set out the following criteria for judging capoeira competitions. Attacks should be evaluated on the basis of their

> potency (striking attacks), elegance, the degree to which they are sustained, posture, lightness, symmetry, perfection in the entry (for attacks that unbalance an adversary), opportunism, equilibrium, precision, and [the degree to which they are an] automatic reflex (throwing techniques).

Senna writes that the aú, or cartwheel, should be a "perfect circle," an openly geometric ideal that is anatomically impossible for most humans, and that capoeira should be performed with a "smoothness in the style" (ibid.: 58–59). Attacks, defenses, and acrobatic movements are to follow exacting forms, Senna implies, uniform among practitioners. Kicks, for example, are to be thrown at regular velocities and at consistently high angles regardless of an adversary's position. In the resulting games, movements flowed smoothly from start to finish, clearly demonstrating an adept's practiced ease.

Angoleiros, like many academics and folklorists, find much to attack in this style of play. They complain that games using such uniform techniques are boring and repetitive, or that players pay little attention to each other; instead of exchanging counterattacks and escapes in close quarters, players execute solo acrobatics. Some critics readily parody the ginga associated with "whitened" styles: a bounding, unornamented step executed at high velocity. They pump their arms vigorously and clench their fists tightly in parody, sometimes implying that the kinesthetic embodies adepts' insecurities and aggression. Detractors say that the style is devoid of malícia, substituting raw athleticism, speed, and strength for cunning, deception, and an acute sense of timing (e.g., Capoeira 1985: 166–168; Frigerio 1989: 93–94). In Bahia, I frequently heard the charge that this style reflected a racist attempt by light-skinned practitioners to deny the African roots of capoeira, to strip it of its character, and to transform it into an "ethnically cleansed" art form.

While these charges may be warranted in particular cases, playing and talking with practitioners and reading what they write leads me to suspect that critics simplify a complex process of stylistic change. In fact, many practitioners of Capoeira Regional are black Brazilians; labeling them all "whitened" seems fraught with inherent political and logical problems. In addition, many groups of Capoeira Regional are explicitly Afrocentric and antiracist. For these players, the style does not appear to be a symptom of racial false consciousness, a bodily form of brainwashing, or ethnic bleaching. A truly racist student (or racially alienated black student) could choose countless martial arts that bear no taint of African influences. Like the Bahian elite that took up samba because of their impatience with "the constraints of elegant European-style deportment," described by Hermano Vianna (1999: 17), middle-class practitioners are often attracted to capoeira because of its distinctive kinesthetics and playfulness. Players of "whitened" styles frequently attend rodas of Angola, hoping for a chance to play or to join the orchestra, and their teachers invite members of Bahia's old guard of angoleiros to their events, host special workshops for Capoeira Angola, and set aside time in their rodas to play the style. Although cynical observers might suspect exploitation or a racist romance with black artistic expression, this was usually not my impression. Rather, I believe that the ways that capoeira took root in middle-class students' bodies had more to do with how the art intrigued them and which sorts of movements proved most engaging or daunting.

CAPOEIRA FROM MIDDLE-CLASS BODIES

As part of the "entrance exam" for his academy in its early years, Mestre Bimba would place a powerful *gravata*, a "necktie" headlock, on a prospective student. If the novice endured the gravata, he was accepted into the new class (R. Almeida 1994b: 61; cf. Decânio n.d.a.: 99–100). Passing the test was a sign of stamina and also, according to some observers, a way of experiencing a slave's yoke. The implication was that to learn Capoeira Regional, a student had to endure humiliation and hardship. Presumably, not every student passed the entrance exam, nor did all those who passed stay with the art when learning it grew difficult, frustrating, uncomfortable, or even painful.

To this day, instructors insist that to learn capoeira, a student has to face his or her limits—shame, inhibition, fear of injury, weakness, a tendency to grow tense in a confrontation, reluctance to conform to an Afro-Brazilian aesthetic in a white-dominated society.[12] But they also suggest that the chance to transform oneself is one of the strongest motives for taking up the art. Capoeira holds out the promise of pleasure, inspires students to face their inhibitions, summons a desire to exceed personal limits, and offers opportunities for students to shape their own bodies. With so many dimensions to the practice and diverse skills to develop, a student can easily focus on the ones that seem most desirable and try to avoid, for a while at least, the most intimidating. Fellow students, friends, family, and one's own fascinations shape how a person pursues proficiency in the art.

For example, one change worked on capoeira by Bimba's students and frequently criticized is the advent of the *martelo*, the "hammer" kick (similar to what practitioners of many martial arts call a "roundhouse" kick). According to Ângelo Decânio (2001: 14), the martelo can be specifically traced to a single student's tactic for countering an adversary's head butt during a basic technique. Other students adopted the counterattack, too, using it to reach steadily higher and higher until they began to do it when standing up. According to Decânio, Mestre Bimba disapproved of the innovation because he felt the kick was dangerous, overly violent, and out of harmony with the other capoeira movements, almost all of which are "round and spinning." Without more experienced players to demonstrate the movement's vulnerability or a community of veterans to disapprove (because Mestre Bimba discouraged his students from playing elsewhere), the mestre's resistance was not enough to stop the spread of the technique. The martelo was not a conscious attempt to evacuate capoeira of its "essence." The kick developed to solve a problem faced in the game's dynamic, an innovation that arose when conservative restraints that might have discouraged it were absent.

Global changes, like the shift to a "clean aesthetic" or flowing movements, were also creative responses to the challenges of learning, in particular the greater shame, stiffer inhibitions, and more severely limited range of motion of middle-class practitioners. Although critics suspect that middle-class students wish to dominate the art, most of those I met expressed a profound sense of awkwardness and inadequacy when they started training. They admired veterans' styles of moving, even when they thought that they could never copy these styles. Admiration did not necessarily translate into imitation. According to Júlio César de Souza Tavares (1984: 104), Capoeira Regional was better suited to the new initiates:

> Capoeira Regional was more appropriate for the whitening process through which Brazilian society was passing because it was already suited to a greater participation by whites. They were less flexible (with "hard joints," as Mestre Bimba would say) and, therefore, found it more difficult to execute the movements that are demanded in the game of Angola.

Tavares suggests that novices chose Capoeira Regional because it was "already suited" to them. His former students, like Ângelo Decânio and Jair Moura, argue instead that they helped to create the new style. They collaborated with Mestre Bimba to fashion Capoeira Regional, sometimes introducing innovative techniques or ways of moving that the mestre disliked, avoiding movement that demanded more profound change of themselves and their bodies. They did not have to loosen their gait so much, bend their waists so readily, or suffer such a profound transformation.

As Norbert Elias (1978: 139) suggests in his history of European manners, the "frontiers of shame" actually close more tightly on the middle and upper classes as a marker of their social position. The same is true in Brazil. Although elites may have been "seduced" by the allure of Afro-Brazilian culture (Sodré 1983), their own desire to learn capoeira butted up against the lower shame thresholds they had developed to secure the social markers of their status: their comportments and manners.[13] The modified style of movement was not directly a product of class; it was a corporeal solution open to anyone who felt shame or inhibition doing these sorts of movements. Innovations sprang from various comportments that players brought to the roda.

In addition to being shaped negatively by inhibition, Capoeira Regional's distinctive kinesthetic was influenced positively by desire. Mestre Bimba's students wanted to become stronger and to learn to fight so they could defend themselves. Taking up an art to learn self-defense, they diligently explored some opportunities for skills within the repertoire of capoeira, letting others fall into disuse. Young men seeking to experience power and strength, no matter what their class or race, may have neglected to develop some of the slow, cramped, closed movements of capoeira, not because they intentionally rejected them, but from an attraction to contrary dimensions of bodily ability. The "implied violence" of the roda did not satisfy their craving for competence as fully as techniques that generated greater momentum, torsion, and velocity. In fact, moments of flowing movement and open, dynamic attacks exist in every style of capoeira. Some of the movement techniques associated with malandros, laborers, and old Afro-Brazilian men may have been confusing, embarrassing, alien, and even ugly to middle-class students when they first saw the traditional game, although they might later grow to appreciate these aesthetics.[14] Overt strength, in a way new students could most immediately feel and understand it, became elaborated in Capoeira Regional.

Exploring particular experiential possibilities in capoeira movement is not purely a product of a player's race. Sociological explanations of stylistic change along these lines—"white people do whitened capoeira because both are white"—cannot explain the details of the change, why one sort of movement and not another is chosen. When veteran capoeiras, tough guys schooled in the street who had never set foot in Mestre Bimba's academy, generated powerful movements, devoid of ornamentation, with a speed and strength suited for fighting, were they practicing a "whitened" style of capoeira? When Mestre Bimba developed devastating hand attacks for the prizefighting ring or found ways to escape from the techniques of other martial arts, was he behaving "white-ly"? Some critics seem to suggest this. In fact, capoeiristas use a language of race, not to reveal the truth about the biological source of differences in movement style, but as an evocative way to discuss these kinesthetic changes, no matter on what color body they appear.

Like all capoeiristas, practitioners of supposedly "whitened" styles are exploring the potential offered by their own bodies, seeking solutions to situations in the roda, and developing their skills. They may focus their energy on qualities of movement consistent with their normal comportment outside the roda. Or they might pursue a trait that they feel they lack in everyday life—strength, velocity, elegance, physical prowess. Changes in capoeira movement styles are not just a symptom of changed philosophy among practitioners or a demographic trend in the identity of players. Different movements result from a shift in the opportunities that practitioners explore, individually or as part of a group. Bimba's students played off one another, learned from each other, provoked each other, and successfully developed tendencies within capoeira, perhaps even beyond what their mestre could have taught them. Flying kicks and gravity-defying flips now seen in some rodas no more spring naturally from white bodies than cunning feints and tightly closed head rolls spring from black ones. They arise from a community's attempts to learn and to develop a bodily art.

12   Tearing Out the Shame

Proponents of Capoeira Angola argue that they preserve a traditional style of moving, and, ultimately, that this provides a foundation for social action and political consciousness-raising. Members of the Grupo de Capoeira Angola Pelourinho, for example, hold that to do the ginga in the group's distinctive fashion—twisting, low to the ground, with sudden stops, starts, and stutters in rhythm—helps to alter students' identities, increasing pride and awareness of their African heritage. Mestre Moraes contended that diluted (*descaracterizado*) forms of capoeira had "Cartesian" aesthetics: straight lines, direct attacks, upright postures, and symmetrical forms. In contrast, an angoleiro should not form geometrically pleasing shapes. He or she should play closed and low, "break" movements, tumble upside down and off balance, and conform to an adversary no matter how awkward the resulting position. This was an African aesthetic, according to Moraes, a "deformed form" in his words, that provided a firm ground for a collective campaign against racism.

In fact, the aesthetic of Capoeira Angola *is* strange at first glance. Its slow movements, quirky danced steps, unusual postures, and inverted acrobatics do not obviously appear strong, dexterous, or even martial to many observers. For example, one mestre told me that when he first saw Capoeira Angola, he thought it looked like "contortionism." Although he later came to admire the style, he couldn't understand it initially, or see how it might be used for self-defense. The sentiment was widely shared by naïve spectators. Proponents, like Alejandro Frigerio, insist that Capoeira Angola's distinctive aesthetics "faithfully reflect . . . the art's social and cultural origin" (1989: 85). Historians and practitioners debate about whether this aesthetic is really African or a more recent invention. A more pressing question for a phenomenology of contemporary capoeira, however, is how it feels for modern capoeiristas to take up styles of moving that are unfamiliar, awkward, or even anachronistic.

One irony of the revival of the Angola style is that a wide range of people participated: black, brown, tan, and white, working class and well educated, Brazilian and foreign (just as dark-skinned capoeiristas play styles that critics decry as "whitened"). A person's movement may be seemingly out of step with his or her identity. For example, at the same time that there were dark-skinned workers and street children in GCAP, the executive committee that oversaw it included a university professor, a librarian, and many women. While I was with them, the group numbered graduate students and dedicated white middle-class enthusiasts among its members. In New York City, traditionalist angoleiros are even more diverse than in Bahia; strong Brazilian, American, and Japanese contingents play there, as well as students from the Caribbean, Africa, and Spanish-speaking Latin America. One Brazilian even joked uneasily that the next generation of "traditional" angoleiro mestres might include many foreigners.

If the art's traditional kinesthetic reflects its origin among African slaves and workers in Salvador's port, modern practitioners include many groups for whom the movements must seem alien. Trained by different occupations, conditioned by diverse religious practices, childhood games, and pastimes, motivated by new politics and theories of education, and including unprecedented numbers of women, students come to the roda out of step with the generation who created Capoeira Angola.

Since part of the appeal of the way of the angoleiros is its respect for tradition, practitioners insist that novices be ready to change physically if they are to learn Capoeira Angola. Adepts cannot trust that the style will emerge naturally from students' bodies, even among those who see it as an expression of their racial identity. This process throws into high relief how achieving identity, even one that is self-fashioned, may be a long-term project, requiring people to invest great energy in learning skills and patiently cultivating themselves. The struggles that students face demonstrate convincingly that the revived Capoeira Angola—whether traditional or a modern invention—demands corporeal change from all novices, forcing them to overcome fears, inhibitions, and old habits. In the process, students develop latent physical potential and transcend learned limits on movement such as manners, poise, or restraint.

The case of Capoeira Angola seems to support Michel Foucault's (1980: 56) suspicion that bodily regimes that instill "mastery and awareness of one's body" can develop a momentum of their own. The desire to become ever more proficient, for instance, may lead a student to violate previous visceral limits on movement. Technical demands placed on the body can transform it. As Roberto DaMatta (1993: 16) argued in the case of soccer, for example, the requirement to refrain from using the hands while playing may bring about the "disinhibited use of the body." To understand this removal of inhibition and its effects, one must note both the forms of inhibition and the ways in which they are overcome.

This chapter examines the specific traits, some controversial, that members of the Grupo de Capoeira Angola Pelourinho consider crucial to an authentic angoleiro aesthetic. These traits include inverted postures, techniques that use the head, a deep squatting stance called the *cocorinha*, movements that are "broken" (*quebrado*), and bodily "softness" (*moleza*). Closely examining how these characteristics might affect a person suggests ways that social identity is lived: capoeira training runs headlong into the movement qualities that distinguish different sorts of people. By examining these characteristics, we can see what is at stake for the individual in bodily transformation.

If Capoeira Angola has the potential to raise consciousness and radicalize students, it is not merely because of the art's faithfulness to tradition or wedding to explicit political programs. The revived style of Capoeira Angola seems almost intentionally calculated to abrade against customary ways of moving and to attack the most basic physical habits. The shame and discomfort that students feel when learning indicates the profundity of the changes demanded of them.

HANDS, HEAD, AND LEGS

Among capoeira's most distinctive characteristics is that practitioners' preferred weapons are generally the legs and head. Although Mestre Bimba taught some hand attacks, and even angoleiros affirm that an adept should be ready to use any weapon when necessary, the arms are seldom used to strike in the roda. Instead, a player typically uses his or her arms to distract, to deflect attacks, to interrupt another players' techniques, to sense an opponent's position, and to support the body, but seldom to punch or hit (although one is likely to catch an "unintentional" elbow to the head from time to time). The vast majority of attacks, instead, are kicks, trips, leg sweeps, and head butts.

Scholars of capoeira have offered many historical explanations for the absence of hand techniques, some more plausible than others.[1] Whatever the historical origin or the initial function of restrictions on punching, the custom of using predominantly the head and feet as weapons affects how practitioners come to experience their bodies. Not surprisingly, outsiders have long found this use of the body upsetting, scandalous, or just plain bizarre. Sensationalist nineteenth-century accounts of fighting by the *capoeiras*, for example, refer extensively to kicks and head butts in lurid prose about battles between gangs. Descriptions list these techniques alongside razor blades, knives, and clubs as signs of the ruffians' depravity and fearsomeness (see Bretas 1991: 240). Apparently, the journalists' audience was expected to find the use of the head and legs to attack, like the treacherous straight razor, shocking proof that the *capoeiras* flouted the most basic social norms. Renowned sociologist Gilberto Freyre (1986b: 322, 325) went so far as to associate *capoeiras'* kicking techniques with sexual perversion.

In particular, when outside observers strive to describe capoeira in the most startling, exotic terms, they refer especially to the head butt and the *rabo de arraia*, the "stingray's tail" kick (e.g., A. Vianna 1984: 134; cf. Freyre 1986b: 322–326). The rabo de arraia is unusual because it demands that the hands be placed on the ground, and that the person doing it either look upside down, peer between the legs, or crane the neck around to see a target, since the body is inverted to attack.[2] Capoeiristas told me that in no other martial art did practitioners use the arms so frequently as support or did they attack from this position. A non-capoeirista would be surprised by the technique, even if trained in another fighting discipline.

Normal bodily comportment for many Brazilians is also upended by the "cabeçada," a group of strikes using the front, top, or side of the head. Capoeiristas consider head butts particularly treacherous attacks. Lamaratine Costa (1962: 77) writes: "Although [the cabeçada] is simple to execute, it is one of the most dangerous attacks, frequently causing deaths." The head is terribly hard, it was explained, and an experienced capoeirista could generate enormous force to drive it into a target: "like a big rock on the end of a stick" in one mestre's grim description. Angoleiros are especially adept, I was told, at using the head as a weapon, a tactic that other players might feel reluctant, even afraid, to employ.[3] Calling a person a "cabeceiro" (head butter), such as in the warnings sung before a game, implies that the player is especially treacherous. Cabeceiros are so cunning that they land the art's most difficult attacks and are so unconcerned about personal well-being that they will slam their heads into an adversary.

Members of GCAP and some other angoleiros also use their heads extensively to support their bodies and consider it a characteristic of the traditional art (a point others dispute). When moving close to the ground, they employ the head as a fifth limb, putting their weight on it in moves such as the *bananeira na cabeça* ("banana tree on the head," or

Students learn how to apply a cabeçada (head butt) when a target prepares for a meia-lua, or crescent moon kick. (*Photo by C. Peçanha*)

headstand) and the *aú na cabeça* (a cartwheel done with the head on the ground). The head also holds up the body in acrobatic flourishes such as the *pião* (the "top," in which the body spins upside down, balanced on the top of the head) or the *escovão* (the "big brush" or "push-broom," a horizontal slide on the top of the head across the floor), as well as a host of transitional moves and unnamed variants on the headstand.[4]

Academic researchers have tended to treat capoeira movements in which the head supports the body as signs to be interpreted. For example, the upside-down body is considered a symbol of social inversion, when the lowly, like the feet, are raised up. Others treat inversion as a carnivalesque reversal of daily order, when concerns of the "mind" and work obligations that normally dominate are temporarily subordinated to bodily pleasure. Or, some scholars suggest that inverted bodily posture is a reference to the "upside-down" world of the afterlife or African spirituality.[5] The first two interpretations treat the body as a "natural symbol," as Mary Douglas (1966, 1970) phrases it, as if a person's understanding of his or her own body was unaffected by patterns of use. In addition, treating the body as a "symbol" is a view from the outside looking in; people doing movements, especially an engrossing, interactive game like capoeira, do not typically experience themselves as signs.

No doubt, the upside-down body serves as a powerful symbol for some players. But tracing out how people talk about inversion or use it as a symbol does not necessarily tell us how it feels to use one's head to strike, or to place it on the ground for the purpose of holding one's body aloft. In fact, tracing out symbolic connections or "meanings" may take us further and further away from considering what a technique might feel like in its palpable immediacy, leaving the bodily experience with which we start an empty center in webs of significance. Instead, we might ask how the head and neck are trained and how patterns of behavior shape the experience of standing on one's head or attacking with it. This requires us to ask how adepts use their heads and necks, not what they "mean."

WORKING WITH BODIES

Until late in the twentieth century, manual laborers in Bahia used their heads to carry things. Travelers' accounts of daily life in Salvador always offer picturesque accounts of Bahians carrying atop their heads heavy loads, some so large that they astonished foreigners. Frede Abreu recounted a nineteenth-century traveler's story of seeing a team of slaves bearing a piano on their heads up the steep slope from Salvador's "lower" to "upper city," an almost incomprehensible feat to anyone familiar with the rise of over seventy meters (more than two hundred feet). Antônio Vianna (1984: 134) recognized a link between work and the art in a description he offers of the "*capoeiras* of yesteryear." Vianna describes one heroic *capoeira*, probably a stevedore in Salvador's port, dispensing police officers with violent cabeçadas, even knocking them from a pier. "On the following day, the *capoeiras* were at their posts, the workers in the process of conducting atop their heads, among other things, heavy packages of dried meat stacked high, muscles tensed, sweating, athletic, and jovial."

While turning upside down may have been unusual for these laborers, bearing the body's weight on the neck or using the head to strike was affected by skills used for carrying. For example, when a player jumps into a headstand during a game, he or she often has to scoot around to get the head and arms under the body's center of gravity.[6] For a raw novice unaccustomed to carrying anything on the head, teetering and adjusting on the neck can be extremely disconcerting as well as difficult.

For many Bahians, using the head as a limb is part of everyday life. (Photo by C. Peçanha)

Presumably, someone accustomed to carrying sacks of cement atop his head, as Mestre Bimba reportedly did, might not experience such discomfort. The extensive use of the head as a limb in Capoeira Angola appears to be a clear case of what Frigerio (1989: 87) described as an "aesthetic . . . that faithfully reflects the art's social and cultural origin," in this case, among people whose bodies were conditioned by their work habits.

Although some Brazilians—like some anthropologists—may treat the head as a "natural symbol" for the intellect, this, too, reflects their patterns of physical activity rather than a necessary order. For example, when I visited a capoeira group that met at a private university in Rio de Janeiro, I was told solemnly that putting one's head on the ground was very dangerous. These students, unaccustomed to bearing loads, were convinced that the head and neck were fragile, prone to injury or breaking. The warning clearly indicated how these participants experienced the bodily potential of their necks; they felt viscerally a strong fear of disaster when they contemplated, or actually tried, putting their weight on their heads. Elsewhere I had seen players lifting their arms so that their whole weight rested on the head alone. Moreover, some veterans in GCAP did asymmetrical headstands on bent necks, using the sides of their heads to bear weight, or were able to scoot about the floor while balanced upside down, pushing themselves around with their hands. At first, these postures appeared as frightening to me as they did to the university students who tried to warn me off attempting them. Years of non-capoeira physical conditioning, and countless warnings as a child to be careful or I would "break my neck," led me to cringe whenever a player's neck bent; it appeared to me that it was buckling under the weight. After tentative experiments using my head for support, conditioning my neck muscles and training myself to balance, however, the position grew much more comfortable.

Similar conditioning also affects the *cocorinha*, a deep squatting posture emblematic of traditional capoeira. The position requires a player to sit completely on his or her calves while keeping the feet flat on the ground. For people unaccustomed to it, the deep leg flexing is virtually impossible. When I first tried to keep my heels down in a low squat, I tipped over backward onto my seat; the muscles and tendons were simply not sufficiently flexible. Some analysts have interpreted low postures in capoeira as expressions of an African dance aesthetic of "getting down" (Thompson 1974: 13; 1988; cf., Dossar 1994: 114), or argued that they resonate with spiritual understandings of the earth (e.g., Dossar 1994: 110, 119; Browning 1995: 106).

These interpretations, however, seldom note that many poor people in Brazil habitually squat. For example, one often sees produce vendors in the fair of São Joaquim in Salvador or people waiting for buses in the city's periphery squatting when there are no benches. In "whitened" forms of capoeira, the cocorinha is sometimes discarded. Mestre Camisa (José Tadeu Carneiro Cardoso) reported that he advocated other defensive postures after finding that squatting was not particularly "efficient" for his students in Rio de Janeiro. Camisa observed on another occasion that the "language of the body" changed over time, and capoeira must keep pace.[7]

REVIVING CAPOEIRA ANGOLA

Although the cocorinha may have been difficult, some of the other exercises we did in GCAP were far worse. Instructors had us bounce around the room in the cocorinha, perform the ginga as low as possible, or do Cossack dance–like low kicks while nearly sitting on our heels. The novice students groaned and complained vigorously. My muscles would be traumatized afterward, making it difficult to walk up stairs for days. After one particularly brutal session, I had to climb the slope from the bus stop to my apartment walking sideways, even backward, as I could manage only a few of the steep steps forward before my thighs screamed in pain.

Training for moves done on the head could be similarly agonizing. We performed repeated cartwheels with our heads on the floor, sometimes not even lifting them as our scalps grated on the rough tile. More intimidating still was descending from the middle of a normal cartwheel into a headstand, or leaping over a chair directly into the inverted position. The hard contact of head on floor actually made dead skin flake off my scalp in fingertip-sized pieces. Early attempts to lower myself from a handstand to headstand left me dazed from crashing into the floor. I worried that my cramped neck was a sign of the immanent, accordion-like collapse of my spine or that the momentary disorientation signaled severe head trauma.

Over time, however, my body habituated to these movements. My thighs and scalp hurt less and less. My aversion to lowering my head to the floor from a handstand diminished as my arms learned the height of my head, tensing just before contact so that I touched down gently. The movements seemed to require less effort as skillful finesse replaced brute strength and a tense apprehensiveness ceded control of my body to a sense of relaxed familiarity.

My experience was far from unique; the majority of new students in GCAP, of different backgrounds and skin colors, were unaccustomed before joining the group to using the head to support weight or resting in the cocorinha posture. When Moraes or one of his assistants demanded that we perform movements in squatting positions, many students "cheated up," standing more upright to reduce the strain on their thighs. Our instructors berated us to get lower. When Mestre Moraes led the class in transforming a cartwheel, into a *ponte*, or back "bridge," demanding that we first lower ourselves into headstands, one could sense the hesitation. The thud of skull on tile in the back of the room reminded us that inexperienced players gathered there to hide from too-careful scrutiny. Some initiates seemed to have an advantage—they were better prepared for the movements or quickly adapted to them—but all struggled to incorporate the techniques. One day, for example, a player whose style I admired admitted after a class that she still felt reluctant to put her head on the ground when she played. She was afraid of being injured.

BROKEN MOVEMENTS, SOFTENED BODIES

In the Grupo de Capoeira Angola Pelourinho, we were drilled extensively to "break" our gingas. "Breaking" a movement meant that it did not flow smoothly from start to finish. Instead, we jerked and shifted unpredictably, interrupted our own rhythms, and articulated our bodies at every possible point. Breaking made techniques difficult to anticipate; a player might start one attack, stutter, and switch suddenly to another. Although these irregular nuances may appear awkward to the untrained eye, we were convinced that it made us more mobile, able to break off a technique suddenly and start another if necessary. We would compliment a player with exemplary style and unpredictability for his or her *mandinga* (sorcery).

Our instructors assumed that breaking did not come naturally for students. Rather, novices tended to develop regular, repetitive responses and a consistent velocity. "*Quebra!*" (Break!), teachers in GCAP would shout to students when their movements became overly predictable, stiff, or simplistic. Leopoldo Castedo (1964: 14) writes that traditional capoeira possessed "a baroque style." "Baroque" Capoeira Angola, drawing on Castedo's description, revels in "dynamism, the delight in the curve, the open form, the theatricality, the tension, the breaking up of symmetry." Novice angoleiros, in contrast, seemed to be natural modernists, falling into what my instructors referred to as "Capoeira Regional" (although the neophyte might have no experience with Mestre Bimba's system): a functional, austere style, with standardized elements, clear verticality, and a symmetrical, predictable ginga.

Not all angoleiros play in a "broken" style. The broken kinesthetic is widely criticized, even mocked by some. Several observers credited Mestre João Grande for pioneering the kinesthetic. Proponents and critics alike suggested that João Grande's personal talent and individual style, influenced by samba and Candomblé religious dancing, led him to develop a distracting, unpredictable way of moving. Others insisted that the style faithfully reflected an older African aesthetic.

Whether or not the kinesthetic is authentically African or the result of one individual's idiosyncratic genius, learning it presents an array of challenges for the novice. Whereas some teachers held that every player creates his or her own ginga, Mestre Moraes advised his students, "It is you who must adapt to Capoeira Angola; Capoeira Angola will not change for you." His students were not always proficient at samba or Candomblé dancing; therefore, their bodies did not come to the roda already "broken." The emphasis on breaking under Moraes drove them to develop a realm of bodily potential to move in syncopated ways and to suddenly truncate movements. If left to their own devices, some contemporary angoleiros might discover such corporeal malleability, as Mestre João Grande had done; if they had not pursued the broken aesthetic intentionally, however, many would never reach this goal.

Mestre Moraes focused on "breaking" the waist in one exercise. He would shout "*Quebra!*" leading us to jerk, bend, and contort our bodies from the knees through the ribs, balancing on our toes as we sunk down on bent legs. He told us that if we hoped to learn Capoeira Angola, we must not be afraid to *mexer a bunda* ("shake the ass"). Practitioners of other styles, we were told, were too embarrassed to "mexer a bunda," overly concerned that they might appear to be *viados* (Brazilian slang, probably most closely translated as "faggots"). Being overly *macho*—especially playing with tense muscles that Moraes mocked on another occasion— made a person too rigid to break at the waist or "mexer a bunda."[8]

In one class, Moraes was especially dismayed at us because he said we were *todo duro*, "completely hard." Capoeira Angola required a person to develop *moleza*, "softness." If we were so inhibited, hopelessly rigid, or insecure about our masculinity, we should take up a different martial art, he growled. On another occasion, Mestre Nô (Norival Moreira de Oliveira) said that it was far easier to teach capoeira in Massaranduba, a poor neighborhood in Bahia's lower city, than in Pituba, a wealthy, beachfront community, because the men in Massaranduba were "already soft." Foreigners were worse still; learning Capoeira Angola was not impossible for them, Moraes opined, but a German would have to "sacrifice more" to achieve proficiency. Mestre Moraes felt this difference was a result of what he called *raça*, or "race." When he explained what he meant by "raça," however, he used the term to refer to both physical traits and characteristic habits. Afro-Bahians were softer because they ate *dendê* (palm oil) and *acarajé* (bean fritters fried in dendê),[9] danced the samba, and were accustomed to *mexendo* (mixing) in the street during popular festivals. A Bahian who did not join in these activities would find his or her body, like a foreigner's, unsuitably hard.

In spite of what one might expect, capoeiristas consider middle-class bodies to be harder than those of the lower classes and the swaggering, loose-limbed malandro. Although an outside observer might consider a laborer's muscles or a taut capoeirista's physique to be "hard" in contrast with the flaccid "softness" of a sedentary office worker, capoeira adepts instead use a contrast that derives from the internal experience of the moving body. "Soft" and "hard" are kinesthetic, rather than anatomical descriptions, capturing how it feels to inhabit different styles of movement. A hard body moves stiffly, as rigid muscles are forced into regular rhythms. Softness, in contrast, is an accommodating suppleness that allows a practitioner to slip insidiously into an adverary's movements. A soft player exerts force without strain or "hardness." Although all capoeiristas strive to develop moleza, not all styles instill the exceptional softness that allows adepts seemingly to turn their bodies inside out to avoid being struck and yet remain close to an adversary.

SHAME AND ITS REMOVAL

A range of influences produce hardness, according to members of GCAP, but the most important among them is "shame" (*vergonha*). Fear for one's own safety or physical weakness might slow a student's progress, but these deficits can be overcome through diligent training. Shame, however, can stymie the entire learning process. Some dimensions of Capoeira Regional may be understood as the result of students modifying the art when confronting shame; Capoeira Angola, in contrast, especially the vigorously enforced "broken" kinesthetic in GCAP, forces adepts to overcome these feelings to a greater degree.

Shame seizes and stiffens the flesh, making a person acutely self-consciousness and constricting his or her range of motion (cf. Leder 1990: 83–92). One class each week, during the first half-hour of training, for example, we had "rhythm class," in which we learned capoeira music. During one session, our instructor, Poloca, became dissatisfied with the students' feeble attempts to sing solo ladainhas. He changed pedagogical tactics. Rather than sing the entire ladainha while playing instruments, he instructed us simply to shout the opening syllables with which all ladainhas begin: *Iê!* (pronounced, "ee-yay!"). This call requires a full chest shout. While the veterans shouted enthusiastically and effortlessly, their voices booming, other students found the task extremely difficultly. If their voices were thin, their tone bad, their timing incorrect, or their sustain too short, Poloca made the students shout again and again; several grew more tense and embarrassed until they could only manage to utter strained, half-strangled squeaks.

Poloca told the students who found the task difficult that they needed to relax their faces and bodies. He said that they contorted themselves and impeded the projection of their own voices. According to Poloca, shame was the primary reason that new students—especially middle-class, lighter-skinned, foreign, and female students—had trouble shouting the "Iê!" Shame was a posture with a tightened chest and throat that choked off singing. Similarly, Nestor Capoeira (1985: 56) writes that "people are not in the custom of singing in public and feel extremely inhibited." As a remedy, Nestor advises training the voice just as one would train for other physical techniques.

Most students who take up Capoeira Angola, regardless of their class, race, or position of social origin, confront shame on the road to proficiency to varying degrees. One evening after a training session, a young Afro-Brazilian student from a poor outlying neighborhood, a streetwise and silver-tongued malandro-in-training, admitted to the whole class that he found it difficult to do some of the soft, broken movements of the art. We had done an exercise in which we simply were called on to "dance" before the berimbau. He was visibly upset with himself for being inhibited during the drill, too stiff to move with the fluidity or grace to which he aspired. I had always thought his looseness was exemplary, but he drove home for me that most, if not all, students have to confront some inhibitions.

Mestre Moraes explained that many exercises we did to increase softness and flexibility, like this one, were specifically intended to overcome the fear of appearing foolish, to "tear the shame" (tirar a vergonha) from our bodies. By forcing us to cross frontiers of inhibition, the exercise should help us to rediscover potential movement that our reservations had led us to relinquish. The difficulty many students encounter learning capoeira does not arise simply from the dexterity and strength demanded by the techniques; it results, too, from confronting learned inability, shamed inhibition, and fearful reluctance to try the unfamiliar. Through exercises like shouting "Iê!" and doing the "quebra" dance, as well as descending to our heads from a handstand, our instructors forced us into uncomfortable positions and required us to do unfamiliar actions so that we developed new skills, as well as changed emotional relationships to moving.

Tearing the shame from students' bodies transforms the way they move and see life, no matter what their color; but it may be especially important to dark-skinned people in Brazil, who are told repeatedly by the media that they are ugly. By training in Capoeira Angola, devotees strip shame from their bodies where dominant ideals of beauty suggest they should feel embarrassed; they become soft, supple, and sly, even though, outside the roda, they may be told that they are brutes, inelegant, and unthinking. Some observers, like Michael Hanchard (1994), have warned that "culturalism," an excessive focus on Afro-Brazilian cultural activities as ends in themselves, may dull activists' ability to bring about political change. Larry Crook and Randall Johnson (1999: 10), in contrast, point out that analysts and activists alike need to pay close attention to "both the efficacy and everydayness" of aesthetics in Afro-Brazilian cultural practices. GCAP, like other black activist organizations and Bahia's Afrocentric carnival groups, takes an explicit stand against the "whitening" tide in Brazil and valorizes black culture, but the group also provides concrete experiences of alternative ways of being.

MOVED TO CHANGE

Some outsiders insist that Afrocentric Capoeira Angola groups do not practice authentic traditional capoeira. One well-known mestre, for example, described the revitalized form to me as "Capoeira Angola invented to battle Capoeira Regional," implying that the crucial fights were outside the roda, for public recognition, students, and money. Luiz Vieira (1990: 107–108) argues that the contemporary "traditional" style—its emphasis on certain rituals, conservative music, and traits like a "broken" aesthetic—results from struggles over legitimacy within the community during a "crisis of succession." He interviewed veteran mestres who claimed, like some I talked to, that young angoleiros exaggerated the traits they considered emblematic of the traditional art, creating a hyperbolic aesthetic, or that they emulated only a handful of model players, ignoring the variety that had long existed in the roda. The revived angoleiro style, they imply, renounces "modernized" styles and distills "traditional" traits. The style is not the pure legacy of an unbroken cultural transmission. The process they describe would hardly be unusual: traditionalist movements, faced with hybrid or updated practices, often become hyperconservative, constituting veritable "fundamentalist" innovations.

Practitioners fight bitterly about authenticity. Some adepts insist that fidelity to tradition, or a style's "Africanity," is the sole ground for evaluating a group's potential political importance. Closer scrutiny of the experience of doing capoeira offers another way to understand how it might transform a student's awareness, an explanation that focuses on the embodied learning process rather than on genealogical integrity.

The kinesthetic of Capoeira Angola at the Grupo de Capoeira Angola Pelourinho is a radical reformation of bodily style, not because it is "traditional" or "Afro-Bahian"—although it may be both—but because it conflicts so markedly with novices' prior habits. Like the pain of muscles growing stronger and tendons stretching to achieve unfamiliar postures, emotional discomfort is the sign of the grip old dispositions have on the student's flesh. The demand for softness and broken movements in GCAP, much like the "necktie" choke that Mestre Bimba placed on prospective students, takes hold of the novice's body; if he or she can endure the physical suffering, fear, and shame, that body will be transformed. Physical practice is an effective vehicle for change, in part because reservations about actions, like turning upside down, are held in place by emotions, themselves visceral and physiological, that are provoked by learned, cultural inclinations.

Some characteristics of this kinesthetic, such as using the head to attack or bear weight, and crouching deeply in "traditional" resting postures, may, in fact, "faithfully reflect . . . the art's social and cultural origin," as Frigerio suggests (1989: 85). If so, then they are increasingly out of step with the modes of moving that students bring from everyday life as their customs change. Conserving a kinesthetic in a changing context can be an increasingly radical course of action. Walking in evil, standing on one's hands, "breaking" one's movements, or being a cabaçeiro grow progressively more challenging to the corporeal status quo. Preserving this movement, divorced from the constellation of labor, leisure, and religious activities that produced it, requires creative techniques to teach what may have once felt natural and demands constant attention to, or even exaggeration of, the finest details of practice.

Whether or not contemporary Capoeira Angola is authentic, the style confronts players profoundly on an experiential level, more so than some other forms of the art. Simply put, to learn Capoeira Angola from mestres Moraes or João Grande demands much of the student. Apprenticeship requires that a novice overcome shame, feel strength in new ways, become comfortable when off balance, and change comportment. Because skills and habits shape perceptions, more is at stake when Capoeira Angola tears shame from the body, breaks up players' movements, and makes students soft and pliant in new ways. Learning these gestures opens a substantial breach with the texture of everyday actions. Some of the art's potential for raising political consciousness derives from this clash between old habits and the new skills produced by the art.

A politicized leader like Mestre Moraes may interpret for students what they are feeling, and GCAP may strive to forge a social movement from the energy unlocked when students overcome shame and recognize untapped physical potential in themselves. But capoeira training is an unruly enterprise, liable to lead a player to develop in ways that are unpredictable, even upsetting to an instructor. Where one student might discover racial pride, another might learn all too well the lessons of malícia and refuse to join any collective enterprise without ulterior motives. Although seminars and sermons may try to prune all novices along similar lines, ultimately, in the words of Mestre Pastinha: "Each one is each one."

This account of capoeira's transformative potential better explains certain thorny details about capoeira "politics" than assuming that stylistic authenticity automatically generates a radical posture. First, Afrocentric angoleiros bemoan that many mestres of Bahia's old guard, their technical and aesthetic role models, often disappoint young activists who wish they would take more critical stands on social issues. If political awareness flowed naturally from authentic styles, as alleged, this inconsistency at the very heart of the community would not be possible. Second, some of the most confrontational Afrocentric capoeiristas play Capoeira Regional, the allegedly "whitened" style. Third, many devoted contemporary angoleiros started their training with Capoeira Regional, switching over after gaining substantial proficiency. If the styles were diametrically opposed, this switch would be akin to learning over again. In fact, many former practitioners of "whitened" styles become exemplary angoleiros and find the style alluring, perhaps because they recognize better than naïve observers the challenge of developing the body's latent potential.[10]

A careful study of how style feels reveals that similar experiences—shame, fear, inhibition, the desire for skill, fascination with the body's potential—confront new practitioners, regardless of their background. A variety of styles arises, in part, from the intensity with which people feel these obstacles or inclinations, their willingness to change habitual ways of moving, and what they seek from apprenticeship. This way of understanding stylistic diversity in capoeira offers greater nuance than simply assuming that style is the result of a student's race, social class, or political consciousness. Numerous exceptions need not be ignored, nor whole groups of practitioners written off as in the grips of bodily "false consciousness." In addition, the characteristics of "whitened" or "African" styles appear less arbitrary or lost in the misty past. Their continued relevance for the immediate bodily experience of players, their suffering and enthusiasms, becomes clearer.

At the same time, a phenomenological study of Capoeira Angola's kinesthetic shows that some of its consciousness-raising potential stems from the movements themselves, as teachers encourage students to break from unexamined habits and to develop unexplored dimensions of their bodily potential. A crucial dimension of identity may be shaped by physical discipline, offering a path—hard and long, true, but reaching profound dimensions of daily life and experience—to change a person's perceptions and sense of self. The revival of Capoeira Angola offers its devotees a technology for self-transformation, a set of arduous exercises that take hold of arm, leg, waist, and head, breaking and softening them so that the world might feel different.

Conclusion: Lessons from the Roda

Ethnographers cannot help but be guided by concerns brought from home, as much as by the people among whom we study. We drag our research questions and theoretical arguments with us like baggage, and they go on to influence what we discover in the field. In the hubbub of everyday life and in the swirl of unfamiliar sensations, our ears prick up when we hear something that recalls our research proposals, reminds us of an impressive lecture, or echoes a passage we have read in a landmark book. The interest in physical education that orients this book arises, in part, out of noisy discussions in the United States about exercise and fitness. But interactions with capoeiristas affected how I subsequently came to understand the subject, forcing me to reconsider how important physical education might be to shaping perceptions and experience.

One of the most exciting dimensions of ethnographic field research is that by putting ourselves into close contact with other ways of life, ethnographers make themselves vulnerable to intellectual challenge and change. Working daily with capoeira practitioners, playing and training alongside them, I frequently found the tables turned on me. Instead of posing all the questions and freely steering my own research, they grilled me: what did I think about the game, what had I found, and how did I see their world?

Capoeiristas, in general, are not a shy bunch, and they were often glad to set me straight. They argued with me when they thought I was misled, dismissed questions they felt were wrongheaded, and frequently ran roughshod over my research agenda. My being an anthropologist counted for little in the roda. Accepting the firm guidance of a mestre meant that this person helped plot the course of my project. I had to negotiate with my collaborators. Originally, I went to Brazil intending to study how different movement styles reflected social identity and shaped political views. Like most anthropologists, I planned to split my time between participating and observing, staying close to the roda, but also sitting outside it to watch. When Mestre Moraes and other adepts made it clear that I had a lot to learn in the roda before I could hope to understand their art, immersion as an apprentice became both the object and the method of my research.

This conclusion offers some reflections on more general anthropological topics, such as culture, embodiment, and experience, that emerged from apprenticeship in capoeira. The roda offered few definitive answers, but it frequently provoked me to rephrase basic research questions and challenged me to do without the comfortable explanatory tactics I had brought with me to the field.

PHYSICAL EDUCATION AS ETHNOGRAPHIC OBJECT

So often, physical education in the United States is treated as a way to instill virtues like "determination" or "teamwork," to relieve stress, to improve health, or to make children more easily managed in their afternoon classes after an interlude of "PE" or "recess." Exercise regimens sometimes appear virtually interchangeable, the only relevant differences being their intensity, their efficiency, or the aspect of "fitness" or portion of the body they might improve. Sport may be treated as a field for pure physical competition, where the best athlete or team can be identified.

In contrast to North American ideas about being "in shape," some capoeiristas considered their art to be downright detrimental to their health, complaining that to learn it, they suffered chronic aches and pains—and risked more serious injury. Instead of public sporting events in which a victor was clearly determined, capoeira matches were inconclusive. Whereas other athletes strive to their utmost to demonstrate their ability, capoeiristas hid what they knew and feigned weakness. They rejected the idea that "cross-training" offered any benefit because they saw bodily fitness not as a general capacity; only capoeira training could improve capoeira skills.

Phenomenologist Heather Devine (1984), in a discussion of "the workout," suggests that physical training is best understood as a search for "a new sense of self" rather than as a simple project to improve health. Devine notes that discomfort and injury can actually spur athletes to greater exertion. They are motivated not by longing for pleasure, but by a desire for self-transformation: "Through training we have the opportunity to mold—to recreate—ourselves.... Only the fit person gains the stamina and skill required to bend and prune the body, and we gain this fitness through the rigor of training" (ibid.: 170). Likewise, capoeiristas claimed that capoeira is a set of techniques (or multiple sets of techniques) for cultivating a way of being: a cunning comportment and a concealed readiness for danger.

Students used exercise to reshape their bodies, first, so that they could play, sing, and perform music in the roda; ultimately, however, exercise changed how they walked, stood, and carried themselves in everyday life. Training techniques augmented their ability to transform themselves. They developed self-awareness, bodily skills, and tenacity that they needed to incorporate capoeira's influence throughout their lives. Ideally, if they pursued the art faithfully and received good guidance, they became *capoeiristas* in the full sense: malicioso, playful, wary, without inhibitions curtailing their freedom to move, and possessing a knack for getting the best of any situation.

The vast majority of practitioners are students—not masters—and they spend a disproportionate amount of time preparing for moments in which they play. To describe capoeira as a "performance," focusing attention only on the goal of training, and to treat masters as the paradigmatic practitioners, is to distort how the art is lived. When, after a difficult class, the legendary Mestre João Grande proclaimed that *he* was still learning the art, I realized that even the best practitioners considered their skills to be works-in-progress. All around, colleagues strove to discover capoeira in themselves, to share with the less experienced what they had found, and to cultivate new abilities. Treating capoeira as a form of physical education rather than a performance to be watched from outside was an approach that had been thrust upon me, whether out of necessity, good luck, or a mestre's gruff wisdom.

Capoeira training is not unique among forms of physical education in trying to reshape novices in profound, open-ended ways. In fact, an analysis of capoeira suggests that every society has similar, idiosyncratic modes of training, even if these regimens entail bodily neglect, denial, or intentional weakening. Studying forms of training offers a path to explore other ways of being-in-the-world. Bodily arts provide sites where an ethnographer's collaborators may already be skilled at teaching apprentices to perceive and behave in culturally appropriate ways.

THE PRAGMATISM OF PRACTICE

Unlike some body disciplines, capoeira does not come accompanied by a very elaborate cosmology or philosophy. East and South Asian martial arts often include sophisticated discussions of life energy, the body's chakras, magical practice, or esoteric forms of awareness. In contrast, capoeira instruction is relentlessly practical. The art sometimes speaks almost entirely in an imperative voice, rather than a contemplative one: "Listen to the music. Keep doing the ginga. Loosen your waist. Keep your eyes open. Don't walk too close to corners. Trust no one." Adepts could spin creative answers to a researcher's bald questions proficiently. However, I became suspicious of the suggestion that capoeira was "more profound" than its practice as a result of warnings that "capoeiristas are liars," as well as adepts' playful responses to earnest questions and an occasional impatient admonition that I should ask fewer questions and figure things out for myself. The art's cunning stance and pragmatic approach to personal change is its profundity.

In capoeira instruction, not during outside interviews, veterans gave the most straightforward advice. Teaching was also the forum in which experts shared most intimately and immediately how capoeira felt to them. Although practical instruction in capoeira was often through imitation or technical direction, in certain moments ("Just stand up!") veterans attempted to shape how novices perceived their own bodies, and the world around them, through poetic coaching. Veterans wanted new adepts to feel the roda's rhythms, hear its sinister implications, sense their own vulnerability, and perceive opportunities in an adversary's movements. Teachers sought to help their students play well rather than achieve an abstract understanding of the art.

Capoeira training is a form of what Loïc Wacquant (1995b: 73) has called "body work." In his ethnographic study of boxing, Wacquant describes physical training as:

> a highly intensive and finely regulated manipulation of the organism whose aim is to imprint into the bodily schema of the fighter postural sets, patterns of movement, and subjective emotional–cognitive states that make him into a conversant practitioner. . . .

Wacquant's sensitive description, with its mix of postures, action patterns, and "emotional–cognitive states," could be applied directly to capoeira. In this list, he suggests one reason why boxing, like capoeira training, is so drawn out: diverse elements go into proficiency. A student must learn a repertoire of things: postures for readiness, reactions that link perception and movement, perceptual skills to glean relevant information in the environment, and corporeal states that combine emotion, perception, and posture.

Attention to "practice" has become important in contemporary social sciences, owing especially to the work of Wacquant's mentor, the late sociologist Pierre Bourdieu (see 1977, 1990b). Bourdieu's theories helped to inspire an upsurge of interest in everyday life, habits, and patterns of action, leading many anthropologists to think about the role of mundane activities in producing large-scale social phenomena like class, gender, culture, and ethnic difference. In spite of this interest, however, there is surprisingly little curiosity about the pragmatic details of practices themselves, except in rare cases like Wacquant's rich study of boxers' training regimens. Theorists of "practice" do not ask how habits are acquired, how techniques feel for the person who does them, or how skills function practically, psychologically, and neurologically. Practice theorists tend to steer clear of biology and phenomenology, seldom raising questions about what happens to the body physically, or what a person's subjective experience might be, during habitual action.

Bourdieu suggests that underlying the many different sorts of activities we do is a relatively small set of principles or categories that he called the *habitus*. Bourdieu defines *habitus* as a patterned set of dispositions that undergirds apparently complex and varied behavior. According to Bourdieu, the *habitus* is a simple, inheritable set of dispositions that produces all sorts of practical improvisations in everyday life. He describes habitus as "very systematic: all the elements of his or her behaviour have something in common, a kind of affinity of *style*, like the works of the same painter" (2002: 28).

Even the greenest capoeira novice knows there's no such shortcut to proficiency, however, no principle that, once learned, generates all the action and abilities. Each skill demands its own attention; each technique, its own exercises. Furthermore, within a discipline like capoeira, contradictory tendencies arise in the same moments. Instead of a unified set of simplified principles, capoeira is a loose assembly of multiple skills, diverse postures, and a few principles, incompletely realized and inconsistently applied. Although facets may be related in specific, practical ways, like a link between learning a rhythm on an instrument and trying to use the same rhythm when one dances, capoeira has no single overarching unity (cf. Hunter and Saunders 1995).

Gaining proficiency in capoeira does not mean that a student acquires some uniform substance or unspoken shared principles. As with the discovery of the bananeira, each novice solves practical problems posed by the activity in his or her own idiosyncratic way, even with the same guidance. Stephen Turner (1994: 19) similarly argues that different people can achieve overtly similar behavior in diverse ways. Nothing can guarantee that everyone will learn or perform in the same fashion, even if the majority of capoeira students eventually manage to stand on their hands. Abundant ethnographic evidence of stylistic variety between, and even within schools, makes proposing that capoeira is a uniform *thing* seem ludicrous. Mestre Pastinha himself recognized: "No one plays in the same way I do. Each person is unique."

Similar behavior cannot be assumed; it must be explained. With so many different teachers and schools of capoeira, so many students creating new moves and missing important lessons, we could expect even more variation in the game than we in fact encounter. Alongside the centrifugal tendencies in the learning process, what centripetal forces encourage capoeiristas to come together? This book explores many of these: communal forms of commemorating the past, group songs, signature instruments, shared rituals, widely circulating cautionary tales, moments of face-to-face contact, similar anxieties about safety, common emotional and corporeal problems, and a powerful desire to play together. However, centripetal forces do not automatically produce uniformity. Moments of harmonious interaction are accomplishments, and even the most cohesive group can eventually split apart. When they come together, adepts sometimes find that they cannot play with each other, try as they might.

Capoeiristas argue bitterly about the art's proper form and its significance. This does not mean that one player or group has successfully internalized "capoeira-ness," while the other has not, although some may accuse others of just that. For the same reason, some mestres— including my own teacher—will no doubt reject some ideas put forward in this book. These disagreements are not symptoms that practitioners (or the author) have inadequate knowledge of capoeira. They are a sign that, in the roda, students find different skills, develop diverse tendencies, and discover many things about themselves and their worlds. The roda is not a universal form inscribed on the soul of each devotee; it is an event balancing conflict and cooperation, knit together by song, music, and ritual, where players continually negotiate and discover what the capoeira between them will be. Although this book describes tendencies that are widespread among capoeiristas, practitioners cannot even agree among themselves on what essentially unifies the art.

EMBODIMENT AND EXPERIENCE

Varieties of training shape distinct forms of human embodiment. Tim Ingold (1998) points out that studying bodies requires not just describing how ideals or values are "written" on people's bodies (cf. Csordas 1994: 12). Rather, "throughout life, the body undergoes processes of growth and decay, and . . . as it does so, particular skills, habits, capacities and strengths, as well as debilities and weaknesses, are enfolded into its very constitution—in its neurology, musculature, even its anatomy" (Ingold 1998: 26). Studying physical education, especially an athletic discipline such as capoeira, makes this pervasive process more evident because the art is so demanding and its effects so spectacular; but this difference is one of degree, not kind. Even such seemingly "nonphysical" activities as working at a desk are bodily disciplines with profound effects on a person's physiology. The prevalence of carpal tunnel syndrome and other work-related chronic conditions in white-collar occupations attests to these effects. A discipline need not be vigorous or conscious for it to reshape a devotee's body.

Because each person develops over time in response to behavior and environment, it quickly becomes impossible to distinguish what is "biological" from what is "cultural" in human training. Ingold (ibid: 25–26, 30 ff.) uses walking as an example. To say that a human being has the biological capacity to walk is meaningless. The ability develops only in a supportive environment with specific role models and training techniques; that is, it develops only in a cultural milieu (cf. Oyama 1985; Thelen and Smith 1994). The result is that humans walk in a variety of ways (Mauss 1973). Drawing a distinction between biology and culture suggests that there might be a biological body walking in a vacuum, absent the effects of environmental conditioning, cultural development, and social interaction, its structure and gait determined only by its genes. Such a monster is unimaginable in reality. No biologically predetermined way to walk lies concealed by cultural variations; only particular ways to walk exist, discovered by each person. And each way of walking will shape a person's flesh over time.

For this reason, this book frequently discusses findings in the neurosciences, psychology, and human biology. Some cultural anthropologists may be uncomfortable with these references. For many of us, the specters of racism, simplistic evolutionary explanations, and genetic determinism (the conviction that human genes wholly determine behavior) haunt discussions of the relation between human variation and biology. Some overly ambitious geneticists have done little to calm these fears, treating biology always as a cause—never an effect—of culture. But, as Tim Ingold (1998: 28) goes on to argue: "Cultural differences . . . *are* biological," as long as we recognize that biological processes unfold developmentally and are not genetically preprogrammed. As the body's malleability becomes increasingly evident in a range of fields, cultural anthropologists can see more clearly how different life ways, forms of physical education, and bodily cultivation might affect the physiological development of humans as living organisms.

Although ethnographic research may not yield data of the same sorts that laboratory studies can produce, the field can offer developmental scenarios that no laboratory-based experiment could ever reproduce, ethically or practically. Training regimens have years, even decades, to shape how a person's body matures; the effects can be subtle and slow, but they amass into profound change. For this reason, ethnographic research offers invaluable contributions to the study of human development. Half a lifetime of diligent capoeira practice—regular acrobatic games in the roda, heightened wariness in everyday life, and a cunning comportment—must inevitably "grow" capoeiristas in peculiar ways, shaping neural, perceptual, and physiological development, just as this training provides practitioners with distinctive metaphors and symbols. Placing ethnographic research in dialogue with biological disciplines enriches both fields. The people among whom ethnographers study provide examples of ways humans have been grown, techniques that might be used to shape embodiment, and insight into how it might feel to live different sorts of corporeality.

This last aspect of embodiment—the subjective experience of its variety—most interests me as a cultural anthropologist. I am not content simply to catalog varieties of bodily technology and to theorize about their physiological effects. Different physical techniques, broadly understood, affect a person's sensual experience, including the most basic perceptions, or what Thomas Csordas (1990: 6) refers to as "prereflective" and "preobjective" experience. For capoeiristas, physical changes wrought by training are never ends in themselves; rather, they occur because adepts pursue specific abilities they want to learn. They don't set out to change their bodies, typically, but instead to learn to cartwheel, to play the berimbau, or to sing better. The body is manipulated through exercises, games, and coaching because it is the foundation of perception and a player's means to act. To learn a new technique, for example, a student must come to experience his or her own limbs in new ways, or become alive to the world with new sensibilities.

Although we cannot ever know for certain what any other person feels, we can study closely the skills and behaviors through which others perceive. We can observe what a physical discipline does to a body, ask a practitioner how it feels, and try to triangulate between these observations to envisage the means through which capoeiristas perceive. Putting ourselves into apprenticeship, we can ask veterans to help us discover proficiency for ourselves, and report back to the best of our ability. This requires taking claims about bodily change seriously, rather than assuming that they are just a culture-bound "discourse" or a set of ideas, divorced from any reality that we too might be part of or join. Although we cannot hope to develop identical skills—no two practitioners do—we can at least learn comparable ones so that we better understand, even feel visceral empathy with, what others try to share in words, song, and gesture. At the very least, we might strive to meet capoeiristas in the roda, becoming better aware of the long path they trod to reach it along the way.

NOTES

Prelude

1. This account is a fictionalized narrative based on participating in similar events since 1992; another version appears in Grupo de Capoeira Angola Pelourhino (GCAP) (1996).

Chapter One

1. When "capoeira," following contemporary usage, refers to the activity, the word is not italicized. When *capoeira* is italicized, it refers to the individual practicing, the older denotation. Confusion is less likely to arise in Portuguese because the noun designating a person is masculine, *o capoeira*, whereas the activity is feminine, *a capoeira*. The use of "malta" to describe gangs allegedly arose because laborers were often recruited to Brazil from the Mediterranean island of Malta.

2. Frequently, mestres, or capoeira "teachers," are known publicly only by their title together with a nickname. Mestre Bimba's nickname is a colloquial word for a young boy's penis, allegedly given by the midwife who delivered him because it was proof that the child was not the daughter his mother had expected. Today, *apelidos* (nicknames) are often given to a student at the student's "baptism," a ritual celebrating a player's introduction into the capoeira community. They sometimes humorously refer to a quirk in the new student's playing style, a distinctive physical trait, or some other salient characteristic of the novice.

3. Residents of Salvador frequently refer to themselves as *baianos*, "Bahians," and the city as "Bahia," even though, in fact, the state of Bahia is huge.

4. The English literature on race in Brazil is vast, in part because Brazil provides such a vivid contrast with racial tensions, segregation, and violence in the United States (e.g., Degler 1986; Hellwig, ed. 1992; Skidmore 1993a; Marx 1998). The most influential social scientist to claim that Brazil had overcome racism was Gilberto Freyre (1986a; cf. Wagley, ed. 1952). As early as the work of Roger Bastide and Pierre Van den Berghe (1957), however, scholars noted profound negative stereotypes of

blacks and mulattos among Brazilians, in spite of explicit egalitarian ideals (cf. Turra and Venturi, eds. 1995). The literature on race relations in Brazil is vast. In addition to the works cited in this section, readers might consult collections edited by Larry Crook and Randall Johnson (1999), Michael Hanchard (1999), and Rebecca Reichmann (1999).

5. For a thorough discussion of the UNESCO project, see Marcos Maio (2001).

6. Population geneticists have found that skin color in Brazil, even at the extremes of lightness and darkness, is a poor indicator of ancestry (e.g., Alves-Silva et al. 2000; Parra et al. 2003; cf. Sans 2000). Even "white" Brazilians often have genetic markers associated with African ancestry.

7. Among those who accepted the argument that inequality in Brazil was based primarily on class rather than on race were Donald Pierson (1967), Thales de Azevedo (1953), and Carl Degler (1986). In contrast, studies that demonstrated ongoing structures of racial prejudice include works by Carlos Hasenbalg (1985) and Nelson do Valle Silva (1985, 1999) (cf. Silva and Hasenbalg 1992, 1999), and Charles Wood and Alberto Magno Carvalho (1988).

8. George Reid Andrews (1991) provides an excellent history of Afro-Brazilian political organization in São Paulo (cf. Gonzalez 1985; Hanchard 1994; Butler 1998b).

9. This ambiguity casts doubt on census data on race because Brazilians tend to "lighten" their color classification as they become wealthier, distorting the apparent socioeconomic gap between blacks and whites (Wood and Carvalho 1998; cf. Harris et al. 1993, 1995; Piza and Fúlvia 1999; Telles 1995, 2002).

10. Some current research, including work by Howard Winant (1992) and Thomas Skidmore (1993a), suggests that Brazilian systems of color classification may be changing, owing in part to the efforts of black activists to promote "negro" as an identity. Livio Sansone (1993) found that young Brazilians more often used the term "negro" than their parents; Michael Turner (1985) conjectures that college students shifted from "brown into black," in part as a result of the Black Soul popular culture movement. Skidmore cautions (1993a: 381), however, that the black consciousness movement may not be affecting all Afro-Brazilians, among whom "whitening" aspirations can still be quite strong (see also Twine 1998).

11. Pierre Bourdieu and Loïc Wacquant (1999) criticize activists and intellectuals like Michael Hanchard (1994) for intellectual imperialism when they advocate bipolar concepts of race for Brazil "imported"

from the United States (cf. Sansone 1997; French 2000; Fry 2000; Sansone, ed. 2002). Brazilians, however, adopt and adapt symbols of Africanity at all levels, from the academic to the popular. As many scholars have shown, the transnational exchange of culture and symbols is long-standing throughout the African diaspora (see especially Gilroy 1993). For instance, Salvador's global visibility as a site of black culture inspires what Michel Agier (1998) has called "activist tourism" (cf. Butler 1998a: 168–169). Black North Americans once traveled to Brazil to experience what they saw as a society free of prejudice (see Hellwig 1992); now many make a pilgrimage to Salvador to experience the city's Afro-Brazilian heritage. While I was in GCAP, a constant complement of foreign capoeiristas was in residence, some for months at a time. This intimate, long-term contact between Bahian and foreign capoeiristas, especially African Americans, left a deep imprint on everyone involved.

12. The term "Afrocentric" is not used in the specific sense intended by Molefi Kete Asante (1988), but more loosely to mean a self-conscious practice or ideology that explicitly adopts what it considers African symbols or perspectives (cf. Covin 1990).

13. Diana Brown (1999) suggests that some Brazilian religions have also re-Africanized. Some Candomblé houses have removed Catholic elements from their iconography and adopted practices they consider more faithfully African.

14. Anthropologists influenced by phenomenological philosophy include Thomas Csordas (1990, 1992, 1993, 1994), Robert Desjarlais (1992, 1997), Steven Friedson (1996), Kathryn Geurts (2002a, 2002b), William Hanks (1990), Tim Ingold (2000), Michael Jackson (1989, 1995, 1996, 1998), Thomas Otts (1990, 1994), and James Weiner (1991, 1992, 1993).

15. The objective of this book is to provide a clear example of an analytical approach that might complement others in anthropology: what Thomas Csordas has called "cultural phenomenology" (cf. Friedson 1996: xiii–xvi). Although this makes the book less complete—more one sided—it may better provide an example of phenomenological ethnography, uncluttered by too many tangential digressions into divergent forms of analysis, no matter how interesting they might be.

Chapter Two

1. The colors black and yellow commemorated Mestre Pastinha, who chose them for his students because they were the colors of his favorite soccer club.

2. Neurological mapping techniques, such as magnetic resonance imaging (MRI) and transcranial magnetic stimulation, indicate that as a skill is

learned, the parts of the brain that are most active when performing it change. At first, the cortex or outer brain, the area associated with conscious thought, is recruited; later, as the task becomes better known, activity moves to subcortical areas, as John Ratey (2001: 36–37) describes, freeing up the cortex to focus on other tasks.

3. Bernstein (1996) argues on several grounds that a skill—a kick, cartwheel, or handstand, for example—cannot be a prefabricated object like a deeply ingrained neurophysical "pathway." First, since animal limbs possess many degrees of freedom and muscle fibers are elastic, they do not respond identically every time they are contracted; only through continually monitoring and readjusting can a body control itself. Second, how would a student ever improve a technique if practice were simply the relentless repetition of the action? A person who fell when learning to balance would merely be rehearsing to fall; a wobbly infant would grow up with the same unsteady gait (cf. Reed and Bril 1996). Third, close studies of skilled actions find that even simple rhythmic tasks consist of constantly varying physical means to produce a desired end. For example, slow-motion analysis of a person striking an anvil shows that the trajectory of the limb varies on almost every repetition, even if the hammer falls in the same spot (cf. Ingold 1998: 26; 2000: 353).

4. The implications of embodiment have long occupied the attention of phenomenologists, beginning with Edmund Husserl (1970, 1989; see also Behnke 1997a; Dreyfus 1991). The anthropological literature on the body is far too vast to review adequately here (for overviews, see Lock 1993; Strathern 1996; Csordas 1999).

5. John Ratey (2001: 56) offers the interesting case of his own brother who, in 1958, applied to the United States Naval Academy, but was turned down because he lacked perfect eyesight. His examiners gave him exercises to strengthen his vision, and he passed the same test a month later.

6. Both Erwin Strauss (1966: 198) and John Dewey (1929: 261) note that the objects constituted by perception beckon to us and repulse us even before we "interpret" them (cf. Heidegger 1996: 62–83 passim). Studies of neuropathology confirm this phenomenological insight; patients who have lost the ability to classify or label objects as a result of localized brain lesions often can properly manipulate the same objects when concentrating on a task (cf. Gelder, de Haan, and Heywood, eds. 2001).

7. Recent findings in the brain sciences support this radical redefinition of consciousness. Neuroscientists Rodolfo Llínas (2001) and Alain Berthoz (2000) point out that only organisms that move possess nervous systems,

and most of the brain's abilities are shaped by the demands of movement, not "pure" cognition (cf. Dreyfus 1967).

8. These links are what phenomenologists refer to as "intentional" ties
(see discussion of the "intentional arc" in Merleau-Ponty 1962: 135–136;
cf. Mohanty 1972, 1985).

9. Merleau-Ponty calls the inchoate awareness of the body's potential action
the *schéma corporel*: the "always changing self-awareness that actors have
of their own bodily position in space," as Hanks succinctly describes
(1990: 83). This book does not use "corporeal schema" or a related term
like "bodily image" to designate this background to perception because
these terms might imply a static visual image, like a mental photograph
or picture.

10. Phenomenologists often do not take into account how this bodily basis
of perception might vary. Gail Weiss (1999: 20) criticizes both Merleau-
Ponty and Paul Schilder (1950), for example, because neither "even
acknowledges, much less develops, the ways in which race, gender, sexuality, age, class, and ethnicity factor into the construction of the habit
body (or primary postures)."

11. A number of texts explicitly deal with the cultural conditioning of the body
through physical disciplines, dance genres, and sports training. James
Morley (2001) analyzes yoga breathing, Susan Brownell (1995) writes
on sport in China, Joseph Alter (1992) and Phillip Zarrilli (1998) study
South Asian wrestling and martial arts, Loïc Wacquant (1995a, 1995b, 1998,
2004) writes on boxers in Chicago, Sally Ann Ness (1992, 1996) studied
Southeast Asian dance, and Susan Leigh Foster (1986, 1992) and Cynthia
Novack (1990) provide accounts of western dance.

Chapter Three

1. In contrast to Mestre Bimba's school, Mestre Pastinha's *Centro Esportivo
de Capoeira Angola* (Sporting Center of Capoeira Angola) sometimes
did not even hold formal classes. Instead, like traditional public rodas,
Pastinha's "academy" served both as a teaching center and as a gathering place where veteran capoeiristas from throughout Salvador
came to play (and tourists, to watch). Pastinha's Centro was a hybrid
institution, combining characteristics of the academy and the standing
public roda. Modern academies more closely resemble Mestre Bimba's
school.

2. No universally recognized standard exists for awarding titles such as
"mestre." A capoeirista's transition from student to teacher can be rocky.
Some senior students, believing they have earned the right to teach,
break away from a long-time mentor to ally with another mestre willing
to give them teaching credentials. Some instructors, awarded the title

"mestre" by one organization, may find that other teachers still find their qualifications insufficient. Especially because scarce employment opportunities may hang in the balance (see Araujo 1994), these conflicts can split groups or cause friction between teachers and estranged former students.

3. Developmental studies suggest that humans' ability to learn by mimicry may be heightened by child-rearing techniques. Chimpanzees raised among humans, for instance, perform better on imitative tasks than chimpanzees raised by their own mothers, sometimes approaching the skill of children on simple tool-using tasks (see Tomasello et al. 1993).

4. Foundational research on the imitation of facial expressions appears in the work of Andrew Meltzoff and Kevin Moore (1983, 1999). For a recent sampling of studies of infant imitation, see Jacqueline Nadel and George Butterworth's (1999) edited volume.

5. A range of neurological articles and medical journals discuss imitation behavior, following an early description by James Baldwin (1901; cf. Lhermitte et al. 1986; De Renzi et al. 1996).

6. The original research on mirror neurons (reported initially in Di Pelligrino et al. 1992, and more extensively in Rizzolatti et al. 1996) has been widely cited in brain sciences. The implications of this research are variously discussed in Trevarthen et al. (1999), Jeannerod (1994: 190), and Berthoz (2000: 20).

7. This account of cultural learning borrows heavily from Susan Oyama (1985, 2000) and Esther Thelen and Linda Smith (1994; cf. Smith and Thelen 1993; Thelen 1995).

8. Stephen Turner's critique of theories of "practice" inspired this discussion of centrifugal tendencies in capoeira apprenticeship (1994, 2002).

9. Maurice Bloch (1998: 16) cautions: "when our informants honestly say 'this is why we do such things', or 'this is what this means', or 'this is how we do such things', instead of being pleased we should be suspicious and ask what kind of *peculiar* knowledge is this which can take such an explicit, linguistic form?"

10. The expression "experience-distant," used by Clifford Geertz (1984: 124) and Uni Wikan (1991), was originally proposed by Heinz Kohut.

11. John Miller Chernoff's (1979) landmark account of West African drumming makes a compelling argument for apprenticeship as a research method, as does Loïc Wacquant's (2004) discussion of boxing (cf. Stoller and Olkes 1987; Desjarlais 1992: 3–35). Timothy Jenkins (1994) and James Fernandez and Michael Herzfeld (1998) offer theoretical defenses of this approach. Jean Lave (e.g., 1977, 1982, 1988, 1990) has been one of the most passionate advocates of studying apprenticeship as a form of education in anthropology (cf. Barz and Cooley 1997).

Chapter Four

1. Roberto DaMatta (1991 [1979]) laid the foundation for anthropological understandings of the malandro in Brazilian popular culture (cf. Matos 1982; Oliven 1984; A. Soares 1994; Dias 2001: 153–183).

2. For a discussion of the many possible origins of the word "capoeira," see Lowell Lewis (1992: 42–43) or Waldeloir Rego (1968: 17–29).

3. For many contemporary practitioners, Juca Reis symbolizes that the *capoeiras* represented a wide range of social groups. Police reports from the drive to rid the republic of *capoeiragem* indicate that few were truly "vagrant"; only around one-fifth of those picked up were unemployed (Bretas 1989: 58; 1991: 242–243; Holloway 1989: 654–661; 1991; C. Soares 1994: 144–145).

4. Marcos Bretas (1991: 240–241) reproduces an editorial from the *Gazeta da Tarde*, December 22, 1885, in which columnist Raul Pompéia described how "the razor reigns" over Rio de Janeiro. Pompéia accused the police of themselves using razors as a "vital and characteristic element of administration" (ibid.: 241), implying that it was difficult to distinguish the civil guard from the maltas.

5. On the persecution of black culture in Salvador and Afro-Bahians' techniques for resisting violent repression, see Kim Butler (1998b: esp. 168–209).

6. Quote attributed to Muniz Sodré in a pamphlet produced by the Fundação Mestre Bimba, dated May 1994.

7. Many capoeiristas credit this presentation to Getúlio Vargas with changing the art's status, leading to an embrace by the Vargas government (e.g., J. Oliveira 1989: 23). Critics consider this an attempt by the state to co-opt a vital form of popular culture (e.g., Frigerio 1989; Accurso 1990; GCAP 1993; L. Reis 1993).

8. The earliest reference I found to n'golo is in the work of Luís da Câmara Cascudo (1967: 179–189; 1972: 243), although the term "n'golo" does not appear in the earlier work. Mestre Pastinha made reference to the "dance of the zebras" in interviews given to reporters as early as 1965 (see Felix 1965: 5; Freire 1967: 79; cf. L. Reis 1993). Oddly, no reference is made to n'golo in Pastinha's book, originally published in 1964. Either Pastinha's ghostwriter omitted this crucial detail, or Pastinha did not share it at this time. Other references to n'golo are sparse and may derive from the same principal sources (e.g., Cruz 1973). Jair Moura recorded a description of the n'golo dance by Albano de Neves e Souza, an immigrant from Luanda (Moura 1980b: 15–16). According to an individual who worked with Moura, Souza was also Cascudo's original source. If so, many references to n'golo may originate from this single source

(e.g., V. Oliveira [1971: 68–69] also cites Souza). The existence of similar dances and fighting styles throughout the Americas offers evidence to some researchers of capoeira's African origin (e.g., Thompson 1974, 1987, 1988, 1992; Dossar 1988; Dawson 1996: 4).

The late Mestre Pastinha was circumspect in his own inimitable way on the question: "It's possible that it [the origin in the dance of the zebra] is not true. But contemporary capoeiristas sure would like it if it would have been, such that their victories would have an equal prize" (Freire 1967: 79), referring to the fact that the n'golo victor could choose any unmarried girl as his bride.

9. Preparations for this anniversary might explain the prominence of Zumbi during my field visits. For more detailed histories of Zumbi, Palmares, and other quilombos, see Décio Freitas (1982), R. K. Kent (1979), and Clóvis Moura (1981). The reader is cautioned that I helped prepare the text that is cited here, translating and editing the original work written by the group's executive board.

10. Other popular histories of capoeira that contain discussions of the quilombos and Zumbi include those of Ubirajara Almeida (1986: 14–15:) and Aristeu Oliveira dos Santos (1993: 37–42). Those histories may have been affected by the popular Brazilian movie *Quilombo*, which features dramatic scenes of maroons fighting bush captains using capoeira-like techniques (cf. Browning 1995: 94–95).

11. As some scholars point out, not all those punished under Brazilian law as *capoeiras* were African; as many as a third of those arrested for *capoeiragem* were European descended (Bretas 1989: 58; 1991: 242–243; Holloway 1989: 654–661; C. Soares 1994: 144–145). Although these historians certainly are correct to make the picture more complex, if whites were punished when they associated with gangs of Africans and mixed-raced, working-class men, this was hardly a racially neutral pattern of persecution.

12. The late Jorge Amado, the most influential Bahian artist of the twentieth century, describes Pastinha in his book, *Bahia de Todos os Santos* (1961: 209).

13. There are no thorough biographies of Mestre Pastinha. Practitioners are familiar, however, with Waldeloir Rego's critical profile (1968: 270–275), Pastinha's own book (1988), and well-circulated newspaper articles (including Felix 1965; "Pastinha Chega . . ." 1966; Freire 1967; "Cadê Pastinha?" 1973; Penalva 1973; and Mazzei 1979).

14. Pastinha's account appears in Freire (1967: 81) and in Decânio (n.d.b.: 20–22; cf. L. Reis 1993: 95). Daniel Noronha, one of the other members of this loosely knit group, provides his own version of the founding of the Centro (Coutinho 1993: 17). The two accounts offer similar descriptions

of the transfer of authority to Mestre Pastinha. Why Pastinha was chosen to succeed Amorzinho over other potential candidates, however, is one point of marked disagreement.

15. Several efforts to reopen the academy in new locations apparently took place ("Cadê Pastinha?" 1973: 6; Mazzei 1979: 32), but the center never regained its vitality.

16. Innumerable articles, stretching over several decades, describe the mestre's slow deterioration. The titles alone suggest their themes: "Capoeira, an art without assistance" (Mattos 1967); "The loneliness of the mestre" (Penalva 1973); "It's sweet to die and later become a street name [written in sarcasm while he was still alive]" (Jehová de Carvalho 1979); "In the Pelourinho, a sick and blind man, It's Mestre Pastinha: history repeats itself [after Mestre Bimba died]" ("No Pelourinho . . ." 1979); "Mestre Pastinha seeks help—before it's too late" ("Mestre Pastinha pede . . ." 1981).

17. Those who argue that capoeira is African frequently point out that both mestres Bimba and Pastinha learned capoeira from Africans. During their lifetimes, the two argued about how to understand this relation. Pastinha asserted that capoeira was African. Bimba countered that, although the slaves were from Africa, capoeira was created in the Bahian Recôncavo, the region around the Bay of All Saints (Felix 1965).

18. This interpretation motivates some Brazilian psychotherapists to advocate that their patients do capoeira as therapy (e.g., Freire 1990).

19. A similar but lengthier composition honoring Princesa Isabel appears on a recording made by Mestre Eziquiel (see Pereira and Carvalho 1992: 17–18). At the same time, there are other compositions critical of Princesa Isabel (e.g., ibid.: 100–101).

20. One version of this verse is attributed to Mestre Pastinha (cited in L. Reis 1993: 97).

Capoeira rends the spindle of the torturer
In the conviction of faith against slavery;
Sweet voice, your sons were heroes.
Capoeira loves abolition.

Chapter Five

1. This transcript is based upon the liner notes (GCAP 1996: 24) but was altered to coincide more closely with the recording. Over time, ladainhas like this one have grown more complex and carefully composed, incorporating academic discoveries about the art's history. Lowell Lewis, for example, concludes that most songs about Zumbi and the quilombos are relatively recent creations (1992: 177). The tendency toward greater complexity has been reinforced by the rise of contests for original compositions and a burgeoning literature on capoeira history.

2. Although this song can comment upon a capoeira game, it may have originally described the actions of *caboclos* and other spirits who possess dancers during Afro-Brazilian possession rituals. (Caboclos are the spirits of dead Native Americans.) Songs about "falling," "tripping," "grabbing," or individuals coming to visit, such as "Benvenuto" and "the sailor," according to some observers, may have once referred to possession. Crossover of songs between *Candomblé do caboclo* and capoeira may be more likely because of similarities between the two practices. During festivals for the caboclos, for example, the audience and spirits alike may engage in *samba duro* (hard samba), a dance in which participants trip each other. Caboclos are cunning and playful when they possess dancers, frequently knocking over spectators. Even the instrumental ensemble for Candomblé do caboclo—guitars, *pandeiros* (tambourine), and occasionally a *reco-reco* (scraper) or *agogô* (double bell-gong)—resembles that for *samba de roda* (circle samba), batuque, and capoeira.

3. Challenge singing is common in Brazilian folk musical traditions (e.g., Reily 2002; Travassos 2000). While in Brazil, I rarely witnessed impromptu singing of *sotaque*, challenges and insults in capoeira. Once, in the middle of a vigorous match, two expert players returned to the front of the orchestra and traded humorous taunts in rhyming couplets.

Journalist Ramagem Badaró reported an exchange of sotaque preceding a game between Mestre Bimba and a visitor in "The Blacks Fight Their Mysterious Battles," in 1944 (reprinted in J. Moura 1991: 70–77). According to Badaró, when the visitor challenged Mestre Bimba, the mestre sang the following verse:

On the day that I awoke
Inside of Itabaiana,
No man mounted a horse,
No woman put out a chicken.
The nuns that were praying
Forgot the litany.

The visitor responded to the boast:

The iúna [a bird] was a sorcerer
When it was on the fountain.
It was cunning and quick,
But capoeira killed it.

In return, Mestre Bimba threatened:

Prayer of a strong arm,
Prayer of St. Matthew.
To the cemetery go the bones,
Your bones, not mine.

Not wishing to let the mestre have the last word, the challenger bragged:

I was born on Saturday,
On Sunday I walked,
And on Monday
I played capoeira. (ibid: 72–73)

An even more extensive example of cantigas de sotaque can be found in Luís da Câmara Cascudo's *Vaqeiros e Cantadores* (cited in Rego 1968: 250–254).

4. "Saints" referred to in capoeira songs may not be exclusively Catholic; Catholic saints are often associated with orixás, or African-derived deities.

5. "Her name" is probably a reference to "Our Lady" (*Nossa senhora*); ribbons printed with the names of prominent churches, including many dedicated to incarnations of Mary, are found throughout Bahia. These ribbons are used as *lembranças* (reminders) of petitions, sometimes tied on church railings, devotees' wrists, luggage, the rearview mirrors of cars, or berimbaus.

6. Although GCAP members used this verse to initiate song cycles, structurally, it resembles a quadra rather than a ladainha. The quadra song structure, common outside of GCAP, is generally forbidden inside the group.

7. The idea of "projection" builds upon the work of Karl Bühler (1990), William Hanks (1996), and Vimala Herman (1999).

8. For explanations of deictic projection and its implications, see especially Hanks (1990), Haviland (1996), Jakobson (1971), Jespersen (1965), Rubba (1996), and Silverstein (1976). For early discussions of the experiential effect of quotation in oral performance, see Babcock (1984: 73) and Martin (1989).

9. Emile Benveniste (1971: 217–222) discusses the significance of the instability of the "mobile sign," "I," in his reflections on the nature of pronouns.

10. Many anthropologists offer other examples of how memories are inscribed in geography, including Keith Basso (1984, 1988, 1996), Steven Feld (1990), Steven Feld and Keith Basso, eds. (1997), Fernando Santos-Granero (1998), Edward Schieffelin (1976), and James Weiner (1991, especially Chapter 2).

11. Contramestre Luiz Carlos "K. K." Bonates provided this song when we discussed the ideas elaborated in this chapter.

12. The Parry–Lord theory holds that oral epics, in particular Homer's tales, are composed from a body of formulas. The theory, argued by the father and son classicists Milman and Adam Parry, and Albert Lord (see

A. Parry 1956, 1981; Lord 1960; M. Parry 1971), inspired extensive discussion among classicists (see Foley 1985). The idea that improvised oral narratives are built up from formulas is most widely known to anthropologists through the work of Richard Bauman (1984).

13. Anthropologist Karin Barber describes a similar phenomenon in Yoruba praise poetry. Barber claims that only in their performance context are the historical poems she studied anything other than "a jumble of obscure fragments," offering a way, in her words, of "re-experiencing the past and reintegrating it into the present" (1989: 14). E. Valentine Daniel similarly contrasts the past lived as myth or as history: "In myth we find a way of being in the world, where participation is fundamental" (1996: 52).

14. The idea of language building the roda alludes to Martin Heidegger's often-cited phrase, "Language is the House of Being" (1971a: 132; cf. 1971b; Weiner 1991: 14ff.).

15. Merleau-Ponty also describes speech as generating the phenomenal world in everyday life: "words, vowels and phonemes are so many ways of 'singing' the world" because they express things in "their emotional essence" (1962: 187; cf. Ingold 2000: 409–410).

16. Philosopher Roman Ingarden (1973) argued that the literary work of art was a "purely intentional structure." As William Hanks explained: "We can think of the intentional object as a sort of target toward which the meaningful expression projects, like an arc or vector" (1996: 123). Ingarden assumed that these structures did not wholly determine the "concretization" of an artistic work because they invariably contained "blank spots" that each reader had to fill in.

Chapter Six

1. This material has received a wealth of critical input from Ubirajara Almeida (Mestre Acordeon), Philip Bohlman, Carolyn Johnson, Virginia Gorlinski, and Martin Stokes. Bruno Nettl and two anonymous reviewers read and helped revise an earlier version of this chapter for publication (as Downey 2002b).

2. Lowell Lewis (1992: 133–161) discusses many arguments about capoeira music; for example, as he details, players do not even agree on which berimbau is the "gunga" (ibid.: 233, n. 3). Lewis also provides notation of some toques (ibid.: 146–151).

3. Regardless of the toque, the accompanying instrumentalists play the same rhythms; except in rare, esoteric instances, a difference in toque can be perceived only in the berimbaus' parts. Some mestres demand that the secondary instruments (the atabaque, reco-reco, and agogô) remain silent during certain toques or until after the ladainha, perhaps to avoid making it difficult to hear improvised lyrics.

4. The toque "Apanha Laranja no Chão Tico-Tico" ("Grab oranges from the ground, little bird") takes its onomatopoeic name from a song by the same name.

5. When Waldeloir Rego questioned mestres in the 1960s, they listed from seven to eighteen different toques. Only four names appeared on all the lists (1968: 59–62). When Kay Schaffer returned to the subject years later, however, she found that some of the mestres Rego had questioned could not recall how to play the toques that they had listed earlier (1981: 41–42). In addition, Shaffer discovered that practitioners used the same names to designate different rhythms; sometimes a single mestre even played the "same" toque in diverse ways in successive recording sessions.

6. In GCAP, some experienced musicians played especially difficult retards and improvised counterrhythms when seated next to another veteran, as if to test each other's musical skill. Preserving the music's implicit pulse could be difficult sitting shoulder-to-shoulder with someone pounding out particularly disruptive syncopations. These challenges were often treated as emotional highlights of playing in the orchestra, the musicians slyly smiling as they tried to disorient each other.

    This sort of competitive rhythmic play suggests that, in spite of Alfred Schutz's (1964) treatment of "being in time together" in music, the temporal relationship among ensemble members is not always synchrony (see Clifton 1983: 239–256). Charles Keil suggests that this productive tension, what he calls "participatory discrepancies," occurs widely in dynamic musical interaction (Keil 1987; cf. Keil and Feld 1994).

7. The use of "phantom" is an allusion to Elizabeth Behnke's (1997b) concept of "ghost gestures."

8. According to Alain Berthoz (2000: 214), neurologists have found that "listening to music has the same effect as singing or playing it," in terms of which areas of the brain are deployed. Berthoz suggests that music perception uses the same neurological mechanisms as performing it, although the brain inhibits action when a person is passively listening. In other words, movement is not perception with an additional, other element. Perception already implies action, inhibited or actual, as a result of human neural architecture.

9. This "other body" is not a specific person, but a generalized adversary's body (see Mead 1962: 14, 167). Gail Weiss (1999) elaborates on the concept of "intercorporeality," and both Mead and Alfred Schutz (1964: 160–162) posit a primary, bodily "conversation in gestures" through which individuals achieve a sense of self (see also Behnke 1997b: 194–195).

10. The theoretical contrast between *enskilment* and *enculturation* is taken from Tim Ingold (2000: 323), who draws on the work of Jean Lave (1990).

Chapter Seven

1. Paul Connerton uses the term "habit-memory" to discuss noncognitive remembering (1989: 22–25ff.; cf. Russell 1921; Bergson 1962). Júlio Tavares (1984) proposes a similar concept for capoeira, suggesting that the art forges the body of the adept into an *arquivo-arma*, an "archive-weapon," in which "the heritage of the Afro-Brazilian population" endures alongside oral traditions (ibid.: 71).

2. The terms "ludic" and "agonistic" are borrowed from Johan Huizinga (1955). Gregory Bateson (1972) and Erving Goffman (1986) discuss the concept of "frame."

3. Lowell Lewis (1992: 120) reports that this sequence was called a *chamada de mandinga* (sorcerer's call) or a *chamada de benção* or ("call of blessing," a reference to a kick called a "blessing"). Iria d'Aquino (1983: 58–60) indicates that she heard it referred to as *oferecendo golpe* or *balão fingindo* ("offering a blow" and "feint of a *balão*," a variety of throw or flip). Mestre Acordeon refers to the sequence as a *chamada de mão* (hand call) (U. Almeida 1986: 164), and Alejandro Frigerio (1989: 94) calls the sequence a *pedida de aú* (request for a cartwheel).

4. In his discussion of "Games within the Game," Lowell Lewis (1992: 121) includes the *dá volta ao mundo* (take a turn around the world) with his analysis of the chamada. When a player "takes a turn around the world," he or she stops playing and begins circling the inside of the roda at a jog. The other player follows. During this sequence, as with the chamada, "hostilities" can resume at any time. In some schools, players customarily do a chamada at the end of the "turn around the world."

5. In fact, both these distortions do occur. In folklore and theater presentations, performers often cooperate to do spectacular acrobatics. With the danger diminished—performers often stay so far apart that they cannot hit each other, even accidentally—many capoeiristas criticize "show" forms of capoeira as "folklorization," interesting only to the most inexperienced spectators, such as foreign tourists. In these settings, the chamada is too esoteric for the audience. Similarly, in efforts to turn capoeira into a sport, the chamada is also dropped. With it and other restraints removed, however, the sport versions of the practice can become excessively violent (cf. Downey 2002a).

6. The contribution of instrumental music to the lived roda is especially subtle. Ethnomusicologist John Blacking (1973: 27) has argued that "The essential quality of music is its power to create another world of virtual time," an observation that resonates with capoeira. For example, Mestre Moraes explained to a group of students that when we sing and play the berimbau, we summon our "ancestors"—fallen mestres like Pastinha,

Traíra, Bimba, and Waldemar. He joked that some players are surprised to find that they can do techniques in the roda that they are unable to do outside it. Moraes said that he knew better; the player in the roda was not the author of these movements. Music allowed capoeira ancestors to animate their descendants.

7. Mestre Pastinha also asserted that capoeira was once more sinister: "My friend, long ago a roda of capoeiristas was bitter; they were men without faith, one against the others, only thinking of how they might encourage the horror of their comrades . . ." (quoted in Decânio n.d.b.: 90).

8. The battles of the *capoeiras* may be evoked in song, for example, but there is no indication that a musical fight-game existed among nineteenth-century gang members. Early travelers' accounts of capoeira-like games among slaves portray challenge dances done to drums, not the berimbau (see A. Oliveira 1958: 48; Rego 1968: 58–59; U. Almeida 1986: 75–76; C. Soares 1994: 29–30). The roda probably developed out of African and Afro-Bahian dances, like the tripping games batuque or pernada (J. Moura 1980a, 1991; cf. Carneiro 1957: 90–94).

9. This phrasing borrows from Maurice Bloch (1989: 2).

Chapter Eight

1. On the malandro, see also the work of Antonio Cândido (1995), José Murilo de Carvalho (1989: esp. 27–28), and Luiz Sergio Dias (2001). One of the earliest malandros in literature, analyzed by Cândido, was Leonardo Filho, a principal character in Manuel Antônio de Almeida's *Memoirs of a Militia Sergeant* (1999). See also Robert Stam (1997: 335 ff.) on the malandro and *capoeiras* in Brazilian cinema.

2. Iris Young (1990: 142), similarly, discusses how feminine comportment should lead phenomenologists to consider "differentiation of the modalities of the lived body" (cf. Langer 1989: 173–174; Csordas 1993; Young 1998).

3. Nestor Capoeira, for example, titled one of his books *Capoeira: Os Fundamentos da Malícia* (N. Capoeira 1992; cf. Lewis 1992: 32–33 ff.; Browning 1995). In his discussion of Candomblé, Paul Johnson defines *fundamentos* as "secret, foundational matters" (2002: 4).

4. Some Brazilians did not use "malícia" in the same broad sense that capoeiristas did. However, the sense that cunning is a virtue is pervasive in Brazil (see DaMatta 1991; Barbosa 1995).

5. Roberto DaMatta (1985) contrasted "house" and "street" in the anthropology of Brazilian popular culture. According to DaMatta, the "house" is a realm of personal relationships, and the "street," a forum for impersonal, rule-defined interaction (cf. DaMatta 1986, 1995; Graham 1988). As Paul Johnson suggests (2002: 129), the "street" is also a space of

danger and violence in the Brazilian imagination (cf. Caldeira and Holston 1999; Caldeira 2000).

6. The contrast with other nations' heroic self-imagining can be marked. Historical conflicts in the United States, for example, are often recast as myths of fair competition in which superior ability prevails. Western gunfights, for instance, which often were treacherous, bullet-in-the-back affairs, are refigured as face-to-face showdowns. Capoeira conflicts are recounted as mythic cases of trickery.

7. The waist is not *necessarily* the phenomenal center of gravity, even though the abdomen may be a convenient place to experience a "center." Anyone who has struggled to teach students their "center" in Asian martial arts or dance knows well that this awareness is not automatic. Other physical disciplines train different parts of the body to become the phenomenal anchor for balancing. For example, coaches in sports requiring driving force from the legs, like American football and speed skating, focus on the thighs as a muscular organ of balance. In contrast, in ballet and jazz dance, instructors encourage dancers to use a visual target and line of sight to maintain balance when spinning. Other arts, like some South Asian forms of meditation, cultivate multiple centers or chakras to influence how practitioners inhabit their bodies.

8. Gilberto Freyre (1964, 1986c: 316), like DaMatta, attributes aspects of the Brazilian soccer style to capoeira's influence. Freyre suggests that the Brazilian state promoted soccer to displace *capoeiragem* (1964: s.p. [x]; cf. Rowe and Schelling 1991: 138).

9. The concepts of "disposition" and "comportment" are much like Antonio Damasio's (1999: 52–53) description of "background emotions," Iris Young's (1990) discussion of "styles" of bodily being, and Thomas Csordas's (1993) notion of "somatic mode of attention."

10. According to Muniz Sodré, Mestre Bimba, a legendary prizefighting champion, recommended without hesitation that a wise capoeirista should run from a fight, only stopping to stab an assailant, treacherously, if pursued:

> Bimba would say that "If the loud-mouth is really tough, you run—[the only thing that] endures a tempest is a cliff face." I think that his phrase is ingenious because it's a play with the idea of invincibility . . . everything has its limit. But Bimba also said: ". . . but if he runs after you, he's already abusing you. You stop suddenly and run him through the belly with a knife." (recounted by Muníz Sodre to Nestor Capoeira 1992: 132)

11. Young (1990: 189) describes Euro-American and Hindu models for locating the self in the chest in her discussion of the phenomenology of women's breasts (cf. Young 1998). Ironically, although her work deftly

explores the way that female and male bodies are lived differently, she does not draw attention to diverse styles of embodiment. Ethnographic research on different styles of bodily being would provide a valuable service to phenomenologists, who may otherwise overlook cultural variety in forms of embodiment (Weiss 1999: 20).

Chapter Nine

1. This discussion draws on the theory of affordances put forward by Eleanor Gibson (1982, 1988) and James Gibson (1977).

2. J. Lowell Lewis (1992: 80–82) offers an extensive discussion of the kinesthetic of "accommodation" in daily life in Bahia and in the roda.

3. One reason that skills are biomechanically necessary is that conscious thought is simply too slow to respond to the everyday exigencies of movement, such as balance and adjusting to other moving objects (Klein 2002; Libet 2002), let alone the heightened physical demands of an activity like capoeira. For a discussion of the neurological challenges posed by movement and the development of skills, see Bernstein (1996) and Berthoz (2000).

4. Although capoeiristas may raise concerns about vulnerability to obsessive heights, many theories of how the corporeal sense of self develops place suffering, its anticipation, and its avoidance at the center of this process (e.g., Merleau-Ponty 1968: 137 ff.). The way in which being struck in training creates an awareness of being open is similar to the phenomenology of pain. Pain results from damage to tissue and thus cannot anticipate injury well, or it would prevent it (Damasio 1999: 78). The heightened sensitivity of damaged tissue serves as a reminder and motivation to protect that flesh while it heals. Similarly, being "entered" in training causes a player to hold his or her body differently, shielding vulnerable areas as if they had become more sensitive to contact.

5. Recent studies of Candomblé in English include Michel Agier (1998), Dale Graden (1998), Rachel Harding (2000), Paul Johnson (2002), Reginaldo Prandi (2000), Robert A. Voeks (1997), and James Wafer (1991).

6. Practitioners and ethnographers are fiercely divided about whether Candomblé and capoeira are related. Waldeloir Rego (1968: 38), who studied both, writes: "In order to play the game of capoeira, nothing depends on elements from Candomblé." Numerous capoeiristas echoed this opinion, sometimes to allay parents' fears that their children would be religiously indoctrinated if they took capoeira classes. Other capoeiristas insisted, just as emphatically, that spirituality was a necessary part of capoeira practice. Margaret Wilson (2001: 32) found the relationship between Candomblé and capoeira at once "obvious but problematic," and suggests that it shifted over time, as the two once "protected each other" when they were persecuted.

7. For more discussion of initiation, see accounts by Barbara Browning (1995: 41, 118–119, 176, n. 7) and Paul Johnson (2002).

8. The imagery of bodily opening in Candomblé builds upon metaphors of sexual penetration, eating (a Brazilian metaphor for sexual intercourse), infection, or poisoning (Matory 1988; Wafer 1991; Johnson 2002). In contrast, the metaphor of entry in capoeira is grounded in an image of falling or being stabbed. Although the metaphors share similar roots in the body conceived of as a container (see Lakoff and Johnson 1980, 1999; Johnson 1987), their implications differ significantly.

9. Barros and Teixeira (1993, 30; quoted in Johnson 2002: 129) observe that an increasing number of noninitiates come to Candomblé terreiros in an effort to achieve "closed bodies," often against street violence. These peripheral participants follow a strategy similar to the one capoeiristas employ.

10. Frederico Abreu explained the abbreviation "P.D.N.S.J.Cristo," and this interpretation is based on discussions with him and his notes on the original text (in Coutinho 1993). The term "Cinco Salomão" probably derives from *Signo de Salomão*, a protective symbol frequently inscribed on berimbaus, *patuás* (protective amulets), and other capoeira-related objects. The importance of Solomon may arise from West African Muslim influences. For more information on patuá, see Luis da Camara Cascudo (1972: 686), Jair Moura (1971), and Marcelino dos Santos (1991: 17). On the specific links between Islam and magic in Brazil, João José Reis (1993: 98–99, 102–103) discusses the supernatural powers attributed to Muslims during the Revolt of the Malês in Salvador (cf. Cascudo 1972: 641).

11. Marcel Mauss (1973: 75) argues that instrumental, psychological, and magical dimensions of bodily techniques are often inextricably tied. One finds that in capoeira. For example, capoeiristas use the word *mandinga*, "sorcery," to describe both magic and movements, especially trickery or cunning feints. In many conversations, it is virtually impossible to tell if practitioners attribute supernatural powers to virtuoso players, or if they feel that the sly maneuvers ensorcell an adversary through distraction.

12. Although anthropologists discuss the "intersubjective" dimensions of human experience—that our sense of self is informed or generated by interacting with other people—the "inter-corporeality" of the body has been less well examined (cf. Jackson 1998). Maurice Merleau-Ponty (1962, 1968), James Ostrow (1990), and Gail Weiss (1999) analyze social bodily engagement.

Chapter Ten

1. Daniel Linger (1992: 4–5) suggests that Brazilians are especially concerned with dangerous face-to-face encounters in everyday life. Most

observers note that Brazil has high rates of violent crimes, although Teresa Caldeira (2000: 105–137) warns that these statistics are difficult to interpret and vary across neighborhoods. The Brazilian murder rate was twice as high as the United States in the 1980s (ibid.: 127) and often is ranked second, after Colombia, in Latin America (although police killings in Brazil account for a significant number of homicides). Capoeira heightens awareness of potential danger and provides distinct strategies for confronting it that require *increased* cunning engagement with the world. This comportment contrasts with many Brazilians' worries about safety, with the touchy explosiveness of the *machão*, or "big macho," discussed by Linger (1992), and with the wealthy who withdraw to "fortified enclaves" (Caldeira 2000: 256–296).

2. Scholars familiar with "practice theory" will recognize an overlap between the phenomena discussed here—habits, proclivities, dispositions, ways of perceiving—and the everyday behavior explored by Pierre Bourdieu (1977, 1990b). In brief, the perspective used in this chapter differs from Bourdieu's approach in that it does not assume that, underlying practice, there is a subterranean component, such as "tacit knowledge," "shared presuppositions," "hidden premises," or a "structuring structure" (see Turner 1994). Instead of a unified "structuring structure," this chapter suggests that capoeira resembles a loose assemblage of "miscellaneous" techniques, as described by Marcel Mauss (1973; cf. Hunter and Saunders 1995). Capoeira skills coalesce incompletely, sometimes with contradictions, as they train the adept's body with new abilities and habits.

3. The original text is free verse, almost every line beginning and ending with ellipses. The fragmentary format and dense punctuation suggest incomplete thoughts, interrupted ideas, things concealed or unspoken, and the searching nature of cunning itself. Even though the format is suggestive, in the interest of readability and space, Decânio's free verse is reproduced here as prose.

4. During a trip with GCAP in 1994, we stopped in a crowded bar to await a religious procession. Happy to secure a table on the patio, we all pulled up folding chairs. Paulinha, one of the group's contramestres, laughed and pointed out that all six or seven of us had crowded together on only one side of the table. No one chose to sit with back turned to the entrance. She joked that going out with a group of capoeiristas was "damn difficult" because everyone wanted to sit on the same side of a room.

5. The nickname "traíra" is a regional variant of *traidor*, traitor. Expressing a similar sentiment, Daniel Noronha wrote, "The law of the capoeirista is betrayal" (Coutinho 1993: 27). The adjective "traitorous" may be applied positively to capoeira techniques; an attack is "traitorous" if it catches an adversary off guard or cannot be anticipated.

6. Frederico Abreu first pointed out to the author the centrality of "brin-cadeira dura" in capoeira education.

7. Mestre Moraes did not give his students apelidos, although some al-ready had them when they enrolled in the group. Moraes claimed that nicknames were a *coisa de marginal*, a practice for hoodlums and toughs. For example, an academic colleague suggested that the police sometimes bestowed nicknames on suspects, particularly those killed during appre-hension, to make the suspect seem more shady and suspicious (cf. Dias 2001: 133 for a similar practice in an earlier period). The practice of nick-naming is widespread in Brazil, however, especially among athletes and public figures. Even the current president is known by a one-word nickname.

8. James Gibson (1979: 203) draws a distinction between "looking at" and "looking around," suggesting that, over time, people have come to live "boxed-up" visual lives:

> Our ancestors were always looking around. They surveyed the environ-ment, for they needed to know where they were and what there was in all directions. Children pay attention to their surroundings when allowed to do so. Animals must do so. But we adults spend most of our time *looking at* instead of *looking around*. In order to look around, of course, one must turn one's head. (emphasis in original)

Although the points here are overly simplified, Gibson draws our atten-tion to looking *behavior* and how it shapes what we see.

Anthropologists who study the senses, Tim Ingold (2000: 253; cf. 1998: 38–40) writes, tend to assume that the senses themselves are not subject to cultural modification. That is, a society may be "ocularcentric," or it may privilege hearing: "But just because here vision, or there touch or hearing, have been singled out as vehicles for symbolic elaboration, [anthropolo-gists assume that] this does not mean that people will see, hear or touch any differently in consequence" (ibid.: 283). In fact, capoeiristas can be almost as "ocularcentric" as western intellectuals, but they train their visual systems in significantly different ways. Similarly, one imagines the development of distinctive visual skills by professional photographers, trackers, birdwatchers, impressionist painters, physical therapists, pick-pockets, police interrogators, fossil hunters, jugglers, racecar drivers, and many other sorts of individuals.

9. Other sports also demand heightened or modified senses of sight. For example, "vision" is attributed to superstar running backs in American football or to playmakers in basketball with a talent for seeing team-mates open for passes all over the floor. Loïc Wacquant (2004: 87) dis-cusses how he had to learn to see when sparring in the boxing ring; he

had to anticipate an opponent's punches and see through the distractions of his own gloves and headgear.

10. Ratey (2001: 97–108) discusses the difference between geniculostriate (object and color recognition) and tectopulvinar (movement perception) neural pathways. In the phenomenon of "blindsight," a lesion that damages the brain's geniculostriate system leaves a person unaware that he or she can "see" any objects and unable to describe their color or other qualities. Victims can still pass diverse tests of visual–motor ability, however, such as picking up objects of which they are not "aware" when explicitly asked. Some even play basketball, although they insist they can't "see," apparently relying entirely on the tectopulvinar parts of the brain to orient action (see Weiskrantz 1986, 1997; Berthoz 2000: 51; cf. Gelder, de Haan, and Heywood, eds. 2001). In an experiment to test visual–motor control, Goodale and Humphrey (2001: 334) found that peripheral vision was as accurate at controlling grasping as vision near the fovea.

11. For more extensive discussion of perceptual learning and exploratory behavior, see the work of Eleanor J. Gibson (1963, 1988; cf. Fahle and Poggio 2002).

Chapter Eleven

1. Clandestine centers for instruction had existed in both Bahia and Rio de Janeiro since early in the twentieth century, including Bimba's earliest schools in the Roça do Lobo on Salvador's outskirts (L. Reis 1993: 63; Decânio 2001).

2. The passage appeared in *Diário da Bahia* (March 13, 1936) and is quoted by Raimundo Cesar Alves de Almeida (1994b: 24).

3. Jair Moura (1991: 27), citing an earlier source (1949), claims that Regional has 50 techniques, "22 of which were mortal if well-applied." Almeida's higher number may be justified because he (Mestre Itapoan) studied with Mestre Bimba after Moura, later in the ongoing development of Capoeira Regional, or it may be a result of inflation.

4. Some former students steadfastly assert that Mestre Bimba did not borrow any techniques. Mestre Itapoan, an indefatigable defender of Mestre Bimba, writes:

> For a long time I've heard talk that Mestre Bimba introduced strikes from jujitsu, judo, freestyle wrestling, and so on into his Capoeira Regional. What really happened was that in order to train his students against possible attacks from fighters employing these other modalities, he had to choose some "guinea pig techniques" to work on. . . . Many people who watched the training session, even some of the students, did not understand what had happened and thought that these were movements of Capoeira Regional. (R. Almeida 1994b: 93)

Mestre Bimba claimed that he introduced into Capoeira Regional moves derived mostly from *batuque*, a leg-kicking and tripping dance. Some scholars see batuque as an ancestor of modern capoeira. If so, then these borrowings are better understood as revival of practices fallen into disuse.

5. Barbara Browning asserts that syncretism and borrowing are essential dimensions of capoeira's "genius," rather than an "adulteration" of the art (1997: 73).

6. Mestre Pastinha benefited from similar patronage, but, as one observer pointed out, the number of students who took Mestre Bimba's course over his lifetime was several orders of magnitude greater than those trained by Mestre Pastinha.

7. The perception that Capoeira Regional was inherently violent might have arisen when Mestre Bimba's students were not restrained in public rodas, using their most aggressive techniques when other, more senior adepts engaged in a stylized duel of implied attacks. For example, they may have used hand techniques that Bimba created, like the *godeme*, a backhanded punch (which was christened when an American marine who had received one proclaimed "God damn it!"), or a cupped-hand blow called the "telephone" because it left the victim's ears ringing. Mestre Bimba drew a clear distinction between what was appropriate in a prizefight and in a traditional roda (J. Moura 1991: 21); his students may not have always been so careful.

8. From 1983 until 1987, Alejandro Frigerio conducted research among some of the same groups with which I later did fieldwork. Frigerio's academic arguments resembled "indigenous" criticisms of Capoeira Regional in these groups, as Luiz Vieira (1990: 106–110) observed. Charges of "embranquecimento" have a broader compass, however; the earliest I found was made in 1977 by André L. Lacé Lopes (quoted in Curvelo 1977; cf. Lopes 1984, 1994).

9. Frigerio elides the distinction between contemporary Capoeira Angola and "traditional capoeira," taking at face value practitioners' claims that their style is identical to past ways of playing.

10. Comte Joseph Arthur de Gobineau served as France's ambassador in Rio de Janeiro at the end of the 1850s. Gobineau's observations of mixed-race populations in Brazil contributed to his writings on racial theory. Certain that the children of mixed-raced unions would be weak and infertile within a few generations, Gobineau predicted that Brazil's population "would disappear, to the last man" within centuries unless a "healthy" influx of European immigrants were to arrive (quoted in Fry 2000: 86).

11. Both Jair Moura and Ângelo Decânio pointed to pictures of Mestre Bimba doing the ginga (e.g., J. Moura 1991: 19) that showed the mestre

swaying pronouncedly and maintaining a very low posture, in marked contrast to what some consider the stereotypical movement style of contemporary Capoeira Regional.

12. Many observers assert that capoeira academies served as what Ordep Serra called a "point of liquidation" between classes in Bahia, bringing people into contact and resocializing them into a shared physical culture (see Hermano Vianna [1999: 86 ff.] for a similar discussion of samba's social role). The result was a comportment, heavily influenced by "folk" or "popular" practices, which has since been treated as paradigmatically "Brazilian" (e.g., Stam 1997: 32). This has led many to value Afro-Brazilian contributions to Brazilian culture. Lélia Gonzalez (1982: 268), for example, exhorts readers to notice how *African* Brazilian bodily habits are: "Pay attention to this, to the relaxation, the ginga, the 'game of the waist' [jogo de cintura], this way of being so open, so marvelous that the Brazilian attributes to himself. People! This is a Black contribution to the formation of the Brazilian."

13. Norbert Elias (1978) describes how greater restraint emerged in European aristocratic circles as a badge of superior status:

> In court circles ... the growing compulsion to be restrained and self-controlled ... becomes also a "mark of distinction" that is immediately imitated below and disseminated with the rise of broader classes. And here, as in the preceding civilization-curves, the admonition "That is not done," with which restraint, fear, shame, and repugnance are inculcated, is connected only very late, as a result of a certain "democratization," to a scientific theory, to an argument that applies to all men equally, regardless of their rank and status. (ibid.: 159)

Ironically, restraint and inhibition appear to be the phenomenological foundation for a visceral sense of social superiority. Although it may grant great privilege, this poise constricts the body's potential for moving. This experiential dynamic might help explain why some middle-class practitioners strongly associate capoeira with "freedom," instead of traits like cunning or treachery that are more important to the practitioners with whom I worked: their personal experience of bodily liberation from powerful inhibitions is so compelling.

14. This also helps to explain why so many angoleiros started playing Capoeira Regional but later, as they came to appreciate the game's subtleties, converted.

Chapter Twelve

1. Some scholars believe that restrictions on using the hands are a legacy of slavery, either that slaves fought with their hands shackled (Dossar 1994: 75; Evleshin 1986: 7), or that, in mortal combat, only legs and head

proved sufficiently lethal weapons. Lowell Lewis (1992: 91) reports a number of these explanations. Daniel Dawson (1994a: 19) suggests that the restriction arose from a traditional African division of bodily labor, citing a proverb: "Hands are to build, feet are to destroy." Dawson also argues that the use of the head and legs to strike is characteristic of many Afro-Atlantic fighting arts, and thus a vestige of capoeira's African origins (1994b; cf. Thompson 1992: xiii).

2. Two variants of the rabo de arraia exist. The more common resembles what Mestre Bimba called a *meia-lua de compasso* ("compass half-moon," that is, a "half-moon" in which the legs turn like the arms of a compass). To do this arcing kick, the attacker doubles over and places both hands on the ground. The attacker looks, upside down, between the legs and, as the body revolves on the pivot foot, swings the heel of the trailing leg out. An archaic variant of the rabo de arraia required a *capoeira* suddenly to perform a handstand in front of an adversary so that the heels could be brought crashing down on a victim's head. Diagrams of the archaic variant appear in Anibal Burlamaque (1928: 24), Nestor Capoeira (1992: [179, the pages of diagrams are not enumerated]), and Lamaratine Pereira da Costa (1962: 73–74).

3. Although capoeiristas claim that the cabeçada is characteristic of *all* styles of the art, a video analysis by Mestre Lucas (Carlos 1994) revealed that it is seldom used in contemporary games. Of more than a thousand offensive techniques used in matches, the majority held outside Bahia, not one head butt was attempted (ibid.: 46). In contrast, in *every* roda at GCAP, players attempted multiple cabeçadas.

4. The "top" is sometimes called *parafuso* (screw). The names of movements are only included for their descriptive value. In fact, my instructors did not use them. I learned these names from published sources, only after practitioners in the United States asked me what these techniques were called.

5. For examples of this sort of interpretation, see Barbara Browning (1995, 1997), Ken Dossar (1994: 88, 95, 114), Lowell Lewis (1992: 83–84), Letícia Reis (1993: 217, 236–237), and Robert Farris Thompson (1988).

6. Dance scholar Maria da Conceição Castro Rocha (1985: 137) suggests that carrying loads atop the head prepares the spines of Afro-Bahian dancers, making them able to assume an exemplary uprightness of posture.

7. Luís de Câmara Cascudo (1976: 183–184) argued that Brazilians were slowly losing the capacity to rest in the cocorinha. Cascusdo alleged that changes in the built environment, including everything from street vendors' stalls to indoor plumbing, made the ability to squat no longer necessary. He implied that this obsolescence was relatively recent. Euclides da Cunha (1923), however, found the custom of squatting

among rural Brazilians remarkable as early as 1902, calling it "ridiculous and adorable" in his landmark work *Os Sertões*. One might conclude that Brazilian elites have long seen the cocorinha as an archaic custom when, in fact, laborers and rural residents still regularly use the ability.

Marcel Mauss (1973: 81) remarked that world cultures could be divided into those that do and do not rest squatting. Nearly every young child can rest in the cocorinha comfortably until, in some societies, disuse gradually makes the posture more and more awkward. Since the nineteenth century, biological anthropologists have suggested that habitually squatting can leave distinct patterns of bone development, including facets on the knee joints (see Rao 1966; Satinoff 1972). Repeated activity remodels the skeleton, just as it does softer tissue like muscle and tendons (cf. Ubelaker 1979; Kennedy 1998; Steen and Lane 1998). Theya Molleson (1989: 357) points out that an absence of squatting facets may make it almost impossible for people who normally sit in chairs to squat for any length of time. (Thanks to Susan Sheridan and Jamie Ullinger for their advice on studies of skeletal markers of activity-related stress.)

8. One of Mestre Pastinha's students described capoeira as a "feminine" martial art because it uses avoidance, trickery, and cunning. Although their bodies might be weaker, he said, women have a much easier time learning malícia; he felt that most already brought it with them to the roda. The question of gender and sexuality in capoeira, especially now that women have begun to practice in large numbers, is not easily addressed here, in part because it is changing. Presentations addressing "the woman in capoeira," became commonplace in the 1990s, focusing on sexism, health concerns, and the art's distinctive benefits for women. "Middle-class" "whitened" styles of the art created the space for the entry of women.

9. Acarajé is a signature Bahian dish sold by street vendors. A well-known corrido uses "dendê" to mean that something is appropriate for capoeira. For example, the "berimbau viola" or the "toque 'Angola'" have "dendê" if they are especially good.

10. The most persuasive evidence that a kinesthetic change wrought by capoeira might bring about social transformation, ironically, is the art's adoption by the Bahian middle and upper classes, the very process politicized angoleiros react against. Although critics may assail it as a "whitening" of the art, Capoeira Regional changed its elite adepts. For many, their apprenticeship led them to participate in street festivals, Afro-Bahian dance, and popular religion. Capoeirista Ângelo Decânio (n.d.a.: 110) describes the change:

> The implanting of capoeira in Brazilian society was an event that profoundly marked our youth, impregnating our imagination and comportment with

the suave African cultural essence! ... There was no acculturation of capoeira to our society; there was a transformation of society by the African philosophy contained in the rituals of capoeira and of Candomblé, the apparent origin of Afro-Brazilian culture!

Although these accounts run the risk of reinstating a romanticized view of Brazil as a "racial democracy," where shared culture breeds social harmony, I heard too many personal accounts and saw too much evidence of this process to simply ignore that this possibility existed.

BIBLIOGRAPHY

Abreu, Frederico. 1994. *Breves notícias sobre a iúna: Apontamentos* 1: 1–10 (pamphlet published by the Fundação Mestre Bimba, Salvador).

———. 1999. *Bimba é bamba: A capoeira no ringue.* Salvador, Brazil: Instituto Jair Moura.

Accurso, Anselmo da Silva. 1990. *Capoeira: Um instrumento de educação popular.* Unpublished manuscript, Universidade do Vale do Rio dos Sinos, São Leopoldo, Brazil.

Agier, Michel. 1998. "Between Affliction and Politics: A Case Study of Bahian Candomblé." In *Afro-Brazilian Culture and Politics: Bahia, 1790s to 1990s.* Edited by Hendrik Kraay. Armonk, NY: M. E. Sharpe, pp. 134–157.

Almeida, Manuel Antônio de. 1999 (1852–1853). *Memoirs of a Militia Sergeant.* Translated by Ronald W. Souza. New York: Oxford University Press.

Almeida, Raimundo Cesar Alves de (Mestre Itapoan). 1982. *Bimba: Perfil do mestre.* Salvador, Brazil: Centro Editorial e Didático da UFBA.

———. 1994a. "Ginga psíquica." *Negaça: Boletim da Ginga Associação de Capoeira* 2: 9–11.

———. 1994b. *A saga do Mestre Bimba.* Salvador, Brazil: Ginga Associação da Capoeira.

Almeida, Ubirajara (Mestre Acordeon). 1986. *Capoeira, A Brazilian Art Form: History, Philosophy, and Practice.* Berkeley, CA: North Atlantic Books.

———. 1999. *Água de beber, camará! Um bate-papo de capoeira.* Salvador, Brazil: EGBA.

Alter, Joseph S. 1992. *The Wrestler's Body: Identity and Ideology in North India.* Berkeley: University of California Press.

Alves-Silva, Juliana, Magda da Silva Santos, Pedro E. M. Guimarães, Alessandro C. S. Ferreira, Hans-Jürgen Bandelt, Sérgio D. J. Pena, and Vania Ferreira Prado. 2000. "The Ancestry of Brazilian mtDNA Lineages." *American Journal of Human Genetics* 67: 444–461.

Amado, Jorge. 1961 (1951). *Bahia de Todos os Santos: Guia das ruas e dos mistérios da Cidade do Salvador,* 9th ed. São Paulo: Livraria Martins Editôra.

Andrews, George Reid. 1991. *Blacks and Whites in São Paulo Brazil, 1888–1988.* Madison: University of Wisconsin Press.

Araujo, Rosângela Costa. 1994. "Profissões étnicas: A profissionalização da capoeira em Salvador." *Bahia: Análise & Dados: O Negro* 3(4): 30–32.

Areias, Almir das. 1983. *O que é capoeira.* São Paulo: Brasiliense.

Argyle, Michael, and Mark Cook. 1976. *Gaze and Mutual Gaze.* Cambridge: Cambridge University Press.

Asante, Molefi Kete. 1988. *Afrocentricity: The Theory of Social Change.* Buffalo, NY: Amulefi.

Azevedo, Thales de. 1953. *As elites de cor: Um estudo de ascensão social.* São Paulo: Companhia Editôra Nacional.

Babcock, Barbara A. 1984 (1977). "The Story in the Story: Metanarration in Folk Narrative." In *Verbal Art as Performance,* by Richard Bauman. Prospect Heights, IL: Waveland Press, pp. 61–79.

Baldwin, James Mark. 1901. *Dictionary of Philosophy and Psychology.* London: Macmillan.

Barber, Karin. 1989. "Interpreting Oriki as History and Literature." In *Discourse and Its Disguises: The Interpretation of African Oral Texts.* Edited by Karin Barber and P. F. de Moraes Farias. Birmingham, UK: University of Birmingham, African Studies Series, pp. 13–24.

Barbieri, Cesar. 1993. *Um jeito brasileiro de aprender a ser.* Brasília: DEFER, Centro de Informação e Documentação sobre a Capoeira (CIDOCA/DF).

Barbosa, Lívia Neves de H. 1995. "The Brazilian Jeitinho: An Exercise in National Identity." In *The Brazilian Puzzle: Culture on the Borderlands of the Western World.* Edited by David Hess and Roberto DaMatta. New York: Columbia University Press, pp. 35–48.

Barcelos, Luiz Claudio. 1999. "Struggling in Paradise: Racial Mobilization and the Contemporary Black Movement in Brazil." In *Race in Contemporary Brazil: From Indifference to Inequality.* Edited by Rebecca Reichmann. University Park: Pennsylvania State University Press, pp. 155–166.

Barros, José Flávio Pessoa de, and Maria Lina Leão Teixeira. 1993. "Corpo fechado/corpo curado." *Revista do Rio de Janeiro– Universidade do Estado do Rio de Janeiro* 1(2): 23–32.

Barthes, Roland. 1977. "The Grain of the Voice." In *Image-Music-Text.* Translated by Stephen Heath. New York: Noonday Press, pp. 179–189.

Barz, Gregory F., and Timothy J. Cooley, eds. 1997. *Shadows in the Field: New Perspectives for Fieldwork in Ethnomusicology.* New York and Oxford: Oxford University Press.

Basso, Keith H. 1984. "'Stalking with Stories': Names, Places, and Moral Narratives Among the Western Apache." In *Text, Play and Story.* Edited by Edward Brunner. Washington, DC: American Ethnological Society Publications, pp. 19–55.

———. 1989. "'Speaking with Names': Language and Landscape Among the Western Apache." *Cultural Anthropology* 3(2): 99–130.

———. 1996. *Wisdom Sits in Places: Landscape and Language Among the Western Apache.* Albuquerque: University of New Mexico Press.

Bastide, Roger. 1978 (1960). *The African Religions of Brazil: Toward a Sociology of the Interpenetration of Civilizations.* Translated by Helen Sebba. Baltimore: Johns Hopkins University Press.

Bastide, Roger, and Pierre Van den Berghe. 1957. "Stereotypes, Norms, and Interracial Behavior in São Paulo, Brazil." *American Sociological Review* 22: 689–694.

Bateson, Gregory. 1972. *Steps Toward an Ecology of the Mind*. New York: Ballantine.

Bauman, Richard. 1984 (1977). *Verbal Art as Performance*. Prospect Heights, IL: Waveland Press.

Baumann, Max Peter. 1997. "Preface: Hearing and Listening in Cultural Context." *World of Music* 39(2): 3–8.

Behnke. Elizabeth A. 1997a. "Body." In *Encyclopedia of Phenomenology*. Edited by Lester Embree et al. Dordrecht and Boston: Kluwer Academic Publishers, pp. 66–71.

———. 1997b. "Ghost Gestures: Phenomenological Investigations of Bodily Micromovements and Their Intercorporeal Implications." *Human Studies* 20: 181–201.

Benveniste, Emile. 1971 (1966). *Problems in General Linguistics*. Translated by Mary E. Meek. Coral Gables, FL: University of Miami Press.

Berger, John. 1972. *Ways of Seeing*. London: BBC and Penguin Books.

Bergson, Henri. 1962. *Matter and Memory*. Translated by N. M. Paul and W. S. Palmer. London: G. Allen & Unwin.

Bernstein, Nicholai A. 1996. "On Dexterity and Development." Translated by Mark L. Latash. In *Dexterity and Its Development*. Edited by Mark L. Latash and Michael T. Turvey. Mahwah, NJ: Lawrence Erlbaum Associates, pp. 1–244.

Berthoz, Alain. 2000 (1997). *The Brain's Sense of Movement*. Translated by Giselle Weiss. Cambridge, MA: Harvard University Press.

Blacking, John. 1973. *How Musical Is Man?* Seattle: University of Washington Press.

———. 1985. "The Context of Venda Possession Music: Reflections on the Effectiveness of Symbols." *Yearbook for Traditional Music* 17: 64–87.

Bloch, Maurice. 1989. *Ritual, History and Power: Selected Papers in Anthropology*. Atlantic Highlands, NJ: Athlone Press.

———. 1998. *How We Think They Think: Anthropological Approaches to Cognition, Memory, and Literacy*. Boulder, CO: Westview Press.

Bonates, Luiz Carlos (K. K.). 1999. *Iúna mandingueira: A ave símbolo da capoeira*. Manaus, Brazil: Instituto Jair Moura, Fenix.

Bourdieu, Pierre. 1977 (1972). *Outline of a Theory of Practice*. Translated by Richard Nice. New York: Cambridge University Press.

———. 1984 (1979). *Distinction: A Social Critique of the Judgement of Taste*. Translated by Richard Nice. Cambridge, MA: Harvard University Press.

———. 1990a. *In Other Words: Essays Towards a Reflexive Sociology*. Translated by M. Adamson. Stanford, CA: Stanford University Press.

———. 1990b (1980). *The Logic of Practice*. Translated by Richard Nice. Stanford, CA: Stanford University Press.

———. 2002. "Habitus." In *Habitus: A Sense of Place*. Edited by Jean Hillier and Emma Rooksby. Burlington, VT: Ashgate, pp. 27–34.

Bourdieu, Pierre, and Loïc Wacquant. 1999. "On the Cunning of Imperialist Reason." *Theory, Culture & Society* 16(1): 41–58.

Bretas, Marcos Luiz. 1989. "Navalhas e capoeiras: Uma outra queda." *Ciência Hoje* 10(59): 55–64.

———. 1991. "A queda do império da navalha e da rasteira (a república e os capoeiras)." *Estudos Afro-Asiáticos* 20: 239–256.

Brown, Diana De G. 1999. "Power, Invention, and the Politics of Race: Umbanda Past and Future." In *Black Brazil: Culture, Identity, and Social Mobilization.* Edited by Larry Crook and Randall Johnson. Los Angeles: UCLA Latin American Center Publications, pp. 213–236.

Brownell, Susan. 1995. *Training the Body for China: Sports in the Moral Order of the People's Republic.* Chicago: University of Chicago Press.

Browning, Barbara. 1995. *Samba: Resistance in Motion.* Bloomington: Indiana University Press.

———. 1997. "Headspin: Capoeira's Ironic Inversions." In *Everynight Life: Culture and Dance in Latin/o America.* Edited by Celeste F. Delgado and José E. Muñoz. Durham, NC: Duke University Press, pp. 65–92.

Bühler, Karl. 1990 (1934). *Theory of Language.* Translated by Donald Fraser Goodwin. Amsterdam and Philadelphia: John Benjamins.

Burdick, John. 1998. *Blessed Anastácia: Women, Race and Popular Christianity in Brazil.* New York: Routledge.

Burlamaqui, Anibal. 1928. *Gynástica nacional (capoeiragem) methodizada e regrada.* Rio de Janeiro: mimeograph.

Butler, Kim D. 1998a. "Afterword: *Ginga Baiana*—The Politics of Race, Class, Culture, and Power in Salvador, Bahia." In *Afro-Brazilian Culture and Politics: Bahia, 1790s to 1990s.* Edited by Hendrik Kraay. Armonk, NY: M. E. Sharpe, pp. 158–175.

———. 1998b. *Freedoms Given, Freedoms Won: Afro-Brazilians in Post-Abolition São Paulo and Salvador.* New Brunswick, NJ: Rutgers University Press.

"Cadê Pastinha?" *Tribuna da Bahia* (Salvador) (January 14, 1973): 5.

Caldeira, Teresa P. R. 2000. *City of Walls: Crime, Segregation, and Citizenship in São Paulo.* Berkeley: University of California Press.

Caldeira, Teresa P. R., and James Holston. 1999. "Democracy and Violence in Brazil." *Comparative Studies of Society and History* 41(4): 691–727.

Cândido, Antônio. 1995. *On Literature and Society.* Translated and edited by H. S. Becker. Princeton, NJ: Princeton University Press.

Capoeira, Nestor. 1985. *Galo já cantou: Capoeira para iniciados.* Rio de Janeiro: Cabicieri Editorial.

———. 1992. *Capoeira: Os fundamentos da malícia.* Rio de Janeiro: Editôra Record.

Carlos, Luiz (Mestre Lucas). 1994. "Rasteira já foi sinônimo de capoeira." *Negaça* 2: 45–47.

Carneiro, Edison. 1957. *A sabedoria popular.* Rio de Janeiro: Ministério da Educação e Cultura, Instituto Nacional do Livro.

Carpenter, Edmund. 1972. *Oh, What a Blow That Phantom Gave Me!* Toronto: Bantam Books.

———. 1973. *Eskimo Realities.* New York: Holt, Rinehart, & Winston.

Carpenter, Edmund, and Marshall McLuhan. 1960. "Acoustic Space." In *Explorations in Communication: An Anthology.* Edited by Edmund Carpenter and Marshall McLuhan. London: Beacon Press, pp. 65–70.

Carvalho, Jehová de. 1979. "Doce é morrer e depois virar um nome de rua." *A Tarde* (Salvador) (July 24, 1979) 2: 1.

Carvalho, José Murilo de. 1989. *Os bestializados: O Rio de Janeiro e a república que não foi.* São Paulo: Companhia das Letras.

Cascudo, Luis de Câmara. 1967. *Folclore do Brasil: Pesquisas e notas.* Rio de Janeiro: Editôra Fundo de Cultura.

———. 1972. *Dicionário do folclore brasileiro,* 3rd ed. Rio de Janeiro: Ediouro.

———. 1976. *História dos nossos gestos: Uma pesquisa na mímica do Brasil.* São Paulo: Edições Melhoramentos.

Casey, Edward S. 1987. *Remembering: A Phenomenological Study.* Bloomington: Indiana University Press.

Castedo, Leopoldo. 1964. *The Baroque Prevalence in Brazilian Art.* New York: Charles Franz Publications.

Chernoff, John Miller. 1979. *African Rhythms and African Sensibility: Aesthetics and Social Action in African Musical Idioms.* Chicago: University of Chicago Press.

———. 1997. "'Hearing' in West African Idioms." *World of Music* 39(2): 19–25.

Clark, Herbert H., and Richard J. Gerrig. 1990. "Quotations as Demonstrations." *Language* 66(4): 764–805.

Clifton, Thomas. 1983. *Music as Heard: A Study in Applied Phenomenology.* New Haven, CT: Yale University Press.

Connerton, Paul. 1989. *How Societies Remember.* New York: Cambridge University Press.

Costa, Eraldo Dias Moura (Mestre Medicina). 1969. "Capoeira." *Notícias Esportivas* (Salvador) 1: 24 (April 14, 1969): 27.

Costa, Lamaratine Pereira da. 1962. *Capoeira sem mestre.* Rio de Janeiro: Edições de Ouro.

Costa, Reginaldo da Silveira (Mestre Squisito). 1993. *O caminho do berimbau: Arte, filosofia e crescimento na capoeira.* Brasília: Thesaurus.

Coutinho, Daniel (Mestre Noronha). 1993. *O ABC da Capoeira Angola: os manuscritos do Mestre Noronha/Daniel Noronha.* Frederico José de Abreu, org. Brasília: DEFER, Centro de Informação e Documentação sobre a Capoeira (CIDOCA/DF).

Covin, David. 1990. "Afrocentricity in O Movimento Netro Unificado." *Journal of Black Studies* 21(2): 126–144.

Coy, Michael. 1989. "From Theory." In *Apprenticeship: From Theory to Method and Back Again.* Edited by Michael W. Coy. Albany: State University of New York Press, pp. 1–11.

Coy, Michael, ed. 1989. *Apprenticeship: From Theory to Method and Back Again.* Albany: State University of New York Press.

Crook, Larry N. 1993. "Black Consciousness, *samba reggae,* and the Re-Africanization of Bahian Carnival Music in Brazil." *World of Music* 35(2): 90–108.

Crook, Larry, and Randall Johnson. 1999. "Introduction." In *Black Brazil: Culture, Identity, and Social Mobilization.* Edited by Larry Crook and Randall Johnson. Los Angeles: UCLA Latin American Center Publications, pp. 1–13.

Crook, Larry, and Randall Johnson, eds. 1999. *Black Brazil: Culture, Identity, and Social Mobilization.* Los Angeles: UCLA Latin American Center Publications.

Cruz, José Luiz Oliveira. 1973. "Origem da Angola." *Tribuna da Bahia* (Salvador) (July 29, 1973): 8.

Csordas, Thomas J. 1990. "Embodiment as a Paradigm for Anthropology." *Ethos* 18(1): 5–47.

———. 1992. "Introduction: The Body as Representation and Being-in-the-World." In *Embodiment and Experience: The Existential Ground of Culture and Self.* Edited by Thomas J. Csordas. New York: Cambridge University Press, pp. 1–24.

———. 1993. "Somatic Modes of Attention." *Cultural Anthropology* 8(2): 135–156.

———. 1994. *The Sacred Self: A Cultural Phenomenology of Charismatic Healing.* Berkeley: University of California Press.

———. 1997. *Language, Charisma, and Creativity: The Ritual Life of a Religious Movement.* Berkeley: University of California Press.

———. 1999. "The Body's Career in Anthropology." In *Anthropological Theory Today.* Edited by Henrietta L. Moore. Cambridge: Polity Press, pp. 172–205.

Cunha. Euclides da. 1923 (1902). *Os sertões.* Rio de Janeiro: Livraria Francisco Alves.

Curvelo, Ivan. 1977. "Capoeira: A falta de rumos e o processo de embranqueci-mento." *Jornal dos Sports* (Rio de Janeiro) (April 24, 1977): s.p. (clipping without pagination).

Damasio, Antonio. 1999. *The Feeling of What Happens: Body and Emotion in the Making of Consciousness.* San Diego and New York: Harcourt.

DaMatta, Roberto. 1985. *A casa e a rua: Espaço, cidadania, mulher e morte no Brasil.* São Paulo: Brasiliense.

———. 1986. *O que faz o Brasil, Brasil?* Rio de Janeiro: Rocco.

———. 1991 (1979). *Carnivals, Rogues, and Heroes: An Interpretation of the Brazilian Dilemma.* Translated by J. Drury. Notre Dame, IN: University of Notre Dame Press.

———. 1993. "Brasil: Um belo jogo de cintura." *Correio da UNESCO* 21(2) (February 1993): 16–17.

———. 1995. "For an Anthropology of the Brazilian Tradition or 'A virtude está no meio." In *The Brazilian Puzzle: Culture on the Borderlands of the Western World.* Edited by David J. Hess and Roberto DaMatta. New York: Columbia University Press, pp. 270–292.

DaMatta, Roberto, Luiz Felipe Baeta Neves, Simoni Lahud Guedes, and Arno Vogel. 1982. *O universo do futebol: Esporte e sociedade brasileira.* Rio de Janeiro: Pinakotheke.

Daniel, E. Valentine. 1996. *Charred Lullabies: Chapters in an Anthropology of Violence.* Princeton, NJ: Princeton University Press.

D'Aquino, Iria. 1983. *Capoeira: Strategies for Status, Power, and Identity.* Ph. D. dissertation. Department of Anthropology, University of Illinois at Urbana-Champaign.

Dawson, C. Daniel. 1994a. "Capoeira: An Exercise of the Soul." In *Celebration: Visions and Voices of the African Diaspora.* Edited by Roger Rosen and Patra McSharry Sevastiades. New York: Rosen Publishing Group, pp. 13–28.

———. 1994b. "Capoeira: An Exercise of the Soul." Presentation made at the Primeiro Encontro Internacional da Capoeira Angola, the Grupo de Capoeira Angola Pelourinho, Salvador, Bahia (August 19, 1994).

———. 1996. Essay in the liner notes from Grupo de Capoeira Angola Pelourinho (CD) *Capoeira Angola from Salvador, Brazil.* Washington, DC: Smithsonian/Folkways Recordings SF CD 40465: 4–5.

Decânio, Ângelo. 2001. "Vim aquí falar de Bimba: História da Regional: Locais de treinamento e ensino/As sedes." Edited by "AADF." *Cordão Branco* 1(2): 14–15.

———. n.d.a. *A herança de Mestre Bimba: A filosofia e a lógica africanas da capoeira.* Manuscript.

———. n.d.b. *A herança de Pastinha: A metafísica da capoeira. Commentários de trechos selecionados do Mestre.* Manuscript.

———. n.d.c. *A herança de Mestre Bimba: A filosofia e a lógica africanas da capoeira.* An earlier version of the above-mentioned manuscript (n.d.a.).

De Casper, Anthony J., and Melanie J. Spence. 1986. "Prenatal Maternal Speech Influences Newborns' Perception of Speech Sounds." *Infant Behavior and Development* 9: 133–150.

Degler, Carl. 1986 (1971). *Neither Black nor White: Slavery and Race Relations in Brazil and the United States.* Madison: University of Wisconsin Press.

De Renzi, E., F. Cavalleri, and S. Facchini. 1996. "Imitation and Utilisation Behavior." *Journal of Neurology, Neurosurgery, and Psychiatry* 61(4): 396–400.

Desjarlais, Robert R. 1992. *Body and Emotion: The Aesthetics of Illness and Healing in the Nepal Himalayas.* Philadelphia: University of Pennsylvania Press.

———. 1997. *Shelter Blues: Sanity and Selfhood Among the Homeless.* Philadelphia: University of Pennsylvania Press.

Desmond, Jane C. 1997. "Embodying Difference: Issues in Dance and Cultural Studies." In *Everynight Life: Culture and Dance in Latin/o America.* Edited by Celeste F. Delgado and José E. Muñoz. Durham, NC: Duke University Press, pp. 33–64.

Devine, Heather. 1984. "The Workout: The Phenomenology of Training." *Phenomenology and Pedagogy* 2(2): 163–177.

Dewey, John. 1929. *Experience and Nature,* 2nd ed. Chicago: Open Court.

Di Pelligrino, G., Fadiga, L., Fogassi, L., Gallese, V., and Rizzolatti, G. 1992. "Understanding Motor Events: A Neurophysiological Study." *Experimental Brain Research* 91: 176–180.

Dias, Luiz Sergio. 2001. *Quem tem medo da capoeira?: Rio de Janeiro, 1890–1904.* Rio de Janeiro: Prefeitura da Cidade do Rio de Janeiro, Secretaria Municipal das Culturas, Departamento Geral de Documentação e Informação Cultural, Arquivo Geral da Cidade do Rio de Janeiro, Divisão de Pesquisa.

Donald, Merlin. 1991. *Origins of the Modern Mind: Three Stages in the Evolution of Culture and Cognition.* Cambridge, MA: Harvard University Press.

Dossar, Kenneth Michael. 1988. "Capoeira Angola: An Ancestral Connection?" *American Visions* 3(4): 38–42.

———. 1994. *Dancing Between Two Worlds: An Aesthetic Analysis of Capoeira Angola.* Ph.D. dissertation, Temple University, Philadelphia.

Douglas, Mary. 1966. *Purity and Danger: An Analysis of the Concepts of Pollution and Taboo.* Boston: Routledge & Kegan Paul.

———. 1970. *Natural Symbols: Explorations in Cosmology.* New York: Random House.

Dowling, W. Jay. 2001. "Perception of Music." In *Blackwell Handbook of Perception.* Edited by E. Bruce Goldstein. Malden, MA: Blackwell Publishers, pp. 469–498.

Downey, Greg. 2002a. "Domesticating an Urban Menace: Efforts to Reform Capoeira as a Brazilian National Sport." *International Journal of the History of Sport* 19(2): 1–32.

———. 2002b. "Listening to Capoeira: Phenomenology. Embodiment, and the Materiality of Music." *Ethnomusicology* 46(3): 487–509.

Dreyfus, Herbert L. 1967. "Why Computers Must Have Bodies in Order to Be Intelligent." *Review of Metaphysics* 21(1): 13–32.

———. 1991. *Being-in-the-World: A Commentary on Heidegger's 'Being and Time, Division I.'* Cambridge, MA: MIT Press.

Dunn, Christopher. 1992. "Afro-Brazilian Carnival: A Stage for Protest." *Afro-Hispanic Review* 11(1–3): 11–20.

Elias, Norbert. 1978 (1939). *The History of Manners. The Civilizing Process:* Vol. 1. New York: Pantheon Books.

Evleshin, Catherine. 1986. "*Capoeira* at the Crossroads." *UCLA Journal of Dance Ethnography* 10: 7–17.

Fahle, Manfred, and Tomaso Poggio, eds. 2002. *Perceptual Learning.* Cambridge, MA: MIT Press.

Feld, Steven. 1990. *Sound and Sentiment: Birds, Weeping, Poetics, and Song in Kaluli Expression,* 2nd ed. Philadelphia: University of Pennsylvania Press.

Feld, Steven, and Keith H. Basso, eds. 1997. *Senses of Place.* School of American Research Advanced Seminar Series. Sante Fe, NM: School of American Research Press.

Felix, Anísio. 1965. "Bimba x Pastinha: Duelo de idéias sobre capoeira." *Diário de Notícias* (Salvador, Bahia) (October 31 and November 1, 1965): 5.

Fernandes, Florestan. 1969. *The Negro in Brazilian Society.* New York: Columbia University Press.

Fernandez, James W., and Michael Herzfeld. 1998. "In Search of Meaningful Methods." In *Handbook of Methods in Cultural Anthropology.* Edited by H. Russell Bernard. Walnut Creek, CA: AltaMira (Sage), pp. 89–129.

Ferrara, Lawrence, and Elizabeth A. Behnke. 1997. "Music." In *Encyclopedia of Phenomenology.* Edited by Lester Embree et al. The Hague: Kluwer Academic Publishers, pp. 467–473.

Foley, John M. 1985. *Oral-Formulaic Theory and Research: An Introduction and Annotated Bibliography.* New York: Garland.

Foster, Susan Leigh. 1986. *Reading Dancing: Bodies and Subjects in Contemporary American Dance.* Berkeley: University of California Press.

———. 1992. "Dancing Bodies." In *Incorporations.* Edited by Jonathan Crary and Sanford Kwinter. New York: Zone, pp. 480–495.

Foucault, Michel. 1980. *Power/Knowledge: Selected Interviews & Other Writings: 1972–1977.* Edited by Colin Gordon. New York: Pantheon Books.

————. 1988. "Technologies of the Self." In *Technologies of the Self: A Seminar with Michel Foucault.* Edited by Luther Martin, Huck Gutman, and Patrick Hutton. Amherst: University of Massachusetts Press, pp. 16–49.

Freire, Roberto. 1967. "É luta, é dança, é capoeira." *Revista Realidade* (February, 1967): 79–82.

Freire, Roberto. 1990 (1977). "É luta, é dança, é capoeira." In *Viva eu, viva tu, viva o rabo do tatu,* 8th ed. São Paulo: Global Editora: 237–250.

Freitas, Décio. 1982. *Palmares: A guerra dos escravos,* 5th ed. Rio de Janeiro: Edições Graal.

French, John D. 2000. "The Missteps of Anti-Imperialist Reason: Bourdieu, Wacquant and Hanchard's *Orpheus and Power.*" *Theory, Culture, and Society* 17(1): 107–128.

Freyre, Gilberto. 1964. "Prefácio." In Mário Filho, *O negro no futebol brasileiro,* 2nd ed. Rio de Janeiro: Civilização Brasileira, pp. ix–xii.

————. 1986a (1933). *The Masters and the Slaves: A Study in the Development of Brazilian Civilization,* 2nd English ed. Translated by S. Putnam. Berkeley: University of California Press.

————. 1986b (1936). *The Mansions and the Shanties: The Making of Modern Brazil.* Translated by H. de Onís. Berkeley: University of California Press.

————. 1986c (1959). *Order and Progress: Brazil from Monarchy to Republic.* Translated by R. Horton. Berkeley: University of California Press.

Friedson, Steven M. 1996. *Dancing Prophets: Musical Experience in Tumbuka Healing.* Chicago: University of Chicago Press.

Frigerio, Alejandro. 1989. "Capoeira: De arte negra a esporte branco." *Revista Brasileira de Ciências Sociais* 4(10): 85–98.

Fry, Peter. 1982. *Para Inglês ver: Identidade e política na cultura brasileira.* Rio de Janeiro: Zahar Editores.

————. 1995. "O que a Cinderela negra tem a dizer sobre a 'política racial' no Brasil." *Revista USP* 28: 122–135.

————. 2000. "Politics, Nationality, and the Meanings of 'Race' in Brazil." *Dædalus* (Special Issue: *Brazil: The Burden of the Past; The Promise of the Future.*) Issued as Volume 129 (number 2) of the *Proceedings of the American Academy of Arts and Sciences* (Spring 2000): 83–118.

Ganem, Admon. 1948. "Coisas típicas da Bahia: A capoeira." *Revista da AABB* (Associação Atlética do Banco do Brasil) (September 1948): 13–21.

Geertz, Clifford. 1976. "Art as a Cultural System." *Modern Language Notes* 91: 1473–1499.

————. 1983. *Local Knowledge: Further Essays in Interpretive Anthropology.* New York: Basic Books.

————. 1984 (1974). "'From the Native's Point of View': On the Nature of Anthropological Understanding. In *Culture Theory: Essays on Mind, Self, and Emotion.* Edited by Richard A. Schweder and Robert A. LeVine. Cambridge: Cambridge University Press, pp. 123–136.

Gelder, Beatrice de, Edward H. F. de Haan, and Charles A. Heywood, eds. 2001. *Out of Mind: Varieties of Unconscious Processes*. Oxford and New York: Oxford University Press.

Geurts, Kathryn Linn. 2002a. *Culture and the Senses: Bodily Ways of Knowing in an African Community*. Berkeley: University of California Press.

———. 2002b. "On Rocks, Walks, and Talks in West Africa: Cultural Categories and an Anthropology of the Senses." *Ethos* 30(3): 1–22.

Gibson, Eleanor J. 1963. "Perceptual Learning." *Annual Review of Psychology* 14: 29–56.

———. 1982. "The Concept of Affordances in Development: The Renascence of Functionalism." In *The Concept of Development: The Minnesota Symposia on Child Psychology*, Vol. 15. Edited by W. Andrew Collins. Hillsdale, NJ: Lawrence Erlbaum Associates, pp. 55–81.

———. 1988. "Exploratory Behavior in the Development of Perceiving, Acting, and the Acquiring of Knowledge." *Annual Review of Psychology* 39: 1–41.

Gibson, James J. 1966. *The Senses Considered as Perceptual Systems*. Boston: Houghton Mifflin.

———. 1977. "The Theory of Affordances." In *Perceiving, Acting, and Knowing*. Edited by Robert E. Shaw and John Bransford. Hillsdale, NJ: Lawrence Erlbaum Associates, pp. 67–82.

———. 1979. *The Ecological Approach to Visual Perception*. Boston: Houghton Mifflin.

Gilroy, Paul. 1993. *The Black Atlantic: Modernity and Double Consciousness*. Cambridge, MA: Harvard University Press.

Goffman. Erving. 1986 (1974). *Frame Analysis: An Essay on the Organization of Experience*. Boston: Northeastern University Press.

Gonzalez, Lélia. 1982. "Alocução." *Estudos Afro-Asiáticos* 6–7: 267–268.

———. 1985. "The Unified Black Movement: A New State in Black Political Mobilization." In *Race, Class, and Power in Brazil*. Edited by Pierre-Michel Fontaine. Los Angeles: UCLA Center for Afro-American Studies, pp. 120–134.

Goodale, Melvyn A., and G. Keith Humphrey. 2001. "Separate Visual Systems for Action and Perception." In *Blackwell Handbook of Perception*. Edited by E. Bruce Goldstein. Malden, MA: Blackwell Publishers, pp. 311–343.

Goody, Esther N. 1989. "Learning, Apprenticeship and the Division of Labor." In *Apprenticeship: From Theory to Method and Back Again*. Edited by Michael W. Coy. Albany: State University of New York Press, pp. 233–256.

Graden, Dale T. 1998. "'So Much Superstition Among These People!': Candomblé and the Dilemmas of Afro-Bahian Intellectuals, 1864–1871." In *Afro-Brazilian Culture and Politics: Bahia, 1790s to 1990s*. Edited by Hendrik Kraay. Armonk, NY: M. E. Sharpe, pp. 57–73.

Graham, Sandra Lauderdale. 1988. *House and Street: The Domestic World of Servants and Masters in Nineteenth-Century Rio de Janeiro*. Cambridge: Cambridge University Press.

Grupo de Capoeira Angola Pelourinho (GCAP). 1989. "Capoeira Angola/ Resistência negra." *Exu* 11: 33–41.

———. 1993. *GCAP: 10 anos gingando na mesma luta. VII Oficina e Mostra de Capoeira Angola.* Salvador, Brazil: Comissão de Documentação e Acervo (GCAP).
———. 1994. *O Universo Musical da Capoeira.* Salvador, Brazil: Comissão de Documentação e Acervo (GCAP). [cited version without pagination]
———. 1996. Liner notes from CD *Capoeira Angola from Salvador, Brazil.* Washington, DC: Smithsonian/Folkways Recordings SF CD 40465.
Grupo de Capoeira Angola Pelourinho, Rio de Janeiro nucleus (GCAP/Rio). n.d. "Grupo de Capoeira Angola Pelourinho." Photocopied pamphlet.
Guillermoprieto, Alma. 1990. *Samba.* New York: Alfred A. Knopf.
Hanchard, Michael. 1993. "Culturalism Versus Cultural Politics: *Movimento Negro* in Rio de Janeiro and São Paulo, Brazil." In *The Violence Within: Cultural and Political Opposition in Divided Nations.* Edited by Kay Warren. Boulder, CO: Westview Press, pp. 57–85.
———. 1994. *Orpheus and Power: The Movimento Negro of Rio de Janeiro and São Paulo, Brazil, 1945–1988.* Princeton, NJ: Princeton University Press.
———. 1999. "Introduction." In *Racial Politics in Contemporary Brazil.* Edited by Michael Hanchard. Durham, NC: Duke University Press, pp. 1–29.
Hanchard, Michael, ed. 1999. *Racial Politics in Contemporary Brazil.* Durham, NC: Duke University Press.
Hanks, William F. 1990. *Referential Practice: Language and Lived Space Among the Maya.* Chicago: University of Chicago Press.
———. 1996. *Language and Communicative Practices.* Boulder, CO: Westview Press.
Hardin, C. L. 1988. *Color for Philosophers: Unweaving the Rainbow,* expanded ed. Indianapolis: Hackett Publishing.
Harding, Rachel. 2000. *A Refuge in Thunder: Candomblé and Alternative Spaces of Blackness.* Bloomington: Indiana University Press.
Harris, Marvin. 1952. "Race Relations in Minas Velhas, a Community in the Mountain Region of Brazil." In *Race and Class in Rural Brazil.* Edited by Charles Wagley. Paris: UNESCO, pp. 47–81.
———. 1964. "Racial Identity in Brazil." *Luso-Brazilian Review* 1: 21–28.
———. 1970. "Referential Ambiguity in the Calculus of Brazilian Racial Identity." *Southwestern Journal of Anthropology* 26: 1–14.
Harris, Marvin, Josildeth Gomes Consorte, Joseph Lang, and Bryan Byrne. 1993. "Who Are the Whites? Imposed Census Categories and the Racial Demography of Brazil." *Social Forces* 72(2): 451–462.
———. 1995. "A Reply to Telles—Who Are the Morenas?" *Social Forces* 73(4): 1613–1614.
Hasenbalg, Carl. 1985. "Race and Socioeconomic Inqualities in Brazil." In *Race, Class, and Power in Brazil.* Edited by Pierre-Michel Fontaine. Los Angeles: UCLA Center for Afro-American Studies, pp. 25–41.
Haviland, John B. 1996. "Projections, Transpositions, and Relativity." In *Rethinking Linguistic Relativity.* Edited by John J. Gumperz and Stephen C. Levinson. Cambridge and New York: Cambridge University Press, pp. 271–323.

Heidegger, Martin. 1971a. *Poetry, Language, Thought*. Translated by Albert Hofstader. New York: Harper & Row.

———. 1971b. (1959). *On the Way to Language*. New York: Harper & Row.

———. 1996. *Being and Time*. Translated by Joan Stambaugh. Albany: State University of New York Press.

Hellwig, David J., ed. 1992. *African-American Reflections on Brazil's Racial Paradise*. Philadelphia: Temple University Press.

Herman, Vimala. 1999. "Deictic Projection and Conceptual Blending in Epistolarity." *Poetics Today* 20(3): 523–541.

Holloway, Thomas H. 1989. "'A Healthy Terror': Police Repression of *Capoeiras* in Nineteenth-Century Rio de Janeiro." *Hispanic American Historical Review* 69(4): 637–676.

———. 1993. *Policing Rio de Janeiro: Repression and Resistance in a 19th Century City*. Stanford, CA: Stanford University Press.

Huizinga, Johan. 1955. *Homo Ludens*. Boston: Beacon Press.

Hunter, Ian, and David Saunders. 1995. "Walks of Life: Mauss on the Human Gymnasium." *Body & Society* 1(2): 65–81.

Husserl, Edmund. 1970. *The Crisis of European Sciences and Transcendental Philosophy: An Introduction to Phenomenological Philosophy*. Translated by David Carr. Evanston, IL: Northwestern University Press.

———. 1989. *Ideas Pertaining to a Pure Phenomenology and to a Phenomenological Philosophy, Second Book*. Translated by R. Rojcewicz and A. Schuwer. Dordrecht: Kluwer Academic Publishers.

IJsseling, Samuel. 1997. *Mimesis: On Appearing and Being*. Kampen, the Netherlands: Kok Pharos Publishing.

Ingarden, Roman. 1973 (1965). *The Literary Work of Art: An Investigation on the Borderlines of Ontology, Logic and Theory of Literature*. Translated by George G. Grabowicz. Evanston, IL: Northwestern University Press.

Ingold, Tim. 1991. "Becoming Persons: Consciousness and Sociality in Human Evolution." *Cultural Dynamics* 4(3): 355–378.

———. 1998. "From Complementarity to Obviation: On Dissolving the Boundaries Between Social and Biological Anthropology, Archaeology and Psychology." *Zeitschrift für Ethnologie* 123(1): 21–52.

———. 2000. *The Perception of the Environment: Essays in Livelihood, Dwelling and Skill*. London and New York: Routledge.

Jackson, Michael. 1989. *Paths Toward a Clearing: Radical Empiricism and Ethnographic Inquiry*. Bloomington: Indiana University Press.

———. 1995. *At Home in the World*. Durham, NC: Duke University Press.

———. 1998. *Minima Ethnographica: Intersubjectivity and the Anthropological Project*. Chicago: University of Chicago Press.

Jackson, Michael, ed. 1996. *Things as They Are: New Directions in Phenomenological Anthropology*. Bloomington: Indiana University Press.

Jakobson, Roman. 1971. "Shifters, Verbal Categories, and the Russian Verb." In *Selected Writings*, Vol. 2, *Word and Language*, pp. 130–147. The Hague: Mouton.

Jeannerod, Marc. 1994. "The Representing Brain: Neural Correlates of Motor Intention and Imagery." *Behavioral and Brain Sciences* 17: 187–245.

Jenkins, Timothy. 1994. "Fieldwork and the Perception of Everyday Life." *Man* (n.s.) 29(2): 433–455.

Jespersen, Ejgil. 1997. "Modeling in Sporting Apprenticeship: The Role of the Body Itself Is Attracting Attention." *Nordisk Pedagogik* 17(3): 178–185.

Jespersen, Otto. 1965 (1924). *The Philosophy of Grammar*. New York: W. W. Norton.

Johnson, Mark. 1987. *The Body in the Mind: The Bodily Basis of Meaning, Imagination, and Reason*. Chicago: University of Chicago Press.

Johnson, Paul Christopher. 2002. *Secrets, Gossip, and Gods: The Transformation of Brazilian Candomblé*. Oxford: Oxford University Press.

Keil, Charles. 1987. "Participatory Discrepancies and the Power of Music." *Cultural Anthropology* 2(3): 275–283. Reprinted in *Music Grooves*, C. Keil and S. Feld. Chicago: University of Chicago Press, pp. 96–108.

Keil, Charles, and Steven Feld. 1994. *Music Grooves: Essays and Dialogues*. Chicago: University of Chicago Press.

Kennedy, Kenneth A. R. 1998. "Markers of Occupational Stress: Conspectus and Prognosis of Research." *International Journal of Osteoarchaeology* 8: 305–310.

Kent, R. K. 1979. "Palmares: An African State in Brazil." In *Maroon Societies: Rebel Slave Communities in the Americas*, 2nd ed. Edited by R. Price. Baltimore: Johns Hopkins University Press, pp. 170–190.

Klein, Stanley. 2002. "Libet's Timing of Mental Events: Commentary on the Commentaries." *Consciousness and Cognition* 11(2): 326–333.

Kottak, Conrad. 1990. *Prime-Time Society: An Anthropological Analysis of Television and Culture*. Belmont, CA: Wadsworth Publishers.

Kubik, Gerhard. 1979. *Angolan Traits in Black Music, Games, and Dances of Brazil: A Study of African Cultural Extensions Overseas*. Lisbon: Centro de Estudos de Antropologia Cultural.

Lakoff, George, and Mark Johnson. 1980. *Metaphors We Live By*. Chicago: University of Chicago Press.

———. 1999. *Philosophy in the Flesh: The Embodied Mind and Its Challenge to Western Thought*. New York: Basic Books.

Langer, Monika M. 1989. *Merleau-Ponty's Phenomenology of Perception: A Guide and Commentary*. Tallahassee: Florida State University Press.

Lave, Jean. 1977. "Cognitive Consequences of Traditional Apprenticeship Training in West Africa." *Anthropology and Education Quarterly* 8: 177–180.

———. 1982. "A Comparative Approach to Educational Forms and Learning Processes." *Anthropology and Education Quarterly* 13: 181–188.

———. 1988. *Cognition in Practice*. Cambridge and New York: Cambridge University Press.

———. 1990. "The Culture of Acquisition and the Practice of Understanding." In *Cultural Psychology: Essays on Comparative Human Development*. Edited by J. W. Stigler, R. A. Shweder, and G. Herdt. Cambridge: Cambridge University Press, pp. 309–327.

Leder, Drew. 1990. *The Absent Body*. Chicago: University of Chicago Press.

Lemle, Marina. n.d. "30 anos de capoeira senzala." (newspaper clipping without publishing information or pagination, published in the early 1990s)

Lewis, J. Lowell. 1992. *Ring of Liberation: Deceptive Discourse in Brazilian Capoeira.* Chicago: University of Chicago Press.

———. 1995. "Genre and Embodiment: From Brazilian *Capoeira* to the Ethnology of Human Movement." *Cultural Anthropology* 10(2): 221–243.

Lhermitte, F., B. Pillon, and M. Serdaru. 1986. "Human Anatomy and the Frontal Lobes. Part 1. Imitation and Utilisation Behavior: A Neuropsychological Study of 75 Patients." *Annals of Neurology* 19(4): 326–334.

Libet, Benjamin. 2002. "The Timing of Mental Events: Libet's Experimental Findings and Their Implications." *Consciousness and Cognition* 11(2): 291–299.

Linger, Daniel Touro. 1992. *Dangerous Encounters: Meaning of Violence in a Brazilian City.* Stanford, CA: Stanford University Press.

Llinás, Rodolfo R. 2001. *I of the Vortex: From Neurons to Self.* Cambridge, MA: MIT Press.

Lock, Andrew. 1980. *The Guided Reinvention of Language.* London: Academic Press.

Lock, Margaret. 1993. "Cultivating the Body: Anthropology and Epistemologies of Bodily Practice and Knowledge." *Annual Review of Anthropology* 22: 133–155.

Lopes, André Luiz Lacé. 1984. "O embranquecimento da capoeira." *Pasquim* (September 27– October 3, 1984): 8–9.

———. 1994. *Administração Esportiva, inclui a mandinga da capoeira; Admininstração Pública e outras administrações.* Rio de Janeiro & Brasília: DEFER, Centro de Informação e Documentação sobre a Capoeira (CIDOCA/DF).

Lord, Albert B. 1960. *The Singer of Tales.* Cambridge, MA: Harvard University Press.

Machado, Manuel dos Reis (Mestre Bimba). 1989. *Curso de Capoeira Regional: Mestre Bimba.* RC Discos/Fita (booklet that accompanied record *Curso de Capoeira Regional: Mestre Bimba*).

Maio, Marcos Chor. 2001. "UNESCO and the Study of Race Relations in Brazil: Regional or National Issue?" *Latin American Research Review* 36(2): 118–136.

Martin, Luther H., Huck Gutman, and Patrick H. Hutton, eds. 1988. *Technologies of the Self: A Seminar with Michel Foucault.* Amherst: University of Massachusetts Press.

Martin, Richard P. 1989. *The Language of Heroes: Speech and Performance in the Iliad.* Ithaca, NY: Cornell University Press.

Marx, Anthony W. 1998. *Making Race and Nation: A Comparison of South Africa, the United States, and Brazil.* Cambridge: Cambridge University Press.

Matory, J. Lorand. 1988. "Homens montados: Homossexualidade e simbolismo da possessão nas religiões afro-brasileiras." In *Escravidão e invenção da liberdade: Estudos sobre o negro no Brasil.* Edited by João José Reis. São Paulo: Brasiliense, pp. 215–231.

Matos, Cláudia Neiva de. 1982. *Acertei no milhar: Malandragem e samba no tempo de Getúlio.* Rio de Janeiro: Paz e Terra.

Mattos, Florisvaldo. 1967. "Capoeira, uma arte sem auxílio." *Jornal do Brasil,* (Rio de Janeiro) (June 30, 1967), B: 1.

Mauss, Marcel. 1973 (1935). "Techniques of the Body." Translated by B. Brewster. *Economy and Society* 2(1): 70–87.

Mazzei, Raymundo. 1979. "Pastinha: 90 anos, cego, mas ainda um mestre da capoeira." *O Globo* (May 2, 1979): 32.

Mead, George Herbert. 1962 (1934). *Mind, Self, and Society, from the Standpoint of a Social Behaviorist.* Chicago: University of Chicago Press.

Meltzoff, Andrew N., and M. Keith Moore. 1983. "Newborn Infants Imitate Adult Facial Gestures." *Child Development* 54: 702–709.

———. 1999. "Persons and Representation: Why Infant Imitation Is Important for Theories of Human Development." In *Imitation in Infancy.* Edited by Jacqueline Nadel and George Butterworth. Cambridge and New York: Cambridge University Press, pp. 9–35.

Merleau-Ponty, Maurice. 1962. *Phenomenology of Perception.* Translated by Colin Smith. London: Routledge.

———. 1964. *The Primacy of Perception, and Other Essays on Phenomenological Psychology, the Philosophy of Art, History and Politics.* Edited by James M. Edie. Evanston, IL: Northwestern University Press.

———. 1968 (1964). *The Visible and the Invisible.* Translated by Alphonso Lingis. Edited by Claude Lefort. Evanston, IL: Northwestern University Press.

"Mestre Pastinha pede ajuda—antes que seja tarde demais." *Tribuna da Bahia* (Salvador) (September 15, 1981): 9.

Mitchell, Michael J., and Charles H. Wood. 1999. "Ironies of Citizenship: Skin Color, Police Brutality, and the Challenge of Democracy in Brazil." *Social Forces* 77(3): 1001–1020.

Mohanty, Jitendranath. 1972. *The Concept of Intentionality.* St. Louis: Warren H. Green.

———. 1985. "Intentionality and the Mind–Body Problem." In *The Possibility of Transcendental Philosophy.* Edited by Dordrecht: Nijhoff, pp. 121–138.

Molleson, Theya. 1989. "Seed Preparation in the Mesolithic: The Osteological Evidence." *Antiquity* 63: 356–362.

Morley, James. 2001. "Inspiration and Expiration: Yoga Practice Through Merleau-Ponty's Phenomenology of the Body." *Philosophy East & West* 51(1): 73–82.

Moura, Clóvis. 1981. *Rebelões da senzala: Quilombos insurreições guerrilhas.* São Paulo: Ciências Humanas.

Moura, Jair. 1971. "Capoeirista de antigamente não 'brincava em serviço.'" *A Tarde* (Salvador) (July 10, 1971): 2.

———. 1980a. *Capoeira: A Luta Regional Baiana.* Cadernos de Cultura No 1. Salvador, Bahia: Secretaria Municipal de Educação e Cultura, Departamento de Assuntos Culturais, Divisão de Folclore.

———. 1980b. *Capoeiragem: Arte & malandragem.* Cadernos de Cultura No 2. Salvador, Bahia: Secretaria Municipal de Educação e Cultura, Departamento de Assuntos Culturais, Divisão de Folclore.

———. 1985. "Evolução, apogeu e declínio da capoeira no Rio de Janeiro." *Caderno RioArte* 1(3): 86–93.

BIBLIOGRAPHY 253

―――. 1991. *Mestre Bimba: A crônica da capoeiragem*. Salvador, Brazil: Zumbimba.

Nadel, Jacqueline, and George Butterworth, eds. 1999. *Imitation in Infancy*. Cambridge and New York: Cambridge University Press.

Ness, Sally Ann. 1992. *Body, Movement, and Culture: Kinesthetic and Visual Symbolism in a Philippine Community*. Philadelphia: University of Pennsylvania Press.

―――. 1996. "Dancing in the Field: Notes from Memory." In *Dancing Knowledge, Culture and Power*. Edited by Susan Leigh Foster. New York: Routledge, pp. 129–154.

"No Pelourinho, um homen doente e cego, é mestre Pastinha: A história se repete." *Tribuna da Bahia* (Salvador) (October 20, 1979) 2: 11.

Novack, Cynthia J. 1990. *Sharing the Dance: Contact Improvisation and American Culture*. Madison: University of Wisconsin Press.

Oliveira, Albano Marinho de. 1958. *Berimbau: O arco musical da capoeira*. Salvador, Brazil: Comissão Bahiana de Folclore.

Oliveira, José Luis (Mestre Bola Sete). 1989. *A capoeira Angola na Bahia*. Salvador, Brazil: EGBA/Fundação das Artes.

Oliveira, Valdemar de. 1971. *Frevo, capoeira e passo*. Recife, Brazil: Companhia Editôra de Pernambuco.

Oliven, Ruben George. 1984. "A malandragem na música popular brasileira." *Latin American Music Review* 5(1): 66–96.

Ortiz, Renato. 1978. *A morte branca do feiticeiro negro; Umbanda: Integração de uma religião numa sociedade de classes*. Petrópolis, Brazil: Editôra Vozes.

―――. 1985. *Cultura brasileira e identidade nacional*, 3rd ed. São Paulo: Editôra Brasiliense.

Ostrow, James. 1990. *Social Sensitivity: A Study of Habit and Experience*. Albany: State University of New York Press.

Otts, Thomas. 1990. "The Angry Liver, the Anxious Heart and the Melancholy Spleen: The Phenomenology of Perceptions in Chinese Culture." *Culture, Medicine and Psychiatry* 14: 21–58.

―――. 1994. "The Silenced Body—The Expressive *Leib*: On the Dialectic of Mind and Life in Chinese Cathartic Healing." In *Embodiment and Experience: The Existential Ground of Self*. Edited by Thomas Csordas. New York: Cambridge University Press, pp. 116–136.

Oyama, Susan. 1985. *The Ontogeny of Information: Developmental Systems and Evolution*. Cambridge and New York: Cambridge University Press.

―――. 2000. *Evolution's Eye: A Systems View of the Biology–Culture Divide*. Durham, NC: Duke University Press.

Parra, Flavia C., Roberto C. Amado, José R. Lambertucci, Jorge Rocha, Carlos M. Antunes, and Sérgio D. J. Pena. 2003. "Color and Genomic Ancestry in Brazilians." *Proceedings of the National Academy of Sciences* 100(1): 177–182.

Parry, Adam. 1956. "The Language of Achilles." *TAPA* 87: 1–7.

―――. 1981. *Logos and Ergon in Thucydides*. Reproduction of Harvard Ph.D. dissentation, 1957, with introduction by D. Kagan. New York: Arno.

Parry, Milman. 1971. *The Making of Homeric Verse: The Collected Papers of Milman Parry.* Edited by Adam Parry. Oxford: Oxford University Press.

Pastinha, Vincente Ferreira (Mestre Pastinha). 1988 (1964). *Capoeira Angola,* 3rd ed. Salvador, Brazil: Fundação Cultural do Estado da Bahia.

"Pastinha chega aos 78 anos numa cadeira de rodas vendo cair a tarde no Pelourinho." *Jornal da Bahia* (Salvador) (August 10, 1966) 2: (incomplete pagination).

Penalva, Ruy. 1973. "A solidão do mestre." *Tribuna da Bahia* (Salvador) (July 19, 1973): 8.

Pereira, Carlos (Charles), and Mônica Carvalho. 1992. *Cantos e ladainhas da capoeira da Bahia.* Salvador, Brazil: Edições Via Bahia.

Perrone, Charles A. 1992. "Axé, Ijexá, Olodum: The Rise of Afro- and African Currents in Brazilian Popular Music." *Afro-Hispanic Review* 9(1–3): 42–50.

Pierson, Donald. 1967 (1942). *Negroes in Brazil: A Study of Race Contact at Bahia.* Carbondale, IL: Southern Illinois University Press.

Pires, Antônio Liberac Cardoso Simões. 2002. *Bimba, Pastinha e Besouro de Mangangá: Três personagems da capoeira baiana.* 2nd ed. Tocantins and Goiana, Brazil: NEAB/Grafset.

Piza, Edith, and Fúlvia Rosemberg. 1999. "Color in the Brazilian Census." In *Race in Contemporary Brazil: From Indifference to Inequality.* Edited by Rebecca Reichmann. University Park: Pennsylvania State University Press, pp. 37–52.

Póvoas, Ruy do Carmo. 1989. *A linguagem do Candomblé: Níveis sociolingüísticos de integração afro-portuguesa.* Rio de Janeiro: José Olímpico.

Prandi, Reginaldo. 2000. "African Gods in Contemporary Brazil: A Sociological Introduction to Candomblé Today." *International Journal of Sociology* 15(4): 641–664.

Rao, P. D. Prasada. 1966. "Squatting Facets on the Talus and Tibia in Australian Aborigines." *Archaeology and Physical Anthropology in Oceania* 2: 51–56.

Ratey, John J. 2001. *A User's Guide to the Brain: Perception, Attention, and the Four Theaters of the Brain.* New York: Vintage Books.

Reed, Edward S., and Blandine Bril. 1996. "The Primacy of Action in Development." In *Dexterity and Its Development.* Edited by Mark L. Latash and Michael T. Turvey. Mahwah, NJ: Lawrence Erlbaum Associates, pp. 431–451.

Rego, Waldeloir. 1968. *Capoeira Angola: Ensaio sócio-etnográfico.* Salvador, Brazil: Editôra Itapuã.

Reichmann, Rebecca. 1999. "Introduction." In *Race in Contemporary Brazil: From Indifference to Inequality.* Edited by Rebecca Reichmann. University Park: Pennsylvania State University Press, pp. 1–35.

Reichmann, Rebecca, ed. 1999. *Race in Contemporary Brazil: From Indifference to Inequality.* University Park: Pennsylvania State University Press.

Reily, Suzel Ana. 2002. *Voices of the Magi: Enchanted Journeys in Southeast Brazil.* Chicago: University of Chicago Press.

Reis, João José. 1993 (1986). *Slave Rebellion in Brazil: The Muslim Uprising of 1835 in Bahia.* Translated by A. Brakel. Baltimore: Johns Hopkins University Press.

Reis, Letícia Vidor de Sousa. 1993. *Negros e brancos no jogo da capoeira: A reinvenção da tradição.* Master's thesis: Universidade de São Paulo.

Risério, Antonio. 1981. *Carnaval Ijexá: Notas sobre afoxés e blocos de novo carnaval afrobaiano*. Salvador, Brazil: Corrupio.

———. 1999. "Carnival: The Colors of Change." In *Black Brazil: Culture, Identity, and Social Mobilization*. Edited by Larry Crook and Randall Johnson. Los Angeles: UCLA Latin American Center Publications, pp. 249–259.

Rizzolatti, Giacomo, Luciano Fadiga, Vittorio Gallese, and Leonardo Fogassi. 1996. "Premotor Cortex and the Recognition of Motor Actions." *Cognitive Brain Research* 3(2): 131–141.

Rocha, Maria da Conceição Castro. 1985. "A dança afro-brasileira e as técnicas do corpo." In *Os Afro-Brasileiros: Anais do III Congresso Afro-Brasileiro*. Edited by R. Motta. Recife: Fundação Joaquim Nabuco and Editôra Massangana, pp. 136–137.

Rodrigues, Fernando. 1995. "Racismo cordial." In *Racismo cordial: A mais completa análise sobre o preconceito de cor no Brasil*. Edited by Cleusa Turra and Gustavo Venturi. São Paulo: Editora Ática (*Folha de São Paulo*/Datafolha), pp. 11–55.

Rolnik, Raquel. 1989. "Territorios negros nas cidades brasileiras (ethnicidade e cidade em São Paulo e no Rio de Janeiro)." *Estudos Afro-Asiaticos* 17: 29–41.

Rowe, William, and Vivian Schelling. 1991. *Memory and Modernity: Popular Culture in Latin America*. New York: Verso.

Rubba, Jo. 1996. "Alternate Grounds in the Interpretation of Deictic Expressions." In *Spaces, Worlds, and Grammar*. Edited by Gilles Fauconnier and Eve Sweetser. Chicago: University of Chicago Press, pp. 227–261.

Russell, Bertrand. 1921. *The Analysis of Mind*. New York: Macmillan.

Salaam, Yusef A. 1983. *Capoeira: African Brazilian Karate*. Hampton, VA: United Brothers and Sisters Communications Systems.

Sanjek, Roger. 1971. "Brazilian Racial Terms: Some Aspects of Meaning and Learning." *American Anthropologist* 73: 1126–1143.

Sans, Mónica. 2000. "Admixture Studies in Latin America: From the 20th to the 21st Century." *Human Biology* 72(1): 155–177.

Sansone, Livio. 1992. "Cor, classe e modernidade em duas areas da Bahia (algumas primeiras impressões)." *Estudos Afro-Asiáticos* 23: 143–173.

———. 1993. "Pai preto, filho negro: Trabalho, cor e diferenças de geração." *Estudos Afro-Asiáticos* 25: 73–98.

———. 1997. "The New Blacks from Bahia: Local and Global in Afro-Bahia." *Identities* 3(4): 457–493.

Sansone, Livio, ed. 2002. *As artimanhas da razão imperialista: Comentários a Bourdieu e Wacquant*. Special issue of *Afro-Asiáticos* 24 (Special Issue 1, January–April). Rio de Janeiro: Universidade Candido Mendes.

Santos, Aristeu Oliveira dos (Mestre Mestrinho). 1993. *Capoeira: Arte-Luta brasileira*. Curitiba, Brazil: Imprensa Oficial do Estado.

Santos, Jocélio Teles dos. 1998. "A Mixed-Race Nation: Afro-Brazilians and Cultural Policy in Bahia, 1970–1990." In *Afro-Brazilian Culture and Politics: Bahia, 1790s to 1990s*. Edited by Hendrik Kraay. Armonk, NY: M. E. Sharpe, pp. 117–133.

Santos, Marcelino dos (Mestre Mau). 1991. *Capoeira e mandingas: Cobrinha Verde*. Salvador, Brazil: A Rasteira.

Santos-Granero, Fernando. 1998. "Writing History into the Landscape: Space, Myth, and Ritual in Contemporary Amazonia." *American Ethnologist* 25(2): 128–148.

Satinoff, Merton I. 1972. "Study of the Squatting Facets of the Talus and Tibia in Ancient Egyptians." *Journal of Human Evolution* 1: 209–212.

Schaffer, Kay. 1981. *Monografias folclóricas: O berimbau-de-barriga e seus toques.* Rio de Janeiro: Ministério da Educação e Cultura, FUNARTE.

Schieffelin, Edward L. 1976. *The Sorrow of the Lonely and the Burning of the Dancers.* New York: St. Martin's Press.

Schilder, Paul. 1950. *The Image and Appearance of the Human Body: Studies in the Constructive Energies of the Psyche.* New York: International Universities Press.

Schutz, Alfred. 1964. "Making Music Together." In *Collected Papers II.* Edited by Arvid Brodersen. The Hague: Nijhoff.

Scott, James C. 1985. *Weapons of the Weak: Everyday Forms of Peasant Resistance.* New Haven, CT, and London: Yale University Press.

Senna, Carlos. 1994. "A vida vegetativa da capoeira." *Negaça* 2: 12–13.

Serra, Ordep. 1988. "Ao Mestre Pastinha, com carinho." *A Tarde* (Salvador) (August 9, 1988): 6.

Sheets-Johnstone, Maxine. 2000. "Kinetic–Tactile–Kinesthetic Bodies: Ontogenetical Foundations of Apprenticeship Learning." *Human Studies* 23: 343–370.

Silva, Gladson de Oliveira. 1993. *Capoeira: Do engenho à universidade.* São Paulo: published by the author.

Silva, Nelson do Valle. 1985. "Updating the Cost of Not Being White in Brazil." In *Race, Class, and Power in Brazil.* Edited by Pierre-Michel Fontaine. Los Angeles: Center for Afro-American Studies, UCLA, pp. 42–55.

———. 1999. "Racial Differences in Income: Brazil, 1988." In *Race in Contemporary Brazil: From Indifference to Inequality.* Edited by Rebecca Reichmann. University Park: Pennsylvania State University Press, pp. 67–82.

Silva, Nelson do Valle, and Carlos Hasenbalg. 1992. *Relações Racias no Brasil Contemporâneo.* Rio de Janeiro: Rio Fundo Editôra.

———. 1999. "Race and Educational Opportunity in Brazil." In *Race in Contemporary Brazil: From Indifference to Inequality.* Edited by Rebecca Reichmann. University Park: Pennsylvania State University Press, pp. 53–65.

Silverstein, Michael. 1976. "Shifters, Linguistic Categories, and Cultural Description." In *Meaning in Anthropology.* Edited by Keith Basson and Henry Selby. Albuquerque: University of New Mexico Press, pp. 11–55.

Simmel, Georg. 1969. "Sociology of the Senses: Visual Interaction." In *Introduction to the Science of Sociology.* Edited by Robert Park and Ernest Burges Chicago: University of Chicago Press, pp. 356–361.

Simpson, Amelia. 1993. *Xuxa: The Mega-Marketing of Gender, Race, and Modernity.* Philadelphia: Temple University Press.

Skidmore, Thomas E. 1993a. "Bi-racial USA vs. Multi-racial Brazil: Is the Contrast Still Valid?" *Journal of Latin American Studies* 25: 373–386.

———. 1993b (1974). *Black into White: Race and Nationality in Brazilian Thought,* 2nd ed. Durham, NC: Duke University Press.

Smith, Linda B., and Esther Thelen, eds. 1993. *A Dynamic Systems Approach to Development: Applications.* Cambridge, MA: Bradford (MIT Press).

Smith, Steven. 1992. "Blues and Our Mind–Body Problem." *Popular Music* 11(1): 41–52.

Soares, Antônio Jorge G. 1994. *Futebol, malandragem e identidade.* Vitória: Secretaria de Produção e Difusão Cultural, Universidade Federal do Espírito Santo (SPDC/UFES).

Soares, Carlos Eugênio Líbano. 1994. *A negregada instituição: Os capoeiras no Rio de Janeiro.* Rio de Janeiro: Secretaria Municipal de Cultura, Departamento Geral de Documentção e Informação Cultural, Divisão de Editoração.

Sodré, Muniz. 1983. *A verdade seduzida: Por um conceito de cultura no Brasil.* Rio de Janeiro: Editôra CODECRI.

Stam, Robert. 1997. *Tropical Multiculturalism: A Comparative History of Race in Brazilian Cinema and Culture.* Durham, NC: Duke University Press.

Steen, Susan L., and Robert W. Lane. 1998. "Evaluation of Habitual Activities Among Two Alaskan Eskimo Populations Based on Musculoskeletal Stress Markers." *International Journal of Osteology* 8: 341–353.

Stoller, Paul. 1989. *The Taste of Ethnographic Things: The Senses in Anthropology.* Philadelphia: University of Pennsylvania Press.

———. 1995. *Embodying Colonial Memories: Spirit Possession, Power, and the Hauka in West Africa.* New York: Routledge.

Stoller, Paul, and Cheryl Olkes. 1987. *In Sorcery's Shadow: A Memoir of Apprenticeship Among the Songhay of Niger.* Chicago: University of Chicago Press.

Strathern, Andrew J. 1996. *Body Thoughts.* Ann Arbor: University of Michigan Press.

Strauss, Erwin W. 1966. *Phenomenological Psychology: The Selected Papers of Erwin W. Strauss.* Translated by Erling Eng. New York: Basic Books.

Tavares, Júlio César de Souza. 1984. *Dança da guerra: Arquivo-arma.* Master's dissertation, Departamento de Sociologia, Universidade de Brasília.

Tefft, Stanton K., ed. 1980. *Secrecy: A Cross-Cultural Perspective.* New York: Human Sciences Press.

Telles. Edward E. 1995. "Who Are the Morenas?" *Social Forces* 73(4): 1609–1611.

———. 1999. "Ethnic Boundaries and Political Mobilization Among African Brazilians: Comparisons with the U.S. Case." In *Racial Politics in Contemporary Brazil.* Edited by Michael Hanchard. Durham, NC: Duke University Press, pp. 82–97.

———. 2002. "Racial Ambiguity Among the Brazilian Population." *Ethnic and Racial Studies* 25(3): 415–441.

Thelen, Esther. 1995. "Motor Development: A New Synthesis." *American Psychologist* 50(2): 79–95.

Thelen, Esther, and Linda B. Smith. 1994. *A Dynamic Systems Approach to the Development of Cognition and Action.* Cambridge, MA: Bradford (MIT Press).

Thompson, Robert Farris. 1974. *African Art in Motion: Icon and Act.* Los Angeles: University of California Press.

———. 1987. "Black Martial Arts of the Caribbean." *Review of Latin Literature and Arts* 37: 44–47.

————. 1988. "Tough Guys Do Dance." *Rolling Stone* 470: 95–100.

————. 1992. "Forward." In Lowell Lewis, *Ring of Liberation: Deceptive Discourse in Brazilan Capoeira.* Chicago: University of Chicago Press: pp. xi–xiv.

Tomasello, Michael, Sue Savage-Rumbaugh, and Ann Cale Kruger. 1993. "Imitative Learning of Actions on Objects by Children, Chimpanzees, and Enculturated Chimpanzees." *Child Development* 64: 1688–1705.

Travassos, Elizabeth. 2000. "Ethics in the Sung Duels of North-Eastern Brazil: Collective Memory and Contemporary Practice." *British Journal of Ethnomusicology* 33(1): 1–30.

Trevarthan, Colwyn, Theano Kokkinaki, and Geraldo A. Fiamenghi Jr. 1999. "What Infants' Imitations Communicate: With Mothers, with Fathers and with Peers." In *Imitation in Infancy.* Edited by Jacqueline Nadel and George Butterworth. Cambridge and New York: Cambridge University Press, pp. 127–185.

Turner, J. Michael. 1985. "Brown into Black: Changing Racial Attitudes of Afro-Brazilian University Students." In *Race, Class, and Power in Brazil.* Edited by Pierre-Michel Fontaine. Los Angeles: Center for Afro-American Studies, UCLA, pp. 73–94.

Turner, Stephen P. 1994. *The Social Theory of Practices: Tradition, Tacit Knowledge, and Presuppositions.* Chicago: University of Chicago Press.

————. 2002. *Brains/Practices/Relativism: Social Theory After Cognitive Science.* Chicago: University of Chicago Press.

Turra, Cleusa, and Gustavo Venturi, eds. 1995. *Racismo cordial: A mais completa análise sobre o preconceito de cor no Brasil.* São Paulo: Editora Ática.

Twine, France Winddance. 1998. *Racism in a Racial Democracy: The Maintenance of White Supremacy in Brazil.* New Brunswick, NJ: Rutgers University Press.

Ubelaker, D. H. 1979. "Skeletal Evidence for Kneeling in Prehistoric Ecuador." *American Journal of Phystical Anthropology* 51: 679–686.

Vianna, Antônio. 1984. *Casos e coisas da Bahia.* Salvador: Fundação Cultural do Estado da Bahia.

Vianna, Hermano. 1999. *The Mystery of Samba: Popular Music and National Identity in Brazil.* Chapel Hill: University of North Carolina Press.

Vieira, Luiz Renato. 1990. *Da vadiação à Capoeira Regional: Uma interpretação da modernização cultural no Brasil.* Master's thesis, Universidade de Brasília, Departamento de Sociologia.

Vigarello, Georges. 1989. "The Upward Training of the Body from the Age of Chivalry to Courtly Civility." In *Fragments for a History of the Body. Part Two.* Edited by M. Feher, R. Naddaff, and N. Tazi. New York: Zone, pp. 148–196.

Voeks, Robert A. 1997. *Sacred Leaves of Candomblé: African Magic, Medicine, and Religion in Brazil.* Austin: University of Texas Press.

Wacquant, Loïc J. D. 1995a. "The Pugilistic Point of View: How Boxers Think and Feel About Their Trade." *Theory and Society* 24(4): 489–535.

————. 1995b. "Pugs at Work: Bodily Capital and Bodily Labour Among Professional Boxers." *Body & Society* 1(1): 65–93.

————. 1998. "The Prizefighter's Three Bodies." *Ethnos* 63(3): 325–352.

———. 2004. *Body & Soul: Notebooks of an Apprentice Boxer.* New York: Oxford University Press.

Wafer, James W. 1991. *The Taste of Blood: Spirit Possession in Brazilian Candomblé.* Philadelphia: University of Pennsylvania Press.

Wagley, Charles. ed. 1952. *Race and Class in Rural Brazil.* Paris: UNESCO.

Walser, Robert. 1993. *Running with the Devil: Power, Gender, and Madness in Heavy Metal Music.* Hanover, NH, and London: Wesleyan University Press.

Weiner, James F. 1991. *The Empty Place: Poetry, Space, and Being Among the Foi of Papua New Guinea.* Bloomington and Indianapolis: Indiana University Press.

———. 1992. "Anthropology Contra Heidegger. 1: Anthropology's Nihilism." *Critique of Anthropology* 12(1): 75–90.

———. 1993. "Anthropology Contra Heidegger. 2: The Limit of Relationship." *Critique of Anthropology* 13(3): 285–301.

Weiskrantz, Lawrence. 1986. *Blindsight: A Case Study and Its Implications.* Oxford: Oxford University Press.

———. 1997. *Consciousness Lost and Found.* Oxford: Oxford University Press.

Weiss, Gail. 1999. *Body Images: Embodiment as Intercorporeality.* New York: Routledge.

Wikan, Unni. 1991. "Toward an Experience-Near Anthropology." *Cultural Anthropology* 6(3): 285–305.

Wilson, Margaret. 2001. "Designs of Deception: Concepts of Consciousness, Spirituality and Survival in Capoeira Angola in Salvador, Brazil." *Anthropology of Consciousness* 12(1): 119–36.

Winant, Howard. 1992. "Rethinking Race in Brazil." *Journal of Latin American Studies* 24(1): 173–192.

———. 1994. *Racial Conditions: Politics, Theory, Comparisons.* Minneapolis: University of Minnesota Press.

Wittgenstein, Ludwig. 1979 (1967). *Remarks on Frazer's Golden Bough.* Translated by A. C. Miles. Revised by R. Rhees. Atlantic Highlands, NJ: Humanities Press International.

Wood, Charles H., and José Alberto Magno de Carvalho. 1988. *The Demography of Inequality in Brazil.* Cambridge and New York: Cambridge University Press.

Young, Iris Marion. 1990. *Throwing Like a Girl and Other Essays in Feminist Philosophy and Social Theory.* Bloomington and Indianapolis: Indiana University Press.

———. 1998. "'Throwing Like a Girl': Twenty Years Later." In *Body and Flesh: A Philosophical Reader.* Edited by Donn Welton. Oxford: Blackwell Publishers, pp. 286–290.

Yúdice, George. 1994. "The Funkification of Rio." In *Microphone Fiends: Youth Music and Youth Culture.* Edited by Tricia Rose and Andrew Ross. New York: Routledge, pp. 193–217.

Zarrilli, Phillip B. 1998. *When the Body Becomes All Eyes: Paradigms, Discourses and Practices of Power in Kalarippayattu, a South Indian Martial Art.* Delhi: Oxford University Press.

INDEX

The letter *f* following a page number denotes a figure.

CPSIA information can be obtained at www.ICGtesting.com
Printed in the USA
BVOW06s0820141215

430202BV00008B/22/P